D1453206

· JOHN CARTER ·

The Taste & Technique of a Bookman

John Carter, right, with the eminent typographer Stanley Morison at the opening of the Rampant Lions Press exhibition at Monotype House in January 1961.

· JOHN CARTER ·

The Taste & Technique of a Bookman

Donald C. Dickinson

PREFACE BY
Sebastian Carter

Oak Knoll Press

New Castle, Delaware

2004

First Edition, 2004

Published by **Oak Knoll Press**
310 Delaware Street, New Castle, Delaware, USA
Web: http://www.oakknoll.com

ISBN: 1-58456-137-8

Title: John Carter - The Taste and Technique of a Bookman
Author: Donald C. Dickinson
Editor: Joseph Rosenblum
Typography and dust jacket design: Adam Koster
Publishing Director: J. Lewis von Hoelle

Library of Congress Cataloging-in-Publication Data

Dickinson, Donald C.
   John Carter: the taste and technique of a bookman / Donald C.
Dickinson ; preface by Sebastian Carter.
      p. cm.
   Includes bibliographical references and index.
   ISBN 1-58456-137-8 (acid-free paper)
   1. Carter, John, 1905-1975. 2. Bibliographers--England--Biography.
3. Booksellers and bookselling--England--Biography. 4. Antiquarian
booksellers--History--20th century. 5. Book collecting--History--20th
century. 6. Rare books--Bibliography. 7. Book industries and trade--
England--History--20th century. 8. Book industries and trade--United
States--History--20th century. I. Title.

Z1004.C325D53 2004
381'.45002'092--dc22
[B]
                                                    2003070155

This work was printed in the United States of America on 60# natural
archival, acid-free paper meeting the requirements of the American
Standard for Permanence of Paper for Printed Library Materials.

CONTENTS

LIST OF ILLUSTRATIONS

To the grandchildren - Langston Hazen, Bridget Manns, Christopher Manns, Emily Ralston and Eric Yagla

The fabulous five

ACKNOWLEDGMENTS

It is a pleasure to thank those who have supported this study of John Carter. I worked at the Harry Ransom Humanities Center Library at the University of Texas under a C. P. Snow Travel Grant, at the Lilly Library at Indiana University under a Everett Helm Fellowship, and at the libraries of Eton College, Cambridge University, and Oxford University under a Henry E. Huntington/British Academy Exchange Fellowship.

I owe special thanks to a number of people who knew Carter and were willing to talk with me or write me about his life and achievements - among them Gabriel Austin, Nicolas Barker, David Butler, Sebastian Carter, John Collins, John Dreyfus, Frank Herrmann, Anthony Hobson, Lord John Kerr, David McKitterick, Stephen C. Massey, Michael Meredith, Peregrine Pollen, Catherine Porteous, Esther Potter, Ronald R. Randall. Anthony Rota, and James Wells. I owe special thanks to Sebastian Carter who gave me open access to family papers and photographs and to Frank Herrmann who answered countless questions and let me use his working files on the history of Sotheby's. Laura Sayre contributed valuable research assistance at the Princeton University library. Amy Rule prepared the well-organized index.

Four people read the complete draft and made significant contributions to the final text. My thanks go to those diligent readers; Sebastian Carter, proprietor of the

Rampant Lions Press, Cambridge; Jean Dickinson, cataloger at the Hoover Institution, Palo Alto, California; John Collins of Maggs Brothers, London, and James Wells, curator emeritus of the John M. Wing Foundation in the History of Printing at the Newberry Library in Chicago, Illinois. Michael Meredith, Eton College librarian, read those portions of the text pertaining to Carter's affiliation with the College both as a student and as a Fellow.

Over a period of five years, many librarians, collectors, faculty members, and curators have provided advice and encouragement - among them William Baker, Nicholas A. Basbanes, Carl T. Berkhout, Glen Dawson, Christopher de Hamel, Donald C. Gallup, James L. Harner, Eric J. Holzenberg, Michael Ingham, Alan Jutzi, Thomas V. Lange, Margaret F. Maxwell, Marvin Mondlin, Richard W. Oram, Lawrence Clark Powell, Joseph Rosenblum, Joel Silver, Stephen Tabor, G. Thomas Tanselle, and David S. Zeidberg.

Carter seldom wrote about himself and, surprisingly, little has been written about him. Fortunately, he was an active letter writer. The Provost and Fellows of Eton College gave me permission to quote from Carter's published and unpublished work. The following institutions and individuals also gave their consent for quotation from letters and documents - The Syndics of the Cambridge University Library - Frank Herrmann, permission to quote from his working files at Cambridge University Library and his book, *Sotheby's - Portrait of an Auction House* - The Eton College Library - The Harry Ransom Humanities Research Center of the University of Texas at Austin - The Lilly Library at Indiana University, Bloomington - King's College, Cambridge University - Department of Rare Books and Special Collections,

Princeton University Library - The Lewis/Walpole Library, Farmington, Connecticut - The Bodleian Library, Oxford University - The Pierpont Morgan Library, New York, Records of the Director's Office - The Newberry Library, Chicago, Illinois - The Charles E. Young Research Library, Department Special Collections, University of California, Los Angeles, and Sebastian Carter, family letters. I am grateful to the curators and staff members in these institutions who so kindly furthered my research.

Permission to reproduce photographs was granted by the Provost and Fellows of Eton College, Figures 4, 6 and 7; The Harry Ransom Humanities Research Center, University of Texas, Austin, Texas, Figures 16b, 17, 19 and 29; The Henry E. Huntington Library, San Marino, California, Figures 16a, 18a and 18b; The Lewis/Walpole Library, Farmington, Connecticut, Figure 37; The Lilly Library, Indiana University, Bloomington, Indiana, Figures 25, 26 and 27; The Wellesley College Archives, Wellesley, Massachusetts, Figure 30; Sebastian Carter, Figures 1, 2, 3, 5, 9, 10, 20a, 20b, 21, 22, 38 and 39; Esther Potter, Figures 18c and 40; Ronald Randall, Figure 13; and Bertram Rota Ltd's Catalogue 290, The Biblio Boys, 1999, Figure 36.

*"Book collecting is the orchid
in the hothouse of connoisseurship."*

– John Carter –

PREFACE

I have in front of me some of the letters received after my uncle John's death in 1975 by his wife Ernestine. The two of them moved in exalted circles, John in his capacity as bibliographical consultant to Sotheby's, Ernestine as a fashion writer, and so there are the expected letters from Paul Mellon, the Earl of Westmorland, Cecil Beaton and many other wealthy, titled and stylish people. Even allowing for the conventions of the occasion, however, what is striking is the warmth of many of the memories. Typical was the art critic Sir Roland Penrose, founder of the Institute of Contemporary Arts, who was married to the glamorous American photographer Lee Miller: "Jake was a friend of such unique value whom we loved dearly and remember among other things those war-time nights sheltering under each other's stairs as an intimate token of friendship." I think the most moving is from his early collaborator Graham Pollard: "John was the best friend I ever had and the first person who really believed in me. I have never really faced up to the thought of a world in which his steadfastness would no longer be a source of ultimate support." While most of the obituaries in the newspapers stressed his achievements in the rare book world and his writings on the subject, as well as his elegant manners and dress sense, these letters testify to the more human side of his nature.

My father Will was his only brother, and younger by seven years. While John had a distinguished academic career, winning scholarships to the traditional family institutions of Eton and King's College, Cambridge, and finishing with a double first in classics, Will was a craftsman at heart and left school at eighteen for a general apprenticeship at Unwin's printing works. After the war he turned his evening and weekend hobby, the Rampant Lions Press, into a full-time business, run from the basement below the family quarters in Chesterton Road, Cambridge.

Throughout the early years of the Press, John was an active supporter. He suggested the name, which came from the Carter coat of arms, and drew up lists of possible future titles, as well as introducing Will to other contributors and advisers such as John Sparrow and John Betjeman. More importantly, he edited a number of early publications, not only the works of family piety which he sponsored, the booklets on *William Johnson Cory* (1959) and *The Ceremony of the Lilies and Roses* (1961), but also the only Rampant Lions book which has gone into a second edition, the entertaining *Clerihews* (1938 and 1946), and the delightful *Last Chapter of Urne Buriall* (1946), with its cover design by John Piper. In 1939, he had suggested the printing of *Sonnets from the Portuguese*, and persuaded Scribner's to take part of the edition: it was of course the 'Reading Sonnets' edition of this text which was the principal suspect in the Wise forgeries affair. When Will and David Kindersley were designing their roman type for Monotype in the late 1950s, it was John who came up with its name, Octavian. (His postcard listing suggestions also refers to a lunch date with me at the Garrick Club, which was the occasion of the Ordeal by Partridge referred to by Don Dickinson on page 326.)

For all this, his manner could sometimes be distinctly lofty. There are some early Rampant Lions prospectuses with fairly acid handwritten comments by him about their literacy and accuracy. Will was distinctly in awe of him, and relations were made more difficult by the contrasts between the two Carter ménages. John and Ernestine were childless, and Ernestine at least was devoted to her small poodle. Will had four children, it was a fairly noisy household at Chesterton Road, and none of us liked dogs.

Nevertheless, John made determined efforts to be a good uncle. I remember childhood visits to Bedford Gardens, on one of which I was presented with a first edition of *King Solomon's Mines*. As the senior Carter of the next generation, I also carried a heavy burden of ancestral expectation, which he took very seriously, passing on various family heirlooms, and even his father's cape, worn for the lilies and roses ceremony. It did not help that I omitted to go to Eton, but a modicum of honour was retrieved when I won a place at King's. He continued the tradition of presentation copies of his books which he had established with Will, always with light-hearted inscriptions. I woke in my college room one morning after a heavy night out to find a copy of his Housman *Selected Prose* anthology on the foot of my bed, inscribed: "for Sebastian, sensibly still asleep at 10.30, 6 Dec 1961, this ill-margined piece of US offset printing with the compliments of the editor." My first job after university was with the venerable London publishing firm of John Murray, and I suspect family contacts helped there, since John was godfather to Jock Murray's son, John Murray VII. And when I got engaged, John and Ernestine threw a grand party at Carlyle Square for some young things they thought we ought to know. Much of this generosity was fairly daunting, but what I was too young to realise was that John was probably unaware of the barriers which his seniority and eminence had erected: each generation finds it hard to understand the diffidence of the next.

As for the diffidence of his brother, here is a letter John wrote to my father in 1961. Will had had an exhibition of Rampant Lions Press work at Monotype House (at the opening party of which the photograph of John with Stanley Morison which appears opposite the title page was taken), and must have said or written something about how this made him feel rather less in John's shadow. He received this affectionate, self-deprecating, though still elder-brotherly, lecture:

> *My dear old bro –*
> *I am delighted - more than delighted - that time, success, maturity, COMMON SENSE, have between them rid you at last of the preposterous notions which have in the past bedevilled us. I suppose all younger brothers suffer in youth from the expectation, cherished even in the best of families, that they must do everything the same way as their elder brothers, only better. But I have not, for 20 years - well, anyway for 10 years - understood how the inhibitions imposed on you by Pop or King's or any of that stuff could survive the plain facts of your increasingly distinguished achievement and the equally increasing repute & regard in which you are held by a very wide range of good judges. I have been very proud of being your brother, for a long time, as our friends well know: why haven't you been proud of being you? You talk, bless you, about my achievement. What is it? 3 or 4 creditable books, of which one perhaps will be remembered 50 years from now, and that only one half mine; a decent prose style; a few thousand column inches in TLS, already yellow with age; a superficial, though sometimes showy, knowledge of the rare book business; some ability to understand the American language -*

I defy you to name anything much else. And you won't find any unprejudiced person to make 'achievement' out of that little list. It was an achievement to capture Ernestine, whom I have to thank for all that has been happy (& not all has) in my life since. But that was, & remains, more my good luck than my good management.

Whereas you, my dear Rampant Lion, have behind you, and on the stocks, and in front of you a body of creative craftsmanship of a quality and a versatility which it wd be very hard to find, today, a half dozen men anywhere to match.

This is something quite different from a knack for making money for Scribner's or Sotheby's, and you know it. You haven't, in the past, been willing to recognise it: diffidence, no doubt; but high time you shed it. Good, very good, that you have...

– Your loving brother, John

Well, they both had their achievements, and John's are described in this book.

– Sebastian Carter

Other Books by the author:

- Bio-Bibliography of Langston Hughes 1902-1967 (1967)

- Helmut Lehmann-Haupt a Bibliography (1975)

- The Dictionary of American Book Collectors (1986)

- George Watson Cole - Bibliographer (1990)

- Henry E. Huntington's Library of Libraries (1995)

- The Dictionary of American Antiquarian Bookdealers (1998)

INTRODUCTION

During the first three decades of the twentieth century, book collecting was dominated on one hand by wealthy businessmen such as Henry Clay Folger, Robert Hoe, and Henry E. Huntington, and on the other by shrewd, experienced dealers like A.S.W. Rosenbach, George D. Smith, and Gabriel Wells. The collectors concentrated on incunabula, early English literature, color plate books, and fine bindings. Dealers were happy to meet those *needs*. In the midst of the economic depression of the 1930s, several younger book dealers began to search for new directions. John Carter was one of the leaders of that group. Trained at Eton College and King's College, Cambridge to think for himself, Carter introduced new collecting lines: musical scores, science and technology, yellow-backs, modern first editions, and detective stories, lines he and David Randall promoted beginning in the 1930s in a series of groundbreaking Scribner's sales catalogs.

In a related effort, Carter and Graham Pollard, in a stunning example of bibliographic detective work, exposed a collection of nineteenth century pamphlets as forgeries and in the process pointed an accusing finger at Thomas J. Wise, the leading English bibliographer of that day. Their book, *An Enquiry Into the Nature of Certain Nineteenth Century Pamphlets,* remains a classic.

Carter worked in the book trade for forty-five years, first as a rare book specialist in Scribner's London office, then at Sotheby's as their American agent. In these positions, and through his writing, he exerted a considerable influence on the pre-war and post-war Anglo-American rare book trade. He was known for his shrewd sense of the market, his wit, his highly distinctive style of dress and bearing, his talent for friendship, and his ability to translate the pleasures of collecting in a highly readable prose. Much of Carter's writing was directed to amateurs who enjoyed collecting as a stimulating hobby but had little interest in the fine points of bibliographic theory. Without diluting the content, Carter knew how to tell a story.

Although his career was spent working for others - often those with considerable financial and social power - Carter maintained a strongly independent nature. When Lord Bernstein, the director of the Granada media conglomerate, failed to support the Soho Bibliographies, for example, Carter, a member of the editorial board, sent in his resignation with instructions to remove his name from all advertising brochures, catalogs, and the official letterhead.

One way to understand Carter is to see him as an outsider, raised the son of a rural clergyman, and a scholarship boy at Eton and Cambridge. He continued in that role throughout his forty year working career - removed from the centers of power by geographical distance at Scribner's and social distance at Sotheby's. As Carter frequently demonstrated, being an outsider could be used to one's advantage. In 1945 the New York collector, Carl Pforzheimer, rejected a preface Carter wrote for *Between the Lines. Letters and Memorandum Interchanged by H. Buxton Forman and Thomas J. Wise.* Carter told Pforzheimer he was satisfied with the rejection since it would give him more freedom to comment on the book in the journals. His review in *The Times Literary Supplement* was devastating.

Considering his important contributions to the literature of book collecting and bibliography, and his stature in the international rare book trade, it is surprising that Carter has not received more attention. Since his death in 1975 there has been only one brief sketch devoted to his achievements. This biography is an attempt to fill that gap.

Carter was often in the right place at the right time; successful at Scribner's just as the rare book market opened between the wars, and successful at Sotheby's as that firm expanded westward. He was blessed with a keen intellect and a lively wit. Through his essays, monographs, and extensive correspondence, we can savor that wit and that intellect. Reader, enjoy!

– D. C. D.

CHAPTER ONE
Early Days

In 1949, when the post of librarian at Cambridge University fell open, several of John Carter's friends urged him to apply. His credentials were impressive - a Cambridge degree taken with high honors in 1927, a lengthy list of scholarly publications on book collecting and bibliography, and twenty-two years in the rare book business. In addition, in November and December 1947, at the invitation of the Syndics of the University Library, he had delivered the prestigious Sandars Lectures in Bibliography - the first book dealer to be so honored since the lectures were founded in 1894.

The position as University Librarian was certainly a distinguished one, as Carter acknowledged in a letter to his friend A.N.L. Munby, Librarian of King's College, Cambridge. From a personal point of view, however, the drawbacks outweighed the advantages. Carter wrote:

> For to me, if I were to be elected, it would be drastic. It would mean concentrating all my interests and energies into a single channel; whereas my present work affords me the opportunity of a much more varied use of such aptitudes as I possess. . . . It would mean the end of my close personal contact with bookish doings in America, by which I set great store and which enables me to exert some influence on both sides of the Atlantic. It would severely reduce that freedom of movement and of maneuver which

derives from my being more or less master of the allocation of my own time and attention. It would mean
exchanging London for the provinces and the kind of life
my wife and I like for another to which I am not sure we
should either of us take kindly. Finally, the change would
cost me about a thousand a year in income.[1]

After marshaling this array of objections, it is not surprising that the forty-three year old Carter decided to continue as Managing Director of Scribner's, London office.
The letter is revealing. Throughout his life Carter consistently made choices that protected his prized "freedom of
movement and of maneuver." Money was important, as he
frequently reminded his employers, but beyond that was a
need to be "master of the allocation of my own time and
attention." According to the sketch in the *Dictionary of
National Biography*, one of
Carter's dominant traits was
"an inclination to concentrate
only on what he found congenial."[2] That analysis might
easily have been expanded to
include a comment that what
Carter found congenial often
pleased others as well.

1. *Thomas Buchanan Carter and Margaret
Theresa Carter - early 1930s.*

John Waynflete Carter,
Jake to his family and close
friends, was born in the family
home on High Street in Eton
on May 10, 1905, the oldest of
the four children of Thomas
Buchanan Carter and Margaret
Theresa Stone. Carter's sister
Mary, always called "Maria,"

was born in 1907, next came
Elizabeth, "Lisa," in 1908 and
finally William, "Will" in
1912.[3] Carter's father was
trained as an architect, but in
1908 took holy orders at
Cuddesdon College. He followed the usual steps after
ordination, serving first as
curate in St Laurence's church
in Upton, across the river
from Eton, then vicar of
Burnham, four miles north,
and eventually vicar of Little
Faringdon, a hamlet on the
Oxfordshire/Gloucestershire
border. He retired in 1927 and
returned to Eton. His change
of occupation, from architect

*2. Carter (left, back) at Little Faringdon with
members of his family: his father (seated, center),
and mother (in front of JWC), his sisters,
Elizabeth (left, front), and Mary (right, front),
and a cousin, Ralph White (standing rear), and
his daughter Mary (seated, center) - c. 1924.*

to clergyman, was not surprising as teachers and clergymen
dominated the family line for several generations back. John
Carter's great, great grandfather, Thomas Thellusson, was
Rector of Clewer, and his grandfather, Thomas John
Proctor, was an Eton master from 1868 to 1899. Another
ancestor, William Adolphus, the bursar of the college during the middle years of the nineteenth century, was by all
accounts a rather dour individual. He was "not a wit, but
said good things now and then."[4] An early document con-
nects the family to William of Waynflete, a fifteenth century Eton Provost. The Stones, on the other hand, were
inclined toward artistic and literary accomplishments.[5]
Carter's mother, Margaret, grew up in a lively Eton household that produced musicians, writers, and artists. Her

father, Edward D. Stone, a poet, a classical scholar, musician, talented amateur actor and an Eton master, went on to found his own school for boys near Broadstairs on the North Foreland. He and his wife, Elizabeth Theresa "Lily" Vidal, raised a family of ten children - among them Lucy, a professional violinist, Faith, an actress and writer and Christopher, a radio personality and one of the founders, along with his brother-in-law, Montague Compton Mackenzie, of The *Gramophone* magazine. Four of the boys attended Eton and three went on to graduate from King's College, Cambridge. The highly regarded wood engraver, Reynolds Stone, was Carter's first cousin. Everything about the Stone family was lively and spontaneous. Some of that spirit must have rubbed off on Carter's father who was, even as a youth, reserved and inclined to quiet reflection. According to a cherished piece of family lore, he surprised everyone on his wedding day. Faith, Margaret's younger sister, reported the details: "I went down to Abingdon for Margaret's wedding. Helensbourne was a lovely seventeenth century house, at the back a garden and at the end of the garden, a river. The climax of the beautiful wedding would be the departure of the bride and groom by boat - rowed by two Blues up the river to Nuneham. Guests would assemble on the lookout to give them God speed. As the boat drew near (there was) a rending crack - twenty people flung into the water - Row On, cried the bridegroom!"[6]

Conventional wisdom might picture life in a remote country parsonage in the 1920's in various shades of gray, but that was not necessarily the case. From 1922 to 1927 the Carters were fortunate to live in a large Victorian residence just north of Lechlade, outside the village of Little Faringdon. With six bedrooms, a breakfast room, dining room, sitting room, drawing room, study and conservatory, and surrounded by an acre of pleasant lawns and gardens, the house was ideal for the family and guests. The Little Faringdon vicarage was Carter's home during his final years at Eton and his three years at Cambridge. It was a place to bring friends, to relax, read, take walks, and spend time on school vacations with his younger brother and sisters.

Reminiscing about the early period of his life Carter wrote, "I come of a respectable upper middle-class family with no Welsh or Irish blood and an incapacity, which I have inherited, for making money."[7] What *was* in abundance was intellectual stimulation. *The Encyclopedia Britannica, The Concise Dictionary of National Biography*, Fowler's *Modern English Usage*, Smith's *Classical Dictionary*, and a Larousse all commanded a place of honor in the Carter dining room and were consulted regularly to settle disputes arising from word games played around the dinner table. Music and books were as much a part of daily life as prayers before meals.

As the son of a provincial clergyman of modest means, Carter's education followed a somewhat predictable course. As George Orwell explained in his essay "Such, Such Were the Joys," promising students who needed support were sometimes admitted to preparatory schools on a reduced fee basis.[8] Under such an arrangement Carter, age ten, entered the Fourth Form at the Sunningdale School in Berkshire at the beginning of the Lent term of 1915. During Carter's time the school was directed by headmasters F. L. Crabtree and D. M. Smith who, along with a staff of six teachers, provided instruction in mathematics, English, history, scripture, geography, and the classics for some sixty-five boys. The students occupied austere quarters, six to eight living in sparsely furnished dormitory

3. Carter age 10 - c. 1915.

rooms. In a slight concession to comfort, a man came around every morning to fill the wash basins with warm water. Carter compiled an outstanding academic record, winning prizes in classics, geography, mathematics, and English. G. A. Ling, a master who had secured Eton scholarships for many of his students, supervised Carter's classes in Latin and Greek.[9] Carter added to his honors in the classroom with success on the playing fields. During the Michaelmas term of 1915 the school newspaper identified him as the best of the backs and predicted he would be useful in the years to come. By 1916 he secured a place on the first eleven in soccer and the next year became the team's captain and received his colors in both soccer and cricket.

If Carter was to become "useful in the years to come" he would, almost certainly, need to obtain a scholarship at one of the prominent public schools. Counting many ancestors on both sides of his family who had served in college positions, Eton was the obvious first choice. After nearly five hundred years (the college was founded by Henry VI in 1440) Eton emerged in the early decades of the twentieth century as the jewel of the English public school system. The very name, Eton, implies privilege and position. It conjures up pictures of boys in formal dress, Masters in flowing robes, ancient buildings and well-kept playing fields. Eton also implies influence. Before Winston

Churchill, who went to Harrow, nearly every Tory prime minister and most of the cabinet came from Eton. Old Etonians traditionally occupy positions of power in the civil service, literature and the arts, education, business and the military. Eton was and is all this and more - a ponderous maze of tradition and intellectual challenge. In Carter's case there were even college buildings with family connections. As an architect, his father had redesigned the high altar at the east end of the College Chapel, planned The Warre Schools in Common Lane, and Baldwin's End, the home of the distinguished Eton master H. E. Luxmoore. Thomas Carter's most ambitious project, a tower at the North corner of School Yard, planned as a memorial to Eton students and masters who died in World War I, had to be set aside as too costly.

In May 1919 Carter took the traditional two and a half day scholarship examinations held in Eton's Upper School. He did well, but since the college awarded only ten to twelve scholarships to new boys, passing the examinations with high grades was no guarantee of admission. There was relief when Carter's father received a letter notifying him that his son had won a foundation scholarship. For the next five years, Carter was identified as a King's Scholar, K.S., a Colleger, with all the privileges and constraints that designation implied. The seventy King's Scholars were an elite minority, admitted for their academic talents rather than for the depth of their parent's bank accounts. They wore gowns over the traditional formal uniform of tails, and for that reason were derisively called "tugs" by their contemporaries, after togatus, Latin for gowned. The other one thousand boys were Oppidans, so named because they lodged in boarding houses in town (*oppidum*). In his readable history, *An English Education,*

Richard Ollard described Eton as an institution with a "salient class distinction."[10] While it is not fair, as Ollard points out, to stereotype Oppidans as rich, burly athletes and Collegers as small, sensitive intellectuals, a division did exist and had long been a significant part of Eton life.

In the summer of 1919, when Carter took up residence, his living quarters must have been similar to those described by Philip Brownrigg: "Then one day . . . about ten boys arrive in Chamber. It is a long, airy room divided into fifteen stalls, rather like a stable, by dark wooden partitions about ten feet high and carved all over with the names of former occupants. There is a passage-way down the middle, and half way on one side an open space between two stalls with a round and ancient table, a great fireplace, and boot-lockers forming benches. A stall is provided with a burry and chair, a bed that folds up into a sort of cupboard and a washbasin with cold water laid on."[11] In this austere setting J. F. Crace, the Master in College, who was at the same time Carter's tutor, ruled with what was said to be a benevolent, unworldly tolerance. As Carter moved up in seniority he was assigned a room of his own with improved facilities.

The college to which Carter came in 1919 was little different than the one his great-grandfather had known half a century before. It was still - among other things - hierarchical, traditional, patriotic, sentimental, and exclusive. The tutorial system encouraged independence, but the classroom instruction and pressures from senior boys demanded a certain amount of conformity. The majority of the masters maintained high standards. It was to this point that Prime Minister Gladstone addressed himself in a letter to the Eton housemaster A. C. Benson. "At Eton in my day," Gladstone wrote, "a boy might if he chose

4. The King's Scholars - Eton house photograph, 1919. Carter, age 14, standing at the far right in the top row. J. F. Crace, the Master in College and Carter's tutor, is seated in the middle of the front row.

learn something, or might, if he chose learn nothing, but that one thing he could not do, and that was to learn anything inaccurately."[12] One of the chief characteristics of an Eton education was that much was left to choice. If a house master objected to a certain poster on one's wall one had no obligation to take it down but only needed to defend it by saying it was important. A boy might be asked to read Homer's *Odyssey* and discuss it with his tutor, but there was no expectation that he needed to agree with the tutor's interpretation. Individual and even eccentric tastes were encouraged, and provincialism and received wisdom rejected. Boys could join societies for the arts or politics, participate in athletics, row on the Thames, or simply enjoy the solitude of their rooms. It was a matter of finding your place in a world that offered both freedom and conformity alongside formality and informality. Carter, along with all the other incoming Collegers, had to learn how to balance these competing forces. Early academic success helped him adjust to the new environment. For those, like Carter, who achieved at the highest level, the college returned a sense of belonging. There was always, as Penelope Fitzgerald put it, "a discrete respect for brilliance."[13]

At the top of the hierarchy during Carter's years at Eton were two commanding figures, the Provost, Montague Rhodes James, and the Head Master, Cyril Alington. James, a medievalist, expert on early Christian writing, and the author of superb ghost stories, came to Eton in 1918 after serving for two decades as Provost of King's College, Cambridge. He was informal, learned and, according to one observer, "unencumbered by any sense of his own importance."[14] Alington, a prolific writer and stimulating teacher, took up his post as Head Master in

1917. In the division of responsibilities, the Provost and the Fellows managed the estates, and oversaw financial matters. The Head Master was responsible for running the school on a day by day basis. The relationship between James and Alington was "as happy as any in the history of Eton, so that their very different qualities were mutually enhanced."[15] Assistant Masters such as A. S. F. Gow, C. M. Wells, Hugh Macnaghten, George Lyttelton, and Carter's tutor, J. F. Crace, reflected Eton's tradition for intellectual quality both in their individual scholarship and in their classroom teaching. Carter's attitudes were shaped by Eton customs as well as by the direct influence of his masters, tutors and fellow students. He continued to excel in sports as well as in academic work. For recreation, he took part in several theatrical productions. In July 1922 he

5. Carter (center), as "The Messenger" in an extract from Sophocles "Oedipus Rex" performed at Eton College, 4 June 1923. Richard Martineau as "The Herdsman" is on Carter's left and Arthur R. D. Watkins, his future roommate at Cambridge, as "Oedipus" on his right.

had a minor role in Oliver Goldsmith's *She Stoops to Conquer*, and the following summer played Dogberry in Shakespeare's *Much Ado About Nothing*. If all was done with a determinedly blasé attitude, Carter was only demonstrating mannerisms common to public school students of the time.

Carter participated in a variety of field sports. In a letter to his mother he explained how he and his teammates had batted for a "glorious win by 105 runs after a 40 run defeat in 1st innings . . . we are going to have a deuce of a feed on Monday: ices, iced drinks, melons, meringues, biscuits and Fullers' cakes. Not very solid but there is to be a general College Sock supper [a celebratory feast] because of the fellows in the eight & us too. The cup is a beauty presented by Oscar Browning. . . . I feel now that I haven't wasted the half."[16] During the 1923 Michaelmas half Carter's teammates elected him to the distinguished post of Keeper (Captain) of the College Wall and on November 30th, St.Andrews Day, he led his team to a victory over the rival Oppidans.[17] On the day of the game, the *Eton College Chronicle* carried interviews with Carter and W. P. Bull, Keeper of the Oppidan Wall. According to the interview, done in a mock serious style, when a reporter came to Carter's room to ask questions he found only an array of wall caps, wall sacks, old cricket-pads, stockings, books, hat-boxes and talking tortoises. A voice is heard at the door: "Confound it, Wher's my Greek Anthology?" When the reporter asked about St. Andrews Day, the Keeper kicked him down the stairs. An accompanying photograph shows Carter in evening dress, hair slicked back and scowling at the camera as if quite ready to kick a troublesome journalist down the stairs. In a brief biographical note, Carter is described as "Keeper (third),

*6. The Wall Game, Eton College - c. 1914. Carter was Keeper (Captain)
of the College Wall and led his team to victory in 1923.*

11.5lb. As a player he is tremendously strong in attack and
defence, and his great skill and experience made him
admirably suited to his place as pivot of the side: College
owes as much to his indefatigable zeal as a Keeper as to his
inspiring example."[18]

During the Lent term of 1924 the members of the Eton
Society, known as Pop, elected Carter to membership.
The organization was made up of a self-perpetuating group
of twenty to thirty boys with athletic, political, or social
talents. The members awarded themselves a number of
special privileges - the right to carry a rolled-up umbrella,
the right to wear braid on one's coat, the right to have
printed stationery, the right to walk arm in arm with a fellow student, and the right to assign tasks to junior boys. It
was all trivial and snobbish but represented to some the
pinnacle of sophistication. In his autobiography, Cyril

Connolly described the campaign of flattery and subtle persuasion he employed in order to be accepted, "I now admitted to myself my ambition to get into Pop and planned my campaign. My handicap was that I had no athletic distinctions, nor was I in Sixth Form from which a certain number of Pops invariably had to be chosen. My only hope was to be elected as a wit. Although it was but a small section of Pop who thought me funny, they were influential. My tactics were to seem as important as I could in College, so that my Oppidan friends would not feel that I was too powerless in my own fief to deserve recognition abroad. . . . I mention this technique in case others who wish to be elected to things may find it helpful."[19] Carter, who never courted popularity, would have found Connolly's approach tiresome and ridiculous.

There is no shortage of Eton recollections, many of them focused on the unpleasant features of college life, snobbery, humiliations, beatings, class distinctions, and intimidation.[20] Carter seldom wrote about his Eton years, but when he did, the view was decidedly rose-tinted. In an article published in *The Texas Quarterly*, Carter recalled some of his early study habits. On a summer afternoon he would find a secluded spot on a small island in the Thames between Windsor and Eton and read portions of Aeschylus, Demosthenes, Cicero or Lucretius as assigned by his instructors. None of these gentlemen, Carter admitted, would have approved his supplementary reading, the love lyrics of the Roman poet Catullus. For Carter and his classmates, like Cyril Connolly and George Orwell, it was Catullus who articulated "the ideal of ourselves: sensitive, passionate, disillusioned, outspoken and disrespectful of persons; worldly wise yet vulnerable."[21] Carter's interest in Catullus led to his first venture into book collecting.

7. Eton College yard - c. 1911.

Before he left Eton he acquired a copy of Octavianus Scotus's folio edition, edited by Antonius Pathenius, printed in 1491, and Gryphius' Lyons edition of 1573. In the Gryphius he inscribed a self-congratulatory note, "Not in B.M. or Bodley."[22] The future bibliographer was already identifying rarities.

William Johnson Cory, an Eton master who died in 1892, became one of the most influential figures in Carter's life. By all accounts, Cory was an articulate reformer who liked to challenge the morals and ethics of both students and colleagues. What may have attracted Carter's interest in the first place, was the fact that Cory was his great, great uncle on his mother's side of the family. In an approach that was refreshingly novel for the time, Cory insisted that the purpose of education was to open the mind to possibilities rather than to tie it down with cumbersome facts.

In a gracefully written essay, he explained his theory:

> You go to school at the age of twelve or thirteen; and for the next four or five years you are not engaged so much in acquiring knowledge as in making mental efforts under criticism. A certain amount of knowledge you can indeed with average facility retain; nor need you regret the hours that you have spent on much that is forgotten, for the shadow of lost knowledge protects you from many illusions. But you go to a great school, not for knowledge so much as for arts and habits; for the habit of attention, for the art of expression, for the art of assuming at a moment's notice a new intellectual posture, for the art of entering quickly into another person's thoughts, for the habit of submitting to censure and refutation, for the art of indicating assent or dissent in graduated terms, for the habit of regarding minute points of accuracy, for the habit of working out what is possible in a given time, for taste, for discrimination, for mental courage and mental soberness. Above all, you go to school for self-knowledge.[23]

Cory's goals became Carter's own. First at Eton, then at King's College, Cambridge Carter pursued his education with a pronounced independence of thought and action. There were masters to be admired and masters to be scorned. One could become a members of the Eton Society and still maintain an amused disdain for the pomposity of fellow members. Cory's message - the importance of developing habits of self-discipline and self-knowledge - stayed with Carter throughout his career.

In 1949, in honor of "The striking originality of his mind, his strong and deep feeling, the range of his knowledge and interests, his faculty of luminous, pregnant - if sometimes perverse reflection and generalization," Carter compiled and annotated a hand-list of Cory's printed works.[24] As an imaginative and inspiring teacher and the author of *Ionica* (1858), "On the Education of the Reasoning Faculties" (1867) and "The Eton Boating Song" (1865), Cory was a figure to be cherished and admired. In an appropriate gesture of admiration, Carter gave his collection of Cory's published works to the Eton College Library.

At the beginning of the 1924 Michaelmas term, Carter moved to King's College, Cambridge. From the time of their founding in 1440, Eton and King's had been closely allied. Henry VI, following the practice established by William of Wykeham - who joined New College, Oxford to Winchester - made Eton a grammar school for King's. By a decree that held well into the nineteenth century, King's could only fill its vacancies from Eton. According to Ollard, the inbreeding had unfortunate results: "For the first four centuries of their lives, Eton and its sister foundation at Cambridge saw a great deal too much of each other and too little of anyone else."[25] Although things had changed considerably by the time Carter took up residence in Cambridge, there remained a strong bond between the two schools. The sentence, "He went from Eton to King's," can be found in the biographies of dozens of Old Etonians.

Carter entered Cambridge, as he had Eton, supported by scholarships and a long line of family tradition. Both of Carter's grandfathers and three of his uncles on his mother's side of the family had been Kingsmen. With athletics no longer a distraction (a leg injury suffered in his senior year at Eton ended any participation in field sports) Carter focused on his studies and when those grew burdensome, on the pleasures of the University community and town. This was the first time he had been away from home for any extended period, so there was much to see and do. At the time of Carter's enrollment, King's was one of the smaller colleges, with a population of some two hundred students and forty-five fellows, of which only about one-third were in residence. The University grew rapidly during the 1920s, but it was the policy of King's to remain small. According to L. P. Wilkinson, the college historian, "Its object was to retain the ideal of a community whose members knew one another."[26] During his three years at Cambridge, Carter shared spacious, ground-floor rooms in the venerable Gibbs' Building with Arthur R. D. "Ronnie"

Watkins, an Eton classical scholar who had entered King's the previous fall. From their tall windows, looking across the main courtyard, Carter and his friends could see the spires of King's Chapel. The two roommates owned a long-horn BMI gramophone, a gift from Carter's uncle, Christopher

8. *The Gibbs Building, Cambridge University. Carter shared ground floor rooms with Ronald Watkins from 1924-1927.*

Stone, and stacks of classical records including the Brahms piano quintet played by Harold Bauer and examples of the works of Mozart, Brahms and Schubert performed by the Flonzaley Quartet. On the paneled walls Medici Society prints and William Morris designs battled for space with shelves of books and journals. Papers covered every flat surface. Carter's growing collection of sixteenth and seventeenth century editions of Catullus commanded a place of its own in a glass-fronted case.[27]

"The atmosphere of Cambridge in the mid-twenties," Carter recalled, "was fatally congenial to anyone with a budding taste for book collecting."[28] One could visit Gustave David's bookshop in St. Edward's passage on Friday evening, or his stall in the market place on Saturdays, and perhaps find a Ben Jonson folio or a Gibbon quarto brought up earlier in the week from Sotheby's or Hodgson's. David was a Cambridge charac-

ter, wrapped in his long brown coat and smoking the stub of a cigarette, murmuring encourage-ment to the timid and smiling at favorite customers. When he retired, he was asked to choose between an annuity from the col-lege or a splendid dinner. He took the dinner but slept through it and broke down in tears when asked to reply to the speeches. After finishing up with David's, the next stop was likely to be Bowes & Bowes on Trinity Street, then on to Heffer's, Galloway & Porter or Deighton Bell. On these treks, Carter was often joined by fellow Kingsmen Donald Beves, William LeFanu,

9. Carter negotiating with a book dealer at Cambridge, outside the King's Library - c. 1925.

Alan Clutton-Brock and the budding editor and biblio-phile, John Hayward. During his first term, Carter would likely have attended the Sandars Lectures on "Printing for Book Production" given by the eminent typographer Emery Walker. In the fall of 1926, he could have heard A.K.J. Esdaile, Secretary of the British Museum, describe

19

"Sources of English Literature; A Guide for Students" and a few months later attended T. S. Eliot's lecture on "Metaphysical Poetry of the 17th Century with Special Attention to Donne, Crashaw and Cowley." In 1925, Sir Arthur Quiller-Couch presented a series of classes on Aristotle's *Poetics*. The Philological Society and the Cambridge Classical Society sponsored lectures on topics such as "Greek and Roman Numismatics," "Roman Literature," and "Greek and Roman Architecture." There were theatrical productions, pageants and musical programs to attend, and exhibitions of paintings and sculpture at the Fitzwilliam Museum. Literary commentary appeared in the *Cambridge Review,* and for those who enjoyed highly charged satire, there was King's own magazine, the *Basileon,* whose trademark caption, "If We Offend, It Is With Your Good Will," perfectly suggested its content. On the social side, there was the cinema featuring American performers like Buster Keaton, Harold Lloyd, Dorothy Gish, and Mary Pickford, and there were dances and parties, weekends in the country, and occasional trips to London. Out of this variety, Carter chose his activities with care - those to do with books and collecting usually found their way to the top of the list.

King's provided Carter with an ideal environment. In addition to the general interest in collecting and bibliography, promoted during the first two decades of the century by Stephen Gaselee, Arthur Cole, and John Maynard Keynes, founders of the Baskerville Club, there was an atmosphere at once more liberal, stylish, and permissive than that found in many of the other colleges. During the 1920s King's was the Cambridge center for those who identified themselves as members or followers of the Bloomsbury movement. Leaders of the group such as

Roger Fry, Lytton Strachey, and E.M. Forster were all Kingsmen. Partly because of that influence, literary and artistic tastes tended to be more extreme. There was less interest in reading Galsworthy and collecting wax flowers under glass domes than in reading Aldous Huxley and attending the Festival Theatre productions of plays by Ibsen, Strindberg, Yeats and Lady Gregory. *Ulysses* was in vogue as was D. H. Lawrence. Auden caused a sensation when he came to King's and read salacious passages from Christopher Isherwood's "Mortmere" saga. Carter enjoyed the general atmosphere of laissez faire. Shane Leslie's classic comment on the difference between Oxford and Cambridge went to the heart of the issue, "At Oxford they walked as though the streets belonged to them. At Cambridge they walked as though they didn't care to whom they belonged."[29]

During the 1925-1926 academic year Carter sharpened his knowledge of bibliography by offering to catalog the incunabula in the Jesus College library, a task he shared with Harry Richardson Creswick, a young library assistant, who, in 1949 became the Cambridge University Librarian. The project proved daunting and, as Carter later admitted, most discoveries he made had been anticipated fifty years earlier by the scholarly university librarian Henry Bradshaw. A trip to Italy with his godfather in 1925 proved more satisfying. C. H. Turner, an ecclesiastical scholar and Fellow of Magdalen College, Oxford, was an enthusiastic collector and ideal guide. He had visited Italy frequently and knew all the prominent book dealers and librarians. In Florence, the pair visited Olschki's book shop and, for the equivalent of thirty-eight shillings, Carter purchased the 1577 Patisson-Estienne edition of Catullus poetry with notes by

Scaliger. Other treasures followed, in what turned out to be a highly productive book hunting vacation. Turner continued to provide help over the next several years, giving advice on worthwhile purchases and sometimes sharing the cost of books that would have been beyond the young collector's reach.[30]

While Turner helped Carter understand the fine points of early printing, the poet and classical scholar A. E. Housman provided him with an equally useful gift, an appreciation for textual criticism. Following a career that began in the Government Patent Office and continued at University College, London, Housman came to Cambridge in the fall of 1911 as Kennedy Professor of Latin and Fellow of Trinity College. During the 1925-1926 academic year, Carter attended Housman's lectures on Catullus LXIV, a choice made more out of a sense of curiosity rather than part of any formal program. His first impressions of that "austere, precise, uncompromising, intellectually athletic "scholar" stayed with him for decades. "No one with ears in his head" Carter recalled in 1960, "could fail to learn, not merely about the work under dissection but about scholarly method in general."[31] In 1926, in preparation for his final examinations, Carter enrolled in Housman's course in textual criticism. Understanding the subject matter, according to the instructor, called for little more than common sense.

> Textual criticism is a science, and since it comprises recension and emendation, it is also an art. It is the science of discovering error in texts and the art of removing it... First then, it is not a sacred mystery. It is purely a matter of reason and of common sense. We exercise textual criticism whenever we notice and correct a misprint.[32]

Beyond the obvious challenges presented by textual criticism - rigor in examination of texts and scrupulous attention to detail - the study had at least one additional appeal as far as Carter was concerned: it was unabashedly elitist. No one put the case better than Housman himself:

> Textual criticism, like most other sciences, is an aristocratic affair, not communicable to all men, not to most men. Not to be a textual critic is no reproach to anyone, unless he pretends to be what he is not. To *be* a textual critic requires aptitude for thinking and willingness to think; and though it also requires other things, those things are supplements and cannot be substitutes. Knowledge is good, method is good, but one thing beyond all others is necessary; and that is to have a head, not a pumpkin, on your shoulders and brains, not pudding, in your head.[33]

The argument that textual criticism was not for everyone appealed to Carter at a very basic level.

Over a period of forty years Carter's enthusiasm for Housman never diminished. The books and journals that once filled a few shelves in his Cambridge rooms eventually found a place in the Lilly Library at Indiana University as the John Carter Collection of A. E. Housman. Along the way there were articles to write, books to edit, checklists to compile, and talks to give. It was the kind of unswerving loyalty that honored both the poet and the collector.

By the time Carter completed his Cambridge studies in 1927 he could count himself successful on several levels. On the academic side, he achieved an enviable double first in the classical tripos leading to an honors degree. From Turner he learned the joys of bibliophily and from Housman the importance of critical judgment. Socially, he developed a number of close friendships that would serve him well as his career progressed. What that career might be posed a question. As he considered life beyond Cambridge, several possibilities presented themselves - the diplomatic service, teaching, and the library profession. While he was still in his second term at Cambridge he questioned Arthur E. Cowley, the Bodley librarian, about a future in library work. Cowley discouraged him. "How much do you think you would be paid?" he asked, "Two hundred a year?" The amount sounded reasonable, and Carter said so. "Ah," said Cowley, "but what do you suppose you would be getting when you are forty, and irretrievably addicted to wine, women and song? I will tell you: four hundred. Go away, my dear boy, and think again."[34] Carter reconsidered. It would take more time to find his route to success.

CHAPTER TWO

Beginning with Scribner's

According to legend, which may or may not have any basis in fact, when Carter's friends at Cambridge asked him about his future plans, he answered, in a word, "Scribners." If that answer was meaningless to most of those who heard it, so much the better. A little mystery was always more entertaining than a flat factual explanation. Working in the London office of the American publisher and book-seller Charles Scribner's Sons may well have been an early goal, but the circumstances of Carter's achieving that goal followed a haphazard chain of events. During his last term at Cambridge, Carter talked with S.C. Roberts, the Secretary of the Cambridge University Press, about his interests in early printed books, the classics, and collecting. Shortly after that, Charles Kingsley, the Director of Scribner's London office, spoke to the journalist Frank Morley about the firm's need for an assistant who could handle the rare book side of the business. What happened next worked nicely to Carter's advantage. On a visit to the offices of the Cambridge University Press, Morley mentioned the Scribner's opening and Roberts remembered his recent conversation with the young classics scholar. In September 1927, having accepted Kingsley's offer of £200 a year, Carter started work at 168 Regent Street as an assistant in the retail department,

10. *Carter in his Scribner's office in Bedford Square. The painting on the mantelpiece is by his friend Paul Nash - c. 1928.*

with the responsibility for acquiring rare books for the New York store. With a lapse of four years for wartime service, he served the firm until 1953, when the London office closed.

The Scribner's name was well established in London long before Carter joined the firm. Charles Welford, working in partnership with Charles Scribner, began to import books from England in the late 1850s. The business was so successful that Welford established a permanent London office in 1879 for purchasing and export. After Welford died in 1885, his assistant, Lemuel W. Bangs, a bon vivant known as "Bangsy" to his American friends and "The Senator" to the British, took over the management of the office. With a style all his own, Bangs liked to drive up to a bookstore in a cab and wait for one of the staff to bring out rarities for his consideration. He dressed in Saville Row frock coats and had a table permanently reserved in his name at the Garrick Club, where his favorite champagne, chilled to exact specifications, was always on hand. When Bangs retired in 1919, due to ill health, Charles Kingsley, a Yale graduate who had worked for Scribner's in New York, took over as director. Kingsley had lived in England for a time and was, by his own account, familiar with English customs and ways of thought. A less colorful figure than his predecessor,

Kingsley managed the London office with a quiet authority from 1920 to 1940. When Carter started work, the
staff consisted of Kingsley, an office manager, a traveling
representative, an accountant, two secretaries and,
depending on the flow of business, two or three shipping
clerks. The chief business of the office was to export
English books for sale in the United States, import
American books for sale in England, publish selective
works independently and purchase rare books for resale
in New York. These functions were carried out through
the firm's three departments, wholesale export, retail (rare
books) and publishing.[1]

For an ambitious young man eager to learn more about
the inner workings of the antiquarian booktrade, London,
during the decade of the twenties, furnished an ideal classroom. There were shops to visit, collectors and dealers to
meet, auctions to attend and catalogs to examine. A galaxy
of prominent bookshops dotted the central city - Foyle's
on Charing Cross Road, Percy Dobell on Bruton Street, E.
P. Goldschmidt on Old Bond Street, Bernard Quaritch on
Grafton Street, Pickering & Chatto on King Street, Francis
Edwards on Marylebone High Street, H. M. Fletcher at
Cecil Court, Elkin Mathews and Maggs Brothers on
Conduit Street, and Birrell & Garnett in Soho, to touch on
only a few. The auction houses, Sotheby's and Hodgson's,
attracted buyers and sellers from the continent and the
United States. It was one of Carter's tasks to become familiar with the city's rare book distribution system - if the
word "system" can be applied to anything as diverse as the
daily give and take of the secondhand book market. It was
through men like A. W. Evans, Percy Muir, Graham
Pollard, E. P. Goldschmidt and Percy Dobell that he
learned the fine points of the trade.

Elkin Mathews' bookshop on 33 Conduit Street was perhaps Carter's favorite stopping place. The senior partner, A. W. Evans, along with his colleagues Robert and Edward "Eddie" Gathorne-Hardy, Greville Worthington and, starting in January 1930, Percy Muir, supplied a lively mix of bibliographical expertise and shrewd salesmanship.[2] It was a place where one could meet friends, catch up on the gossip (Carter loved gossip) and, in the late afternoon, enjoy a glass of dry sherry. During his early years with Scribner's Carter bought more books from Elkin Mathews than from any other shop in the city. Looking back on the relationship, Muir wrote, "Scribner's always (has) first refusal of anything which I think might be in their line. I have regarded them for a long time as our No.1 customer."[3] Carter replied, "I am glad to think our operations . . . have been as satisfactory to you as they have been to us. As far as I am concerned, the closer our connection the better."[4]

Another regular stop on Carter's London tour was Birrell & Garnett's bookshop at 30 Gerrard Street in Soho. The senior partners, the dramatist and critic Francis Birrell and the novelist David 'Bunny' Garnett, both had links to the Bloomsbury group. For a brief time in the early nineteen twenties, Francis Meynell leased working space in the shop's basement for his Nonesuch Press.[5] Between 1924 and 1938, when it closed, the shop was managed by two knowledgeable bibliographers, Jane Norton and Graham Pollard. When Pollard came down from Oxford in 1925, he was already known as an enthusiastic collector with interests in typography, early writing books, binding, newspaper history and the history of the English booktrade. Carter found Pollard stimulating and shrewd, an uncompromising man with careful, sometimes painfully methodical work habits. Pollard was one of many dealers who supplied stock for Scribner's New York rare book department, a market he viewed with a certain amount of cynicism. In reply to one of Carter's requests he wrote "You asked me for some new ideas. I am afraid I only have one suggestion, a 1st edition of Descartes's *Discours de la Methode* 1637 contemporary vellum. I want 45£ which is not, I think, dear although cogito ergo sum is an obvious lie about most of your American customers. I believe the idea is sufficiently well known to interest them."[6]

In addition to the book shops where bibliophiles and dealers met as a matter of course, there were several private clubs that encouraged collecting. The First Edition Club, founded in 1921 by the colorful A.J.A. Symons, issued the *Book Collector's Quarterly* from 1930-1932, provided rooms for dinners and meetings, arranged exhibitions, published a number of handsome limited editions, and sponsored a "Fifty Books of the Year" competition. Carter and Muir wrote articles for the *Book Collector's Quarterly*, but as bookdealers were not admitted to membership. The Double Crown Club, established in 1924 by Oliver Simon, Hubert Foss and Holbrook Jackson, had no such scruples and, on a selective basis, accepted bibliophiles, typographers, designers, bookdealers and publishers with an interest in the graphic arts. The list of those asked to speak at the club's dinners during its early years included Eric Gill, Stanley Morison, Holbrook Jackson, Michael Sadleir, Emery Walker and A. W. Pollard. Carter was elected to membership in 1932, became Secretary the following year and in that office, according to James Moran, "was to prove the Club's most valuable historiographer," writing "lucid, astringently witty and sometimes irreverent reports of Club meetings."[7]

The Bibliographical Society, founded in 1892, supplied a base for those who preferred the historical approach, while the Roxburghe Club, where no mere bookseller could aspire to membership, furnished an enclave for wealthy collectors. The National Book Council, founded in 1924, was the antithesis of the Roxburghe Club and invited membership from all levels of the book community. The Council, renamed the National Book League in 1944, had as its worthy if somewhat amorphous goal, the promotion of books and reading

Books on book collecting and bibliography found a favored place on the lists of a number of London publishers during the late 1920s and early 1930s. Under the direction of Michael Sadleir, Constable's launched its distinguished Bibliographia Series, and at Cassell's, Desmond Flower began to publish handsomely printed limited editions. Book dealers had abundant stocks of quality rare books, and collectors had money to spend. With the crisis brought on by the New York stock market crash still two years away, Carter could hardly have chosen a better time to enter the booktrade.

By his own admission, Carter knew little about the rare book business when he joined Scribner's and, in fact, had no work experience whatever. In mid-September Kingsley wrote to Charles Scribner II in New York, "Carter has been here for two weeks and I think will work into a satisfactory assistant."[8] Three months later, however, Kingsley's report was less favorable:

> I find it not so easy to form an intelligent estimate of Carter. He is of course well educated and intelligent, but so far he has not shown much initiative, or to put it differently, I have to watch him more closely than should be necessary to feel certain that things are being attended to.

> This is not due to any lack of effort on his part but I think
> largely to Eton and Kings training. I am going to explode
> one of these days and think that may have some effect.[9]

It is easy to understand how Carter's first few months on the
job might have produced Kingsley's negative evaluation. If
adjusting to a daily work routine was difficult for Carter,
adjusting to his new assistant - a young, untrained, somewhat
dandified university graduate - must have been a daunting
challenge for Kingsley. With or without Kingsley's promised
explosion the two soon reached an accommodation. In early
March, Kingsley involved Carter in the forthcoming visit of
John C. Champion, the head of the firm's rare book department in New York, who would be coming to London on a
buying trip. Kingsley wrote to Scribner, "We are looking
forward to Champion's arrival. Carter will devote his entire
time to helping him." From the same letter, it is clear that
Carter was learning from the ground up. "A fine sale at
Sotheby's" Kingsley reported, "Mr. Carter will be in attendance at the sale in order to mark down prices paid and the
buyers."[10] By April the atmosphere had improved to the
point where Kingsley was willing to offer a few carefully
chosen words of praise - "Carter, who seems to be catching
on to things better as the weeks pass, has been around with
him [Champion] and I think they will find each other of
mutual assistance."[11] A year and a half later Kingsley admitted that the Champion visit had not been a complete success.
As he explained to Scribner, "On the first trip Champion
was a bit 'up-stage' and avoided having Carter with him
whenever possible. I think it was prejudice on account of
Carter's Oxford accent."[12]

Since much of Carter's work required a first-hand
knowledge of the American market, Scribner made
arrangements for him to come to New York during the

early months of 1929 for a three month training period. There was much to learn. How was the New York office organized and who ran the various departments? Who were the important private collectors and what were their specialties? How could the London office meet the needs of American librarians? How did the American antiquarian trade work? Which dealers could be trusted? Where did collectors, librarians and dealers meet for business and pleasure? The New York office arranged for Carter's living costs - $12.00 a week for modest accommodations at the Allerton House, and $25.00 more for expenses. Tall, thin and fastidiously dressed, Carter not only looked good but with his Eton and Cambridge pedigree carried impeccable credentials. To his American employers he projected an engaging attitude, deferential, informed, and attentive. A few days after his arrival Scribner wrote back to the London office, "Carter . . . has made a very good impression on everyone here. He seems like a very attractive fellow and interested in his work."[13] As he became familiar with New York, Carter could hardly have imagined that over the next four decades he would spend twelve years in the States - a quarter of his adult life. For the moment the city struck him as rowdy, busy and dirty but, as he reported to his friend Graham Pollard, "I enjoy this perfectly bloody town hugely."[14]

Carter's arrival in New York in early January 1929 coincided with the auction of Jerome Kern's library, one of the finest private collections ever assembled in America. Kern, who had made a fortune as a composer of the popular musical comedies *Show Boat*, *Roberta* and *Swing Time* started to collect books and manuscripts as a hobby shortly before World War I. He concentrated on the so-called high-spots of English literature - special editions of books by recognized authors - particularly those from the eighteenth and nineteenth centuries. His shelves held long runs of Lord Byron, Charles Dickens, Oliver Goldsmith, Thomas Hardy, Samuel Johnson, Rudyard Kipling, Alexander Pope, Percy Bysshe Shelley, Robert Louis Stevenson, and William Makepeace Thackeray. A particular feature of the Kern collection was the large number of presentation copies, letters, diaries, and manuscripts. The pre-auction exhibition set up by the Anderson Galleries the first week of January 1929 struck some as a gaudy display while others found it a trove of mouth-watering opportunities. The president of the Anderson Galleries, the ubiquitous Mitchell Kennerley, saw the Kern sale as an opportunity to gain both fame and fortune. This was Kennerley's final year at the Anderson and he was determined to go out with a bang. Would there ever again appear on the market such treasures as Lord Byron's manuscript of Cantos XIV and XV of *Don Juan,* a perfect 'Pickwick' in parts, or Shelley's own copy of *Queen Mab*? Kennerley thought not and decided to back his opinion with a vast advertising campaign and an elaborate two-volume sales catalog.

Kern built his collection working with some of the most important antiquarian dealers in the world, men such as A.S.W. Rosenbach, Gabriel Wells, Charles Sessler, E. Byrne Hackett, and Bernard Quaritch. These experts and their colleagues took part in the auction for two reasons - to see if the prices they charged Kern would hold up and to look for bargains. It pleased the dealers to see Kern's purchase prices double and triple. No one found any bargains. During the sale's ten sessions, which netted $1,729,462 or an astounding $1,167 per lot, Carter witnessed one of the most remarkable events of American book auction history. Elizabeth Barrett Browning's *Battle of Marathon*, that Kern had purchased for $1,650, brought $17,500 from Rosenbach. The *Pickwick Papers* in parts, that cost Kern $800 at the John Quinn sale in 1923, went to Alwin J. Scheuer for $28,000. Gabriel Wells made headlines on Wednesday, January 23, when he took Shelley's *Queen Mab* for $68,000, an increase of $62,000 over the price Kern had paid in the Buxton Forman sale of 1920. Collectors who submitted modest bids through regular channels had no chance at all. Mrs. J. I. Insley Blair of Tuxedo Park, New York, one of Scribner's valued customers, asked Champion to help her decide on bid levels. Champion replied, "In order to get item *72 Jane Eyre*, (London, 1847) you will probably have to go as high as $500."[15] Blair bid $420 only to see the book go to Scheuer for $3,600. Concerning item 588, Oliver Goldsmith's *She Stoops to Conquer* (1773), Champion commented "This is excessively rare in original wrappers, and for this reason they value it at from $2000 to $2500. It hardly seems possible that this will bring that figure."[16] Champion's analysis again proved faulty as the volume went for $8,000. Extravagant prices continued to control the second part of the sale. On Tuesday evening January 21, Champion entered Blair's bid of $2,200 for item 749, Keats' *Poems* (1817), handsomely bound in a crushed levant morocco solander case, but Barnet J. Beyer, one of the most active bidders, took it for $3,500. This initial exposure to the American book auction scene must have left Carter as astounded as it did seasoned New Yorkers. He remembered the sale as "the most widely publicised, the most theatrical, and the most resoundingly successful ever held, before or since."[17]

While the Kern sale was one of the high points of Carter's visit, the real purpose was to get acquainted with the procedures in the New York office and meet the people who ran it. At the top of the hierarchy were Charles Scribner II, son of the founder and Chairman of the Board, his brother Arthur H. Scribner, who had been elected President of the firm in September 1928, and Charles "Charlie" Scribner III, the firm's vice president. All three men supported the London office and were enthusiastic about plans for its expansion. George McKay Schieffelin, a grandson of Charles Scribner II and the firm's assistant treasurer, introduced Carter to the budget process while Maxwell E. Perkins and John Hall Wheelock, the firm's legendary editors, made themselves available for advice on literary acquisitions.

As manager of the New York rare book department, it was Champion's responsibility to introduce Carter to some of the prominent city bookdealers and collectors. E. Byrne Hackett's Brick Row Bookshop on East Forty-seventh Street was a good starting place, since it offered an outstanding array of fine bindings, first editions, press books, and association copies. The shop attracted the elite of New York collectors, among them Morris Parrish, a specialist in nineteenth century fiction, Carroll A. Wilson, an Alcott, Emerson, Hawthorne, and Holmes collector, H. Bacon Collamore, noted for his A. E. Housman books and manuscripts and Wilmarth S."Lefty" Lewis, the resolute Horace Walpole collector. Carter struck up immediate friendships with Hackett's knowledgeable young assistants, Michael Papantonio and David A. Randall, both, over the next few years, to become prominent members of the New York antiquarian trade; Papantonio in partnership with John S. Van Eisen Kohn at the Seven Gables Bookshop, and Randall, after 1935, as chief of Scribner's rare book department in New York.

Just around the corner from the Brick Row, on Forty-sixth Street and Park Avenue, Max Harzof ran G. A. Baker & Company. Randall, who worked for Harzof after he left Brick Row, described him as a "great bear of a man, about 275 pounds, irreverent, profane in speech, sloppy in dress . . . and withal the finest all-around book-man I have been privileged to know."[18] Harzof may have lacked Hackett's urbane manners but he had no trouble attracting collectors - among them Chauncey Brewster Tinker, Yale's Keeper of Rare Books, Josiah K. Lilly, president of one of the country's largest pharmaceutical firms, and William A. Jackson, soon to be appointed adviser and bibliographer for the distinguished New York collector Carl H. Pforzheimer. These connections would serve Carter well for several decades.

Bookshops like the Brick Row and G. A. Baker & Company catered to the uptown carriage trade but there was another side of the New York book business. During the twenty-year period between the two world wars, collectors of all stripes were drawn downtown to lower Fourth Avenue, an area known as Booksellers' Row. This was the hub of the city's used booktrade, with shops lining the street between Eight and Fourteenth Streets. Run-of-the-mill, secondhand, out-of-print books predominated, but rarities could be found. Carter visited and enjoyed this wildly eclectic array. The legend most frequently repeated on Booksellers' Row was about a browser who paid fifty cents for a tattered pamphlet that turned out to be the *Bay Psalm Book* (1640), the first book printed in British America. The final selling price increased directly in proportion to the rhetorical ability of the storyteller and the gullibility of the audience. The irascible Peter Stammer, one of the first dealers to settle in the area, was said to have torn the covers off a book in front of a customer rather than admit it was under-priced. Samuel Dauber and Nathan Pine, perhaps the best known of the Fourth Avenue dealers, sold old and new books from a stock running between 200,000 to 250,000 volumes. Few of the Fourth Avenue shops published catalogs, but D & P, as it was known, was an exception. When the partners issued Catalogue One Hundred, they asked some of their distinguished customers for comments. Carl Van Doren wrote, "I am a one bookshop man. Dauber and Pine are my one bookshop."[19] Louis Untermeyer, the poet and anthologist, agreed saying, "Your shop has given browsing a definiteness, even a dignity!"[20]

In the 1920s and 1930s, when collectors or dealers wanted to locate a hard to find title they often turned to book scouts, unsung heroes with no permanent business location, who worked the streets hunting for bargains they could resell for a small profit. Among these itinerants, I. R. "Ike" Brussel stood out, a shrewd book hunter from Brooklyn who liked to sign himself "L.O.G.S." - the "Last of the Great Scouts." Brussel had no time for decorum in either dress or language, but he knew where to find important books. It was a skill that kept money in his pocket through the Depression when many of the uptown dealers were forced out of business. In the middle 1930s Brussel produced two well-received bibliographies, *Anglo-American First Editions East to West, 1826-1900* (1935) and *Anglo-American Editions West to East 1786-1900* (1936). When Brussel died in 1972, Carter wrote a warm tribute in the *Book Collector*. Brussel's skill in locating rarities, Carter claimed, was due to "his capacious memory, his lively imagination, his infinite pertinacity and his wide acquaintance in the trade both in his

own country and our own."[21] In spite of his rich
Brooklyn accent and baggy clothes, he was one of the few
Americans welcomed by such diverse literary figures as
Michael Sadleir and A. E. Housman.

During his three-months stay in New York, Carter was
particularly taken with what he called American clubbability. This, in spite of the federal prohibition law that prevented the sale of alcoholic beverages. Exhibitions and parties at the Grolier Club, the Pierpont Morgan Library, and
the New York Public Library brought together collectors,
printers, dealers and librarians in a way that was almost
entirely unknown in England. Among American book dealers and collectors Carter noticed an "insatiable propensity
to gossip" that promoted "a diffusion of news and information throughout the bibliophile community."[22] When A.S.
W. Rosenbach bought Robert Burns' *Poems* (1793) at the
Kern sale for $23,500, many of those present knew the
intended customer was the Philadelphia collector John
Gribbel. All of this contrasted sharply with the top-secret
attitude common in the British Isles. It was not unusual,
Carter claimed, for English dealers to display a "traditional
if not temperamental reluctance ever to tell you where such
and such an item went to, often extended to transactions
with customers thirty or forty years dead."[23]

The exchange of news and information that appealed to
Carter had, beneath the surface, certain limitations. The
majority of dealers, librarians, and collectors could not
claim membership in the Grolier Club, or expect to receive
invitations to the Pierpont Morgan Library exhibitions. In
order to find out when Hackett planned to open his next
branch or what Kennerley expected to do after the
Anderson Galleries closed, one needed to read the
American Book Collector or, more likely, *Publishers' Weekly*.

During its early years, the *American Book Collector* maintained a definite style - opinionated, informative and colloquial; a reflection of its crusading founder, Charles F. Heartman. A typical issue of the monthly consisted of a series of short articles, and a report of auction sales. In his column, "Remarks Called For and Otherwise," Heartman attacked practices that displeased him, often identifying dealers and collectors by name. Through the Depression he preached optimism and, in florid editorials, trumpeted a pride of collecting:

> Every collector, every great bibliophile is conscious of the fact that the pursuit of his great quest is also involving him in the responsibilities of a custodian and a trustee of the great treasures of the world which he must not only preserve for future generations to which he must add is his self-imposed duty and a glorious privilege, the fulfillment of which carries a dignification leading to everlasting canonization.[24]

While the *American Book Collector* served as a pulpit for its editor, *Publishers' Weekly* allowed its readers to choose from a diversity of opinions and news. Frederick G. Melcher, who became editor in 1918, surrounded himself with a group of experienced columnists and reporters. During the 1920s and 1930s, Frederick M. Hopkins wrote a lively column called "Old and Rare Books," John T. Winterich supplied articles on collecting and book values, Hellmut Lehmann-Haupt wrote about early European book illustration, and Walter Blumenthal described technical advances in binding and printing. Subscribers found *Publishers' Weekly* to be an accurate and readable source of information on graphics, printing, illustration, binding, children's books, and library services. A regular feature in the back pages allowed dealers to list books wanted and books for sale - a service that in 1950 became a separate publication, *AB Bookman's Weekly*. As a trade journal, *Publishers' Weekly* was an unrivaled success. Carter became a regular reader and was delighted when Melcher, whom he met socially, asked him to submit an article for publication. This was the beginning of a satisfying professional association that lasted over twenty years and resulted in the dozens of articles, notes and reviews.[25]

In the midst of this New World euphoria, Carter became aware of several disquieting trends. Although the problems were not confined to New York, the concentration of dealers and collectors in that city seemed to give them a particular force. In the late 1920s a few dealer-speculators, notable among them Barnet J. Beyer and Alwin J. Scheuer, promoted certain authors and classes of books as investments. It wasn't enough for a book to have a remarkable text, or literary acclaim, it had to have strong portfolio quality. In this misguided approach, advanced by dealers and accepted as gospel by many collectors, it was thought a certainty that if John Galsworthy's *The Man of Property* (1906) sold for $100 last year, it would bring $200 or more next year. Dealers encouraged customers to buy now because, as they advised, the book would never again be available at such a reasonable price. This approach duplicated Wall Street marketing where optimism overruled good judgment and, as with many of the Wall Street ventures, came to a sudden halt as the New York stock market collapsed on Black Tuesday, October 29, 1929.

Another distortion in the book trade, as Carter saw it, came from zealots known as point-maniacs and condition-purists. These collectors, and the dealers who supported them, turned bibliographic niceties into a game of one-upmanship. If collector "A" found a misprint on page six in the first edition of Conan Doyle's *The Sign of the Four* (1890) collector "B" found two misprints on page twenty-seven and a dropped letter on page fifty, proving that his copy was a true first state of the first printing of the first edition. The matter of condition was equally contentious and again seemed to balance more on an accumulation of minutiae than on common sense. Always an important element in the evaluation of rare books, original condition, as defined by collectors in the late twenties, became a meaningless fetish. It was not only unrealistic but silly, for example, for collectors to demand original binding states - plain paper wrappers or paper-covered boards - in eighteenth and early nineteenth century books, when those forms were originally intended as a temporary protection for the text until it could be passed along to a bookbinder. The purist would be satisfied with nothing less than Sir Walter Scott's *Waverley* (1814) in original boards, with edges untrimmed and uncut, with all the half-titles. As for Scott's *Rokeby: a Poem* (1813), that would only be acceptable if it came in the original boards and included the final eight extra leaves of advertising. Carter spoke out against these affectations in his first published article, "Original Condition." This "Appeal to Reason," as it was subtitled, ended with a rhetorical flourish - "Let us by all means bow down before the really brilliant copy in original condition, and price it up accordingly, but let us not despise the sound rebound copy nor the man who buys it."[26] Why not, he argued, show the beginning collector a reasonably good copy of Anthony Trollope's *He Knew He Was Right* and suggest he wait for some future date to purchase the 1869 issue with the original pictorial wrappers? It followed that part of the dealer's responsibility should be to anticipate the collector's needs and try to meet them at a reasonable price. In ringing tones Carter proclaimed, "It is no good sitting still until a customer comes in and asks for something, or selling him something obvious because everyone else is selling it: we must go out into the highways and byways and compel them to come in, and once they are in, we must treat them as intelligent human beings."[27]

Carter also observed an unfortunate tendency for collectors to copy the latest fashion rather than follow their own tastes. Since Jerome Kern collected Dickens, Goldsmith, Hardy, and Samuel Johnson, many beginning collectors simply followed that lead. This narrowing of focus produced an unhealthy situation wherein large numbers of collectors all wanted the same books. Dealers were only too happy to supply that *need* at ever-increasing prices. Carter had a solution, "If only people would follow their own taste" he mused, "or, if they have none but must collect, try to find some untrodden path in the huge prairie which is literature, they would find that there are quite enough books to go around."[28] He promoted the same idea in 1934 in *New Paths in Book Collecting,* a collection of essays written by several of his friends, to demonstrate the possibilities in a number of overlooked collecting fields such as detective fiction, musical first editions, war books, serial fiction, and yellow-backs.

Carter was pleased that he had been able to carry out the main objectives of his New York trip. In the four months he was there, he had had a chance to observe the workings of the home office and meet the people in charge. In and about the city he had gotten acquainted with a number of influential dealers, collectors, curators, librarians and publishers - a circle of professionals that would prove useful in the future. He had made no attempt to meet A.S.W. Rosenbach or Gabriel Wells, the aristocrats of the New York antiquarian trade, but focused instead on younger men like Randall and Papantonio. Although some New Yorkers may have been put off by Carter's youth, and his somewhat patrician public school bearing, others were impressed by his inquiring mind, his knowledge of books and printing, his quick wit, and his stylish manners. Among those most impressed were Charles Scribner II and his brother Arthur. Before he sailed, Carter talked with Arthur Scribner about a raise saying it would help him meet increased living costs in London. In a letter to Kingsley, Charles Scribner III approved the raise, saying, "My father and uncle both think very highly of him and rather than have him dissatisfied, they would be prepared to give him as much as four hundred pounds a year."[29] After mentioning the needs of other staff members, several of whom had families and had worked longer than Carter, Kingsley agreed, admitting, presciently, "He has of course much larger possibilities than anyone else here."[30]

In addition to adjusting his salary, the Scribner brothers decided to give Carter more independence of operation. In January Arthur Scribner wrote to Kingsley, "I have had a talk with Champion and it has been decided that he will not go to London this winter, and we shall have to rely on Carter's purchases. I believe in giving him a free hand, for he should by this time have an accurate knowledge of the value of the various items and you and he are both well informed as to our present stock. He may, of course, make mistakes, but we all do that and the main thing is to concentrate largely upon the purchase of individual items and avoid sets, this being of course a general statement."[31] Kingsley was happy to give his new assistant a free hand. In September he wrote "Carter has caught on splendidly since his return, he is liked throughout the trade and people begin to speak respectfully of him as a bibliophile. If he sticks to it he will in a few years be recognized as one of the real experts and I am anxious that he find time to do some writing on the subject. . . . I am trying to work him in a bit on the publishing end, but he finds his time pretty well filled with scouting around for Champion. One thing I want him to do when he returns from vacation is to take charge of the typographical arrangement of newspaper advertisement, prospectuses etc."[32] Three months later, Kingsley followed up with more praise, "I look to him to become in a few years time one of the leading lights in the rare book world. I am trying to keep him in general touch with the business at large but his time is pretty fully occupied with the rare books. His trip to America was an invaluable experience and I would suggest that it be repeated every three or four years."[33]

Kingsley's plan to keep Carter informed on matters pertaining to the business at large was a clear indication that the apprenticeship was over. Any doubts on that question were settled during the summer and early fall of 1931, when Carter took full charge of the London office during Kingsley's four month stay in New York. Through June and July, Carter handled a series of sensitive negotiations concerning Winston Churchill's *Marlborough*. Several publishing houses were competing for the manuscript, and offers and counter offers flew between London and New York. In a detailed three-page letter, Carter outlined the situation for Scribner, including the names of the chief participants and their relative strengths and weaknesses.

Scribner replied gratefully, "You did a great deal towards clearing up the Churchill situation. Many thanks for the thorough way in which you handled the matter."[34]

Between the winter of 1929, when Carter first visited New York, and the summer of 1932, the Scribner hierarchy changed drastically. When Charles Scribner II died in 1930, his brother Arthur assumed the presidency, and on his death two years later, Charles Scribner III, who had managed the day to day business of the firm, became President. He was a resourceful manager and an avid reader, with a taste for quality printing and design. As a collector and a member of the Grolier Club, he appreciated the importance of rare books, and the place of that department in the company structure. Scribner respected Carter's abilities because of several complicated negotiations carried out successfully between London and New York while Kingsley was on vacation. As a consequence, when costly rarities were considered or personnel problems weighed, Carter's opinions received close attention from the New York office. This productive relationship lasted until Scribner's death in 1952.

Carter's stock increased on all fronts. He was not averse to using a formidable family connection when it suited his purposes. " I was talking to Compton Mackenzie the other evening," he wrote Scribner, "and he mentioned casually that he had always felt he would like to publish with us. I didn't show too marked an interest, because I don't know how much we want him, if at all."[35] Scribner was dubious, but at the end of the letter added a few words of encouragement "We are all very keen, however, to accede to any suggestions from you and if we do not accept them all with enthusiasm, please don't be discouraged."[36] Carter was not discouraged, and continued to provide suggestions from family and friends. In the summer of 1930, Kingsley reported, "Carter, on a recent weekend visit to some literary friends in the country, ran across some information about an unpublished manuscript of John Donne. . . . I asked Carter to make a memorandum of the facts in the case, and I enclose it herewith."[37] Scribner's reply was negative, but again softened with concern for Carter's feelings, "We might take 250 of a limited edition made in England but, at the risk of disappointing Carter, I had just as soon let the matter slide, letting the Oxford Press publish it in both countries."[38]

Much of Scribner's concern about taking on new projects was based on his reading of the firm's balance sheets. Business was down in all areas. When the market crashed in October 1929, it took almost everybody by surprise and caused immediate after-shocks in England and Europe. British exports fell from £839 million in 1929 to £461 in 1931, while unemployment, a serious problem even before the market crisis, rose from 1,520,000 in January 1930 to 2,500,000 by the end of the year. The new Labour government under Ramsay MacDonald established various councils and commissions to examine the issues, but nothing seemed to help. The steady flow of buying and selling that had been the antiquarian book trade dried to a trickle. Dealers who had invested heavily in high priced rarities watched glumly as they gathered dust on their shelves. There was nothing to do but reduce prices, lay off staff, and offer long term payment plans. Collectors seldom responded, but when they did, it was almost in one voice, "Sorry, out of the market." Even though Carter reported available bargains, augmenting stock seemed foolish. By February 1932, the steady decline in sterling prompted Scribner to propose a variety of options; among them, closing the London office. As a compromise he ordered retail and wholesale departments on both sides of the Atlantic to make drastic cuts in personnel.

Two years before the market crash, with business advancing at an encouraging rate, Kingsley and the Scribner brothers had discussed moving the firm out of its cramped location on Regent Street into larger and more harmonious quarters. By April 1929, when Carter returned from his first trip to New York, a suitable location had been found. The property at 23 Bedford Square seemed ideal. It was two blocks from the British Museum, close to the offices of a number of other publishing houses, and only a few doors from the First Edition Club. Number 23 was a handsome three-story building designed in the neo-classical tradition by Robert Adam, a leading eighteenth century architect. The interior was graced with the hallmarks of Adam's lavish style - carved mantels, painted medallions, elaborate fireplaces, and decorated ceilings. The property faced the north side of the square with space for shipping and stock rooms in the rear on Gower Mews. Kingsley reported that the firm's business could easily be done in the main floor offices, reception area, and stock room, allowing him to rent the upper floors for a substantial gain. It was also his wish to make the new building more of a "book center," with amenities that would attract collectors and dealers. Although that objective was never completely realized, the move to Bedford Square, completed in September 1930, was a success, and provided the London office with a dignified and attractive new home.

While the other members of the firm settled into the new location, Carter made his presence known in the city's bookshops and auction rooms. With encouragement from Scribner and Kingsley, he continued to buy, but at a much reduced level. In February 1932, at Scribner's request, he returned to New York to work with Champion on the inventory and help prepare the fall and winter rare book catalogs. This was an area where Carter had definite ideas for change. During the 1920's, Scribner's, and most of the other rare book firms in London and New York, issued workmanlike but unimaginative lists of books under such bland headings as "American History," "English Literature," and "First Editions Old and New." The catalogs had a cluttered, mechanical look with drab covers, poorly-chosen type faces and overcrowded pages. If notes appeared at all, they seldom went beyond vague descriptions such as "rare," "first edition," "a fine set in original condition" or "presentation copy." It was a lazy way to sell books.

Carter's goal was to reverse these trends and produce catalogs that would stimulate interest in what he liked to call 'new paths' in book collecting. Scribner's Catalog 92, *First Editions of Famous Adventure Stories 1831-1922* (1932) was a good example. It featured books by popular, but hitherto uncollected authors such as Sax Rohmer and Mayne Reid. This was followed by Catalog 94, *Classics of Discovery & Exploration 1773-1933* (1933), and Carter's particular favorite, Catalog 98, *Detective Fiction: A Collection of First and a Few Early Editions* (1934). These efforts were not uniformly successful but they broke with tradition and established Scribner's as a firm willing to go beyond Dickens, Milton and Shakespeare.

The story behind the development of Catalog 98 illustrated Carter's growing skills as a bibliographer and bookdealer. He had started collecting detective fiction as a hobby shortly after joining Scribner's in 1927. Aside from the pure entertainment value of the thrill-packed plots, detective fiction, at that time, was affordable and easy to find. In addition, there was no conflict of interest with Scribner's regular customers. "What I needed." Carter explained, "was something not merely that no one was collecting but that no one seemed likely to consider collecting."[39] From basements and bargain stalls he gathered books not only by such established authors like Edgar Allan Poe, Wilkie Collins and Conan Doyle, but by popular nineteenth century favorites such as Anna Katherine Green, Fergus W. Hume, and William Russell. To capture the spirit of these authors, Carter liked to quote a line from Russell's best known work, *Recollections of a Detective Police Officer* (1856). The hero confronted the villain with steely resolve, "The game is up, my good Mr. Gates, I arrest you for felony."

When other collectors began to show an interest in detective fiction, attracted by the essays of Vincent Starrett and Dorothy L. Sayers, Carter decided to move on. When he offered his collection, now over 350 volumes, to the New York office, Champion agreed to take the books, which he considered trash, but on the condition that Carter oversee the catalog's production and write the notes. This was exactly what Carter had in mind. He found a young graphic artist in the office and encouraged him to come up with something new. The result, an arresting cover design showing a shadowy street dominated by an ominous dark building, set the right tone. In the introduction Carter defended his choice of titles saying "The collector who is interested in a subject, particularly an uncharted subject, will appreciate the mere presence of uncommon but significant titles, at modest prices, for the coherence which they give to the survey of

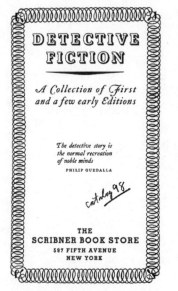

11. *Scribner's catalog 98 (1934). This catalog contained Carter's own collection of detective fiction and featured such little known authors as Fergus Hume, Anna Katherine Green, and William Russell. An American collector bought the collection en bloc. Years later, it came on the market again and David Randall purchased it for the Lilly Library of Indiana University.*

a literary form; he will see certain books which a sound judgment tells him he must have, even if their condition leaves something to be desired."[40] With extended notes on almost every item, and elaborate indexes, including one of detectives names, the catalog was expensive to produce but, as Carter explained, "it was intended as a demonstration piece."[41]

In one embarrassing incident Carter's enthusiasm for producing catalog copy got out of hand. In 1932, as a favor to Muir, he wrote and signed introductions to two Elkin Mathews English literature catalogs. Scribner was not pleased. As he pointed out to Kingsley, advertising a competitor's rare book stock was hardly part of Carter's job description. Kingsley responded, "I was myself considerably annoyed at the Elkin Mathews affair and expressed myself somewhat forcibly. . . . It was pure inadvertence on his part and now he understands quite clearly that nothing of the kind must occur again."[42] Scribner's next letter to Kingsley passed over the Elkin Mathews matter as unimportant, and only asked about the progress of Carter's book on collecting.

Catalog production moved into an even more ambitious phase after March 1935, when David A. Randall, on Carter's recommendation, became head of Scribner's New

York Rare Book Department. Randall brought with him a wide experience in the book trade, a brisk demeanor and a self-confident willingness to experiment. In the thirty-seven catalogs produced between 1935 and 1952, Carter and Randall set new standards for rare book salesmanship. Their first joint effort was Catalog 102, *Familiar Quotations, A Collection of Their Earliest Appearances* (1935). The introduction left no doubt as to the compiler's purpose - "The present catalogue is an attempt to present a "new path in book collecting."[43] It was an original idea - to feature well known quotations by offering the books in which they first appeared. The collector who wanted to own the source of the lines "Be good, sweet maid, and let who will be clever," for example, paid $4.50 for the 1858 edition of Charles Kingsley's *Andromeda and Other Poems.* Many of the books were listed from $10 to $25, illustrating another one of Carter's precepts, that books could be priced within the budget of collectors with modest means. Some of the books were first editions, many were not. According to Carter and Randall "collectors and dealers have long been too snobbish about first editions."[44] The catalog achieved its purpose and brought new customers into the Scribner's fold.

In 1933 the firm issued a catalog of the printed first editions of songs by famous composers. The songs sold so well that Champion asked Carter for more, particularly opera and concert scores. It was a difficult area with few bibliographies and fewer price guides. Carter talked the situation over with Percy Muir, a partner of Elkin Mathews, and C. B. Oldman, a bibliographer at the British Museum. Oldman told the booksellers if they wanted to be successful they would need to spend some time in Germany where several publishers were known to hold stocks of early printed music. Muir agreed to make the trip, financed by Scribner, with the understanding that what the New York publisher didn't want would go to Elkin Mathews. Carter agreed to deal with the home office and write the catalog copy. First, there was the question of what to look for. "Generally speaking," Muir declared, "we observed no other limits than our joint personal enthusiasm; and by the time we had finished we had a dazzling list."[45] It didn't take long for choice items to appear in the Scribner's catalogs. In 1935, Catalog104, *One Hundred Books,* listed a first edition of Bach's *"Königlichen Majestät in Preussen* (1747); Beethoven's *String Quartet in E Flat Opus 74* (1809) and Wagner's *Die Walküre* (1865). The full impact of Muir's buying didn't appear until 1938 with the issue of Catalog 111, *50 Books, Manuscripts, Music,* and Catalog 112, *Bach to Stravinsky.* The catalog was a hard-bound folio, printed on high quality paper, with full page illustrations for each of the offerings. The crown jewel, priced at $20,000, was the original holograph manuscript, in Mozart's hand, of his orchestral score of the *Symphony in D Major* (1782), the so-called Haffner Symphony. Muir had located the wonderful manuscript in Germany with the help of Paul Graupe, a Berlin antiques dealer. Many people were interested, including the Pittsburg collector Charles J. Rosenbloom, but it took over a year to find a buyer, and even then the price had to be reduced. The transaction was complicated. - Scribner's supplied $6,000 for the original purchase and, by agreement, Elkin Mathews realized half the profits. The final selling price of $14,000 yielded $4,000 for each firm, certainly a satisfactory result. [46]

In addition to music, Catalog 111 offered a number of books on the history of science, another new path Carter and Randall believed collectors should consider. There was

Wolfgang Amadeus Mozart

ORIGINAL MANUSCRIPT OF THE HAFFNER SYMPHONY

(K. 385)

This is the original holograph manuscript, in Mozart's hand, of the full orchestral score of the Symphony in D major (the so-called HAFFNER SYMPHONY), Kochel-Verzeichniss No. 385. The superscription is by Leopold Mozart, the father of Wolfgang. It reads: — Synfonia /di /Amadeo Wolfgango /Mozart a Viena nel mese di /Juglio 1782 /.

The Manuscript comprises thirty leaves, in the customary oblong folio, of which fifty-seven pages contain the manuscript. Each page has twelve music staves and is uncut except at the top edge. It is contained in a superb satin-lined, pale blue velvet case, with corners of beaten silver, on the upper side of which is the italic letter "L" (Ludwig II) and an emblem with the Bavarian arms in silver. (*See Frontispiece.*)

The Haffner symphony is the first of the seven composed in Vienna by Mozart. It was written at the end of July and the beginning of August, 1782, shortly after the first performance of *Die Entführung aus dem Serail*. Its origin is due to the wish of his father, Leopold, to grace the festivities in the house of the Salzburg merchant and Burgomeister, Sigmund Haffner (for whom Wolfgang had already, in 1776, written the exquisite *Haffner Serenade*) with an orchestral piece by his son. According to his letter to his father, Mozart, already deeply engaged in other work, undertook to carry out the proposal in the greatest haste, sending each movement separately to his father as it was completed.

The manuscript was one of those bequeathed to Mozart's widow, Konstanze. It was acquired from her in 1800 by Johann André, inherited in 1841 by his son Julius, from whom King Ludwig II of Bavaria, the patron of Wagner, acquired it. He accounted it the most precious of his musical possessions. $20,000.

[32]

12. The entry for the holograph manuscript of Mozart's Haffner Symphony from Scribner's catalog 111 (1938). Carter and Percy Muir were among the first rare book dealers to offer music manuscripts.

a first edition of Agricola's *De Re Metallica* (1556) and his *De Ortu et Causis Subterraneorum Libri V* for $225, Boyle's *The Sceptical Chymist*, first edition (1661) and the second edition (1680) for $1,250 and the first edition of Jenner's *An Inquiry Into the Causes and Effects of the Variolae Vaccinae...* (1798) for $350. All sold quickly, and prompted Carter to prepare Catalog 113, *Science and Thought in the 19th Century*. In the introduction he wrote:

> Of recent years, discriminating collectors have turned their attention increasingly to the first editions of those books which have in one way or another influenced the progress of science or the development of thought and human behavior.
>
> No one who has not dabbled in this kind of collecting can have any idea of the fascination of the search for facts and achievements and their printed origins; the tracking down of a pregnant idea or train of philosophic thought to the mind that first conceived it.
>
> The material is of a character, we believe, to attract the collector of vision, and to command the attention of those libraries and institutions which take the history of science and of thought for their province. [47]

At prices ranging from thirty-five to fifty dollars, the catalog offered Freud's *Die Traumdeutung* (1900), Gray's *Anatomy, Descriptive and Surgical* (1858), and Koch's *Die Aetiologie der Tuberculose* (1882). Few individual collectors responded, but orders from the University of California at Berkeley, the Buffalo Museum of Science, Johns Hopkins University in Baltimore, and the University of Chicago made the catalog a success. Eighty percent of the books sold in the first six months.

Carter and Randall kept coming up with clever ideas to market rare books. Catalog 117, *Scribner's Presents the*

Modern Library in First Editions (1938), was one of their finest efforts. Carter explained the catalog's development, "We began to look for a select list of books, of all kinds, which enjoy not only the accolade of fame but the solid testimony of steady sales, books that the world both admires and *reads*. In the Modern Library we found just such a list."[48] The catalog described first editions of 331 Modern Library books from *The Education of Henry Adams* (1907) to Emil Zola's *Nana* (1880). Carter's notes, while furnishing details on an author's background, sometimes read like a publisher's advertisement. He described Scott Fitzgerald's *The Great Gatsby*, for example, as "the most brilliant and understanding portrait of the first mad days of the bootlegging era. It is by all odds Scott Firtzgerald's best book, and a work that no one interested in the development of American literature or life can afford to overlook."[49] With that kind of promotion it is not surprising that the books sold out quickly. According to Randall, when the partners tried to duplicate that success a few years later with Catalog 123, *The Limited Editions Club in First Editions*, the results were disappointing.

The last catalog Carter and Randall created, number 137, *Fifty Distinguished Books and Manuscripts* (1952), featured an eye-popping array of literary, historical and scientific monuments. Buyers could invest in the original transcript of Winston Churchill's "Iron Curtain" speech for $550; the first edition of Einstein's *Die Grundlage der Allgemeinen Relativitätstheorie* (1916) at $285; six books from Hitler's personal library at $4,500; the first edition of Richard Strauss' *Der Rosenkavalier* (1910) for $825; or the Shuckburgh copy of the Gutenberg Bible - no price listed. Although individual items were unquestionably distinguished, the catalog itself lacked a central theme. It almost seemed a collection of treasures thrown together to clear out the Scribner's vault. Carter reflected his own dissatisfactions to John Hayward,

> The notes for this catalog were put together in haste and I am not proud of them. The format is a disgrace to the Scribner's Press and I am ashamed of it. But some of the contents are, I think, rather nice, though too deliberately mixed a bag to be more than ephemeral in interest. Please do not show it to anyone in or near the trade.[50]

Carter and Randall wanted the Scribner's catalogs to be attractive and readable. They worked with graphic artists to improve the cover designs and page layouts and wrote bibliographically detailed notes intended to give the reader a sense of a book's history and importance. In an address before the members of the Bibliographical Society of America, Carter explained his point of view. "A good catalog note" he claimed, "can do more than summarize the pertinent information, biographical, literary and bibliographical. It can add to our knowledge of the author, the subject, or the book described."[51] With this fresh approach, Carter and Randall attracted a new breed of collectors - younger men and women whose enthusiasm and imagination made up for their limited financial resources. Finally, they wanted to introduce new collecting lines - detective fiction, adventure stories, musical first editions, philosophy, medicine, political economy, and the history of science. Private collectors and institutions responded to the innovations to the extent that the Rare Book Department began to report profits. Carter and Randall's successful techniques attracted the notice of other rare book dealers. It is easy to see reflections of the Scribner's

13. Carter and Randall at work in Scribner's New York office - c. 1950.

style in The Gotham Book Mart's *We Moderns 1920-1940* (1940), Edward Morrill's *American Children's Books* (1941), and the Seven Gables Bookshop's *First Books By American Authors* (1965). Perhaps the most important result of Carter and Randall's efforts was to establish Scribner's as one of the leading antiquarian bookshops in the United States, a place where collectors could be assured an outstanding stock and a high level of professional expertise.

Not all of Carter's assignments centered in New York and London. In June 1932, immediately after his return from four months in New York, Kingsley dispatched him to the Continent. In a closely packed two-week agenda he was to attend an auction of some important nineteenth century French first editions in Lucerne, then meet with bookdealers in Lugano, Geneva, Lyons, and Paris. Kingsley budgeted £600 for the trip and, ever-mindful of the balance sheet, was pleased when Carter spent slightly less than the full amount. In a report to Scribner, he wrote, "Carter returned the first of last week from his trip to the Continent, where I think he has made some very attractive purchases without spending too much money, well under £600."[52] When the books reached New York, Scribner wrote directly to Carter, "Everybody in the Retail seemed more than pleased with your purchases on the Continent. I trust we shall be able to do well enough with them to encourage you to buy more. At the moment things are somewhat brighter in Wall Street but general business is as dead as ever."[53]

Somewhat encouraged by increased sales, Scribner promised Carter a raise in salary from £400 to £500 in 1935, and to £600 the following year. This was of course good news, but it was the last sentence in Scribner's letter that Carter must have read more than once to make sure he understood the implications. With reference to Kingsley, Scribner wrote, "As he says, he is not young and at any time we may have to call on someone else to take charge of the London Office and we all feel strongly that you would be the person who could best do this." [54] The future looked rosy, indeed.

As if to put Carter's management skills to an immediate test, Scribner presented him with a problem - rather a series of problems - that had developed in the retail department in New York . After an exchange of letters in the fall of 1934, Scribner asked Carter to come to New York to help straighten out some of the difficulties. Once on the scene, Carter quickly saw that problems existed throughout the store in personnel, bookkeeping, publicity, and allocation of display space. As a first step, with Scribner's approval, Carter developed a plan to move the rare books from a dingy mezzanine onto a prominent main floor location formerly occupied by the juvenile department. There would be new carpeting and lighting, handsome new shelving, and an attractive office for the new director. Champion, who had been in charge of rare books for a number of years, was good with customers, but lacked basic management skills. It was time to make a change. On Carter's recommendation, backed by Wilmarth S. Lewis, one of the firm's best customers, Scribner offered the position to Randall. It was an excellent choice. With his blunt, determined style of salesmanship he was just the person needed to revitalize Scribner's Rare Book Department. He agreed with Carter that the old reliance on catering to a few wealthy collectors devoted to finely bound standard sets of Trollope, Dickens, and Hardy would no longer support a book business.

With new facilities under construction and a new man in charge, the Rare Book Department was ready to make its mark. Carter and Randall decided to cut prices on several slow-moving categories: color plate books, Cruikshankiana, sporting books, and private press publications. They began to build up collections in areas they felt, given the right kind of publicity, would have more appeal: musical first editions, English translations of foreign classics, and histories of science and thought. In a half-page advertisement headed "Enlargement & Reorganization of the Rare Book Department of the Scribner's Book Store," readers of *The Colophon* were informed that the shop would now feature books "which appeal to the collector with imagination and to those who are a little tired of the familiar offerings."[55] In one final aspect of reorganization, Carter completely revised the department's bookkeeping and filing systems. In order to record their progress, Carter and Randall produced a six-page "Report of the Rare Book Department." It covered financial condition - "more satisfactory than had been expected," and laid out plans for the next few years: "expensive books can be sold, and are being sold, as long as they are the right books and we shall not command the attention of the big collectors until we have some big books."[56] This was an optimistic line to take in the middle of the Depression, but Carter and Randall felt sure they would succeed.

In a letter to Kingsley, Scribner expressed his pleasure with Carter's efforts: "He has done an excellent job here and the retail has been going ahead in fine shape. Everyone in the department seems very enthusiastic. Carter himself took a bag full of music books to a man who wrote to us from Pittsburgh and made a sale of $3,500 out there."[57]

Things were going well. It seemed like a good time to ask for a raise. Since Randall had been hired at $3,500 Carter felt his salary, $2,500, needed adjustment. Besides, as he confided to Scribner, he planned to get married in the near future.[58] Impressed with his young rare book specialist, who seemed to be an adept manager, Scribner agreed that salaries of the rare book specialists in London and New York should be the same.

In the spring of 1935, Scribner asked Kingsley and Carter to look into the costs and legal requirements involved in order to incorporate the London office. The process called for consultations with lawyers, accountants, and various local government officials - a slow and complicated paper trail. When Kingsley mentioned obstacles,

Scribner, two thousand miles away, brushed the questions aside saying he felt sure the whole procedure could be completed easily in a matter of months. It may not have been easy, but by July 1, 1935 all the signatures were in place and Charles Scribner's Sons became Charles Scribner's Sons, Ltd. The letterhead listed three directors, Charles Scribner, Charles Kingsley, and John Carter. The new title meant little to Carter, but it was a welcome recognition of his status with the firm.

Carter's first eight years with Scribner's had been satisfying both professionally and personally. He enjoyed his job, particularly the connections it provided with bookdealers and collectors on both sides of the Atlantic. He had proved himself to be a knowledgeable bibliophile, a capable and lively writer, and a well organized and imaginative manager.

CHAPTER THREE
Early Publications

During the 1930s, as Carter's stature continued to rise, his articles and books on collecting and bibliography began to appear on both sides of the Atlantic. Between 1930 and 1935 his output was impressive. *Binding Variants in English Publishing 1820-1900* came out in 1932, and *An Enquiry Into the Nature of Certain Nineteenth Century Pamphlets* in 1934. In 1932 he edited Sir Thomas Browne's *Urne Buriall* and *The Garden of Cyrus*, and two years later, *New Paths in Book Collecting*. During the same period he published a dozen journal articles and several dozen reviews - all while holding down a demanding full-time job. These early publications covered a variety of subjects - the effect of the economic depression on the antiquarian book trade, nineteenth century publisher's cloth bindings, bibliography, and, in his most ambitious work, co-written with Graham Pollard, the analysis of a group of bibliographic forgeries. His style was forceful, clear, and eminently readable, although sometimes a sentence stretched forward nearly out of control. Considering the state of the rare book trade in the United States during the Depression he wrote:

> It was customary, a year ago, to talk comfortably about the enormously increasing number of collectors: how many of these recruits to the noble army of bibliophiles

were really mercenaries has been abundantly proved by
the recent unloading of books which the boom had made
fashionable, which people did not really want, which they
had only bought to sell - and are now selling (one notes
with some malice) at very unsatisfactory prices."[1]

His sense of humor, never far beneath the surface, often
relieved the flow of this stately prose. "Why," he wondered, with a swipe at A.J.A. Symons, the Secretary and
founder of the First Edition Club, "has nobody started a
Second Edition Club?"[2]

Carter owed much of his early success to the support
given him by Michael Sadleir, one of the directors of the
London publishing firm of Constable & Company. There
is no account of how Carter and Sadleir met, but it is likely to have happened in the late 1920s in one of the many
bookshops they frequented. Sadleir was seventeen years
older than Carter, and by 1927, when Carter started to
work for Scribner's, recognized as a successful publisher,
bibliographer, collector, novelist, and biographer. The
regard of a young man of promise for an older man with a
firmly established reputation, and the older man's respect
for youthful energy and imagination, defined their relationship. Carter once referred to himself as Sadleir's
"avowed disciple."[3] Influences flowed both ways, but in
the decade of the thirties, Carter's writing frequently followed lines already laid down by Sadleir. It was Sadleir, for
example, who first criticized unimaginative collectors who
devoted all their resources to gathering expensive high
spots. He urged collectors to look beyond endorsed rarities and follow their individual interests. The trade itself
had to absorb part of the blame. "Dealers, very short-
sightedly, played up to this snob-demand and (with few
fine exceptions) made little attempt to cater for smaller

people, who, finding their modest wants ignored by persons busy operating on a big financial scale, got tired of the whole business."[4] Carter explored those same themes a year later, urging collectors to trust their own taste and avoid the fashion of the moment. As for dealers, he repeated Sadleir's claim that they had been "only interested in an eclectic list of high spots and when the crash came there was nothing much to fall back upon."[5]

In the spring of 1933, Sadleir and Carter began to plan a publication that would give collectors something to fall back on. The result, a symposium of nine essays appropriately titled *New Paths in Book Collecting*, appeared under Constable's imprint in November 1934. Charles Scribner and Kingsley encouraged Carter to do the book, although they felt a volume of essays on collecting would be difficult to sell, particularly when the contributors, chiefly London bookmen, were almost entirely unknown in the United States. Looking back, Carter remembered Scribner's approach "loyally if dubiously supporting their London agent."[6] In an outline provided for would-be contributors, Carter defined the book's audience and suggested a general style:

Memorandum for contributors,

This book is aimed at the intelligent general collector, not the novice. We must assume, therefore, a knowledge of the rudiments of bibliography; but let us nevertheless avoid the more pedantic forms of bibliographic virtuosity.

You need not bother about general, or even particular, exhortations to collect on new lines: that will be dealt with in the introduction.

The general plan is to combine in readable form -

(a) A literary and historical survey of your field with a delimitation of its extent.

(b) The essential details of the first edition of every book you mention - i.e. author, title, place, publisher, date, binding. Size need only be given if it is larger than 8vo or smaller than 12mo - together, of course, with other bibliographical information where there is any.

(c) Hints to the collector, information about relative scarcities etc; with the minimum of actual price quotations, please.[7]

He asked each contributor to produce a five thousand word literary survey. What he wanted, he said, were essays in method. Given the nature of the undertaking, it is hardly surprising that the authors were chosen from the younger generation of dealers and bibliographers. The antiquarian trade was represented by Carter with "Detective Fiction," Muir with "Ignoring the Flag," and "War Books," and Pollard with "Serial Fiction;" publishing by Sadleir's "Yellow-Backs," and Thomas Balston's "English Book Illustrations, 1880-1900;" bibliography by C. B. Oldman with "Musical First Editions;" and the American scene by David A. Randall, "American First Editions, 1900-1933," and John T. Winterich, "The Expansion of an Author Collection." In his introduction, Carter employed an apt musical parallel to emphasize the importance of the suggested new approaches:

> A collection of "high spots" may sound the chord of C major, which is indeed a fine and resounding noise; yet there are other and more subtle harmonies, the pleasantest of which are those we evolve for ourselves. These are composed of notes which anyone can use and many have used but by our own arrangement of them we can achieve a sound never heard before. So it is with books. By rearranging familiar books according to some constructive

plan, a new significance is added to them, and, which is more, the unfamiliar, the neglected books will acquire significance by their context.[8]

Carter's thirty page essay, "Detective Fiction," based on his own collection, identified some of the classics, beginning with what he called the "Poe-Wilkie Collins-Gaboriau Period," and progressed to a number of less well known names such as Edward J. Reed, author of *Fort Minister, M.P. A Westminister Mystery* (Arrowsmith, 1885) and Victor Whitechurch, who wrote *Shot on the Downs* (Fisher, Unwin, 1927). He identified authors as "interesting," "workmanlike," or sometimes "influential," but rarely subjected them to a closer scrutiny. Obeying his own recommendation, he limited remarks on rarity and bibliographic points. The collector of detective fiction, Carter concluded, would not only have the stimulating opportunity of investigating a neglected area of literature, but would benefit financially by being ahead of the market. Detective fiction was clearly an inviting new path.

In an effort to create publicity for the book, Carter and Sadleir arranged an exhibition "by kind permission of Messrs J. & E. Bumpus" at the Old Court House in Marylebone Lane. For sixpence, visitors could obtain an attractive fifty page annotated catalog. The foreword, unsigned, but undoubtedly by Carter, once again stated the importance of individual taste, and the variety of possibilities open to collectors. The purpose of the exhibition was "to demonstrate that there are many possible kinds of book-collecting beyond the vain and costly pursuit of world-rarities and famous first editions. . . . The fun of book-hunting is the chase; and the pursuit of items not universally known and valued gives a maximum of chase with, at the end, a minimum of expenditure."[9] In addition to listing the books described in the chapters of *New Paths,* the catalog presented what Carter called "several hobby-horses," a twelve-page section devoted to "The Evolution of 'Trade' and Publishers' Binding, 1600-1900," and another on "Books Printed on Coloured Paper or in Coloured Ink." These were added "to suggest to the post-slump generation an *á la carte* approach to book-collecting as an alternative to the *prix fixe* attitude. (Is it on the Grolier, de Ricci, Newton or whosits list?) which had infected bibliography in the late 1920s."[10]

New Paths in Book-Collecting was widely reviewed, but not universally approved. Charles Heartman, editor of *The American Book Collector*, praised several individual essays, but questioned the value of the book as a whole. "What does it mean to the collector," he asked, "inasmuch as new paths in book collecting are concerned? I think very little, for with the exception, perhaps, of yellow-backs, all the other subjects have been and are collected."[11] He also objected to the "strictly literary character of the subjects discussed," and claimed that aside from the essay on yellow-backs, there were no genuine new paths.[12] Simon Nowell-Smith, in a mischievous mood, wrote a sarcastic - Carter called it snotty - review in the *Times Literary Supplement* asking why anyone should care about "two-shilling railway fiction, execrably printed, bound . . . in strawboard, crudely illustrated and carrying advertisements of soap, pills and cocoa."[13] This was too much for Sadleir, who answered in kind, "We are all of us rightly ashamed to have disturbed your reviewer's lofty serenity by vulgar chatter about modern first editions, murder books, yellow-backs and the like. . . . Your reviewer, presumably, would have them collect bird's eggs or postage stamps or go in for wireless - anything rather than show an interest in books unhallowed by the literary approval of the past."[14] Ralph Wright said the essays left the impression that the only thing to do "is to collect worthless books,"[15] while the anonymous reviewer in *Life and Letters* found the essays disappointing and full of errors.[16] Reviews in *The Bookseller, The Manchester Guardian,* and *The New York Times* were generally more favorable. Whether due to the negative reviews, or, more likely, to the depressed economy, the book failed to find a market in either England or the United States. With tens of thousands out of work, book-collecting was hardly a topic of immediate interest. In an effort to salvage some return for his expenditure, Sadleir took the unbound sheets from four of the essays, including Carter's piece on "Detective Fiction,"gave them brick-red paper wrappers, and issued them separately under the series title "Aspects of Book Collecting." Again, buyers failed to respond. Carter looked back with some amusement on the intense sense of mission he and his friends shared during that period: "We thought of ourselves as Young Turks, determined to replace tarnished shibboleths and ritual genuflection to over-worked patterns by fresh ideas, more imaginative approaches, more flexible postures."[17]

In a completely different line of bibliophily, Carter and Sadleir shared an interest in the history and development of nineteenth-century binding styles. Again, Sadleir led the way. As a publisher, it was his daily responsibility to make decisions on type, paper, ink, binding, and illustration. Since his personal collecting interests focused on the nineteenth century, it was natural for him to turn his attention to the binding and printing practices of that period. During the 1820s and 1830s, significant changes took place in book production, particularly in the way books were bound and distributed. Before 1820, a text usually went through three steps, from publisher, to printer, to binder. Toward the end of the chain, the printer passed along his work, in wrappers or original boards, to a binder for a permanent casing. Around 1825 all that changed - publishers began to take responsibility for binding, and by 1840 publisher's cloth had almost entirely supplanted wrappers and boards. This increased production, lowered prices, and expanded the market for books. Sadleir's *Evolution of Publishers' Binding Styles 1770-1900* (1930), a landmark work, described the history of that change, and encouraged bibliographers and collectors to take a new look at nineteenth century book production. In addition to its historical perspective Sadleir's study raised a number of intriguing social questions - How were books distributed in the nineteenth century? In what ways did the reading public change between 1820 and 1890? What effect did the new production methods have on the author/publisher relationship? While it was not Sadleir's purpose to answer these questions, he deserves credit for furnishing a background for their consideration.[18]

Carter was intrigued by Sadleir's views and expanded them in a series of publications of his own. In the 1931 issue of the *Colophon*, he presented evidence "of a very tentative kind," to show that cloth binding may have been introduced in 1825 rather than in 1821, as Sadleir had suggested. Next, he published a short article on the difficulties publishers faced in selling cloth bindings to collectors who remained loyal to wrappers and boards.[19] He used the articles as the basis for his first published monograph, *Binding Variants in English Publishing 1820-1900*, a study he called a "rather swollen appendix" to Sadleirs' *Evolution of Publishers' Binding Styles.*[20] While Sadleir spent a considerable amount of time describing eighteenth century binding styles, Carter took up the history beginning in the 1820's, when publishers' bindings first came into use. He divided the book into two parts, the first, a historical overview including consideration of such topics as the origin of cloth, end papers, spine lettering, labels, advertisements and ornaments, and the second, an illustrative checklist of over one-hundred first editions from the period. A reproduction of the first entry in the checklist will serve to demonstrate Carter's meticulous approach (see figure 14 on the following page).

When it came to setting priorities, Carter's approach was speculative. In a modest preliminary note he set out four general disclaimers:

(1) I do not presume, when describing three variants on a book that there does not exist a fourth.

(2) When I note or draw a conclusion from inserted advertisements, I am no party to the idea that all copies should contain them.

(3) The letters A,B,C etc., attached to the variants described are used for convenience only and are no indication in themselves of any order of priority whatever. . . A, B, C are just three variants observed by me and described for the reader, who is besought to form his own opinion on the evidence presented to him before proceeding to agree or disagree with mine.

(4) The description of colours is by no means easy and though I have done my best to be consistent and reasonably accurate, there are probably some lapses.[22]

Was marbled cloth used before 1850? When was watered silk introduced? When did the publisher's name

W. H. AINSWORTH

THE TOWER OF LONDON. 1840   Bentley

A. Claret-coloured ribbed cloth; spine lettered and blocked in gilt; sides blocked in blind with a 3-line border and large corner ornaments, with different vignettes in gilt on front and back.

B. Claret-coloured morocco; spine exactly the same as A; sides have the same gilt vignettes as A, but these are surrounded by a decorative frame and a 4-line border in gilt.

C. Half-morocco or half-roan, of various colours; spine as A; sides have gilt vignettes only, blocked on the cloth.

The colours of A and B vary slightly: edges of A *generally* uncut, of B *generally* gilt; but see p. 77 for a discussion of edges in books issued in parts.

This is a good example of the alternative bindings usually available for books of this kind. The publishers offered it 'handsomely bound in cloth extra, with designs by George Cruikshank on the cover, 14/6: half-morocco, 17/6: and whole morocco, gilt edges, 21/-.' The only copies I have seen in half-roan had been bound from the parts.

All these bindings occur on copies with first or second states of the altered plates indifferently.

CRICHTON. 1849   Chapman & Hall
(1st edition illustrated by Phiz)

A. Green morocco cloth, uncut; sides blocked in blind with 2-line border and decorated frame; front

89

first appear on a book's spine? Did gilt lettering on cloth exist before 1832? Carter prefaced answers to questions of this kind with cautionary phrases such as "it seems" or "lacking further evidence one may conclude." E. A. Osborne, reviewing the book for *Publishers' Weekly*, approved Carter's restraint, patient research and capacity for clear presentation.[23] In the *Times Literary Supplement*, the reviewer commented favorably on the book's handsome physical appearance, and was particularly taken with the twelve fold-out collotype illustrations.[24] In spite of these positive evaluations, fewer than five hundred copies sold between 1932 and 1938. Although this was disappointing, Sadleir and Carter felt *Binding Variants* had fulfilled its purpose, to illuminate a neglected corner of book production.

With a considerable amount of research already in hand, Carter continued to expand his study of nineteenth century binding styles. In February 1935, R. B. Bowker in New York and Constable in London published his essay *Publisher's Cloth 1820-1900*, a guide prepared to accompany an exhibition at the New York Public Library. The text, which Carter claimed he wrote in a hotel room in forty-eight hours, drew heavily on his earlier work. Again, Sadleir's hand was present and acknowledged. In the preface, Carter wrote, "In the essay which follows, I make no apology for my obvious indebtedness to Mr. Michael Sadleir's published work, since that indebtedness is common to all of us. His unpublished work in this field has recently been so closely involved with my own that I hardly know where one ends and the other begins."[25] Since *Publisher's Cloth* was prepared for the general public, Carter decided "in the spirit of simplicity" to omit detailed bibliographic descriptions - that information, he said, could easily be found in Sadleir's books or his own. The result, a readable introduction to a complex subject, justified that decision.

Carter's next contribution, *More Binding Variants* (1938), was a supplement to his earlier work on the same topic. This time the title page identified Sadleir as a major contributor. *More Binding Variants* not only added titles overlooked in the earlier work, but made modifications and amplifications suggested by readers. Sadleir contributed lengthy descriptions of the variant bindings in J. S. LeFanu's *The House by the Churchyard* (1863), and a ten page section on the binding styles used for Mrs. Henry Wood's novels. The reviewer in the *Times Literary Supplement* wrote "There is in this work ample proof of Mr. Carter's patience and skill; he is never dogmatic, each theory being put forward tentatively. With variant bindings there is unfortunately seldom proof of what style or colour cloth was primarily used, and without this, the best theories may be wrong.No one knows this better than Mr. Carter, and in this book he has boldly given all the evidence he has been able to find. His summing up is brilliantly concise; but no judgment is passed without proof."[26]

Carter's interest in binding styles never diminished. In January 1947, he and Sadleir collaborated on an exhibition of Victorian fiction sponsored by the National Book League. The catalog was of more than passing interest, containing, as it did, a forward by Sadleir, a lengthy introduction by Carter, and extended notes on a variety of topics such as part-issues, three-deckers, illustrators, magazine serials, novels of manners, and the Irish School. An incident connected with the exhibition nicely illustrates Carter's ability to pull success from potential disaster. It was the custom at the National Book League to invite Queen Mary to private showings of all new exhibitions. She enjoyed the displays and often found an item that particularly pleased her. The proper response, of course, would be to offer the book to Her Majesty with the compliments of the League. Problems arose when the chosen piece was the jewel in the collection of a private owner and not available, even for the Queen. Carter gave the problem considerable thought and decided the best solution was to manufacture an eye-catcher. He sent Patricia Herrmann, the director's assistant, to Thomas Thorp's shop on Albemarle Street with instruction to buy the prettiest three-decker she could find. The chosen book had a flower-strewn binding and highly decorated pages. When it was placed in a case in a central area of the exhibition and lit with a small spot, the effect was quite remarkable. The Queen saw it, was enchanted, and graciously accepted it as a gift from the League.[27]

In 1953, Carter and Sadleir collaborated again, writing about the special nomenclature used to describe nineteenth century cloth grains.[28] Four years later, Carter sold his entire collection illustrating the history of publisher's bindings to the Bodleian Library at Oxford. The sale did not diminish his interest in the subject. In 1972 he sent his friend Philip "Pip" Gaskell a two-page closely written letter packed with comments on the section on binding in Gaskell's in progress guide, *New Introduction to Bibliography*.[29] Gaskell responded with gratitude to the man who, along with Sadleir, had given bibliographic legitimacy to the study of bindings.

While Carter's books and articles on binding styles owe much to Sadleir's early work, they stand on their own as unique scholarly contributions. It is easy to agree with

Muir, who said they contributed "a new and important chapter to our knowledge of the history of book production."[30] Taken together, they demonstrate Carter's ability to seize a topic, carry out the research, and present the results in a highly readable prose.

Carter and Sadleir had mutual interests in bibliography, publishing, book collecting, and book history. Why, they wondered, were those topics given so little attention in the press? The *Times Literary Supplement,* a natural place to look for news of the antiquarian book world, was particularly derelict. Readers had to be satisfied with a lackluster column carried from time to time on the back page called "Notes on Sales." Early in 1931, when Simon Nowell-Smith came down from Oxford to work for *The Times,* he was asked to take a look at "Notes on Sales." This was the opening Sadleir had been waiting for. He invited Nowell-Smith, Carter, Pollard, John Hayward, A. W. Evans, Eddie Gathorne-Hardy, Percy Dobell, Percy Muir, and Dudley Massey to a dinner to discuss possible new directions for the *Times* back page. By the time the brandy had been passed around, several of those present had agreed to contribute notes and reviews. This was the first meeting of the Biblio Boys or Biblios as they liked to call themselves. For over forty years, with a brief hiatus during the war, and with an ever-changing membership - but never exceeding fifteen - they met monthly for dinner and conversation, unhampered by a constitution, elected officers, newsletters, annual reports, or rules of order. In 1958 the list of members included Carter, Pollard, Muir, Massey, and Hayward, from the original group, and F. S. Ferguson, Rupert Hart-Davis, Anthony Hobson, Arnold Muirhead, A.N.L. Munby, Howard Nixon, Stanley Sawyer, and John Sparrow as newer recruits. Wilmarth S.

Lewis became the group's American corresponding member. Carter acted as the club's unofficial secretary and sent out postcards announcing the date and place of the meetings. When members died or stopped attending he wrote letters soliciting names to fill the gaps. In one such letter, he sketched out his view of the qualities to be looked for in those under consideration for membership - "a real interest in bibliography and book collecting, a considerable measure of enterprise and a tolerance for slander, scandal and hard words, the essence of our conversation."[31] In a speech before the Bibliographical Society, Carter characterized the Biblio meetings as "informal, convivial, disrespectful, a briskly productive seminar."[32]

It didn't take long for the Biblios to pump life onto the moribund back page of the *Times Literary Supplement*. In the fall of 1931, Muir and A.J.A. Symons, the editor of *Book Collector's Quarterly*, got into a lively debate over the proper meaning of the terms edition and impression. Symons argued that "impression" was misleading, and should be abolished in favor of the more inclusive "edition." Muir based his opinion on an 1898 recommendation from the Publishers' Association to the effect that every printing after the first printing, without change in type, be called an impression and any printing with a change of type be identified as a new edition. Carter provided a thorough analysis of both sides of the debate in a lengthy article appropriately titled "The Edition or Impression Controversy."[33] In the process of supporting Muir's views, Carter inserted strong words of praise for those who were making an effort to improve the quality of the back page. "Notes on Sales" he reported, "has, in the last six months branched into wider bibliographical fields. The scheme is sponsored by several of the most enterprising and distinguished leaders in the English book collecting world."[34] As one of those enterprising leaders, Carter wrote a detailed letter to the *TLS* editor in 1932 questioning the accuracy of some of the pronouncements in Thomas J. Wise's recently published bibliography of Byron - "his rulings seem dogmatic and arbitrary"[35] - an attack he pursued in two lengthy letters in the spring of 1933.[36] By the end of that year Robert Gathorne-Hardy, E. A. Osborne, Carter, and Sadleir had all contributed reviews and comments to a new column called "Bibliographic Notes." At the same time, Muir started writing a series of articles on private libraries in England. As a result of these efforts, the back page began to be consulted on a regular basis by those interested in collecting and bibliography. Starting in 1946, when Stanley Morison was editor, the paper employed Carter on an annual retainer to organize and edit the bibliographical and sales articles and help allocate reviews. He continued as the paper's bibliographical consultant until shortly before his death.

In addition to writing for the *Times Literary Supplement,* several of the Biblios contributed to *Bibliographical Notes and Queries,* (*BN&Q*), a periodical edited by Muir and published irregularly between 1935 and 1939. Muir, Carter, and their friends started *BN&Q* with the idea that collectors and dealers would welcome a publication devoted to the exchange of information on bibliographic problems. Organized in a question and answer format, with no advertising or editorials, the publication was utilitarian in the extreme. The first issue, January 1935, consisted of thirty-seven queries ranging from Viscount Esher's question about inserted advertisements in the 1855 edition of Tennyson's *Maud,* to A. Edward Newton's inquiry - "When were the words 'a novel,' in the modern sense, first used on a title-page? I have said repeatedly, in Congreve's *Incognito* London, 1691. I have a copy; it is rare. I have too, *The Novels of Elizabeth*, London 1680, but here novel means news or history. If I am wrong *re Incognito* let someone set me right."[37] Almost from the beginning, the publication attracted as many contributions from America as from England. In recognition of that fact, the October 1935 issue announced that David A. Randall would serve as American editor and that Charles Scribner's Sons would share publication responsibilities with Elkin Mathews. At the end of the first year, in a burst of misplaced enthusiasm, the editors decided to turn the quarterly into a monthly, a decision that had unfortunate consequences. The April 1936 issue carried an appeal to subscribers:

> It must be emphasized that the success of the journal depends not only on subscriptions but even more on the co-operation of subscribers in the way of contributions. A few subscribers contribute regularly both new queries and answers to old ones. Presumably subscription to this journal pre-supposes an interest in bibliographical investigation, and such an interest surely connotes the existence in the subscriber's mind of unsolved puzzles. Yet many subscribers have never made a single contribution, either query or answer.[38]

Readers were informed that of the 150 queries presented up to that time, only 86 had received answers.[39] The shortage of suitable inquiries also continued to be a problem. When no issues appeared between February 1937 and January 1938 it was clear something had to be done. The January issue announced the appointment of an advisory board made up of contributors from England and the

BIBLIOGRAPHICAL NOTES AND QUERIES

Vol. II. Nos. 4-5. MAY 1936

Edited by P. H. MUIR

American Editor, DAVID RANDALL

✳ ✳ ✳

London Office: ELKIN MATHEWS LTD., 78 Grosvenor Street, W.1
New York Office: CHARLES SCRIBNER'S SONS, 597 Fifth Avenue

WE are gratified by the response to our editorial plea in No. 3. In consequence we are able to issue a double number this time and thus to catch
up with arrears. This leaves very little material in hand for a June issue. Moreover, the response so far has been largely from the faithful few who have kept
the paper going all along.

Apparently some subscribers have indulged in private correspondence with
one another on the subject of queries printed here. There is no objection to
that, but it is hoped that the substance of such correspondence and/or any
further information arising therefrom may be at the disposal of this journal
so that all subscribers may profit by it.

ANSWERS TO EARLIER QUERIES IN NUMERICAL ORDER

Query No. 4. Galsworthy: *Swan Song*

In my copy, page 15 has line 23 "plate", and line 24 "form", presumably instead of line 23
"plat-" and line 24 "form". Otherwise, my copy is as E. B. M.'s copy A, except for the word
"RENCOUNTER" on Contents page, which is as described by me in *B. N. & Q.*, I. 3, p. 1.
It has the correct numeral on p. 77.—Harold E. James.

Query No. 24. John Martin

I have now discovered the steel-engraving "The Highland Fortress of Lessing Cray" (*C*,
not G) in *The Winter's Wreath for MDCCCXXXII* (London: Whittaker, Treacher and
Arnot, and George Smith, Liverpool) where it faces p. 37 and illustrates "A Tale of Second
Sight", by W. B. Chorley. The author states that "Lessing Cray" is a fictitious name.—
T. Balston.

Query No. 48. Leonardo da Vinci MSS.

(1) In 1898 Rouveyre published in Paris the following: *I Manoscritti di Leonardo da Vinci
della Reale Biblioteca di Windsor: Dell' Anatomia, . . . trascritti e annotati di Giovanni
Plumati. . . .*

(2) In 1881–90 Quantin published in facsimile, with a literal transcription, those MSS. of
Leonardo's which are in the Institut de Paris, and also two MSS. then in the possession of
Lord Ashburnham.

(3) In 1894–1904, Hoepli, Milan, issued, in 6 vols., *Il codice atlantico*, the MS. of which
is in the Ambrosian Library in Milan.

1

15. A typical page from 'Bibliographical Notes and Queries.'

United States and, in a final attempt at survival, offered
BN&Q free to all interested parties with the printing costs
to be absorbed by Elkin Mathews and Scribner's. It must
have seemed unlikely, even to those eager for continua-
tion, that such an arrangement would work on any long-
range basis. With a lack of contributions, and the expanding conflict on the Continent, the periodical had little

chance of survival, and in fact only lasted until May 1939. The last issue ended with query 330 signed George Waynflete, Carter in disguise. He asked if the preface to Thackeray's *Pendennis* was always found bound in with volume two. Among those who supplied queries and answers on a regular basis, none was more active than Carter. Questions bearing his own name and his various pseudonyms - Harriet Marlow, Ignoramus, Homlock Shears, and George Waynflete, for example, appeared five or six times in every issue. Carter was unhappy with the publication's demise, particularly when he had counted on support from those in the trade as well as from collectors. In a rare burst of anger he wrote, "It became gradually clear that most book collectors, though willing, even anxious, to be instructed, are too lazy, or too diffident, or too little interested to make a forum go. Meanwhile many subscribers on whom the editors had hoped to rely for many solid contributions remained uncooperative, so that the main burden fell on a small band of devoted supporters who were determined that an institution so potentially valuable to the bibliographical and collecting world should not be allowed to perish of undernourishment in its infancy."[40] When *BN&Q* ceased, Carter and Muir promised to try again after the war. That opportunity came in the spring of 1952 when the first issue of *The Book Collector* appeared. Toward the back of the journal, under the familiar heading, "Bibliographical Notes and Queries," a series of questions appeared with a note announcing the revival of the publication. Again, subscribers were invited to submit questions and supply answers. The first question printed in the Spring 1952 issue came from an old friend, Harriet Marlow, concerning the priority of a certain printing of Dante. The second came from Carter asking about a publisher's mark on an early trade binding, and the third from George Waynflete who, undaunted after thirteen years, still wanted to know about the preface to Thackeray's *Pendennis.*

Sadleir was not as involved in *BN&Q* as some of the other members of the Biblios, but did contribute from time to time when questions arose on Victorian binding styles. Although he and Carter saw less of each other after the war, their friendship continued. They belonged to the same clubs and had many mutual friends. Never an easy man to know or to please, Sadleir respected Carter's abilities and found a rebellious streak in him that matched his own. Neither man hesitated to challenge established wisdom. When Sadleir died in 1957, Carter praised him as "probably the most accomplished book-collector" and "the most influential bibliographer of our time."[41] He recognized Sadleir as one of the most important influences in his early career.

The same year that Constable published Carter's *Binding Variants in English Publishing 1820-1900*, Cassell and Company brought out his edition of Sir Thomas Browne's *Urne Buriall* and *The Garden of Cyrus*. Carter's interest in Browne went back to his senior year at Eton when the enigmatic assistant master George Lyttelton introduced him to the writings of the seventeenth century physician/author in a course with the pleasantly vague title, "extra studies." Carter was impressed with Browne's resonant prose and chose to read a selection from *Urne Buriall* as a contribution to the annual Sixth Form exercise known as "Speeches." During his second year at Cambridge, Carter located a copy of *Urne Buriall* in the Trinity College library with Browne's handwritten corrections. The existence of one corrected copy suggested the possibility of finding others. That proved to be the case, when in 1928 the London book dealer Percy Dobell showed him not one but two copies with marginal corrections. Although the handwriting was similar to Brownes, Dobell, an extremely cautious man, was not willing to claim authenticity, and neither was the prime authority on Browne, the bibliographer Geoffrey Keynes. In spite of this formidable alignment of negative opinion, Carter decided to proceed. He bought the books on approval for Scribner's, and got his superior, Charles Kingsley, to agree to an imaginative scheme. Kingsley promised that if the handwriting proved to be authentic, the firm would buy both copies and give the one in slightly less desirable condition to Carter as a bonus. The challenge was all Carter needed. After several months of research at the British Museum and a careful re-examination of the copy in Trinity College, he convinced both Kingsley and Keynes that the handwriting was indeed authentic.[42]

The next step was almost automatic. Carter wanted to get his research published. During his first years in London he had become acquainted with Desmond Flower, the son of Newman Flower, the director of the publishing firm Cassell and Company. As a junior member of the firm, but one with considerable influence, Flower decided to experiment with a line of fine printing. Encouraged by Carter, he got his father's permission to bring out a luxurious edition of *Urne Buriall* with notes based on six copies showing corrections in Browne's hand. No expense would be spared. Paul Nash, the surrealist painter, agreed to do the illustrations and design the morocco and vellum binding. Oliver Simon's Curwen Press printed a run of two hundred fifteen copies, as the advertisement declared, "for the world." The book was universally admired, particularly for Nash's drawings, but predictably, at fifteen guineas a copy, found only a few buyers.[43] Was it a sumptuous trifle? The *Times Literary Supplement* reviewer thought not. Carter's editorial work was said to be "of outstanding interest from the student point of view."[44]The renowned art critic Herbert Read called the book "one of the loveliest achievements of contemporary English art."[45]

Carter continued his search for annotated copies of *Urne Buriall* through the correspondence columns in the *Times Literary Supplement*. By 1943 he was able to account for nine, and by 1957, twelve. In 1958, Cambridge University Press published a revised edition of the Browne meditations based on Carter's research. This time there were no Nash illustrations or morocco bindings but sales were encouraging. Of the 3,000 copies in the initial print run, the press sold all but 300 by the end of 1966, and, prompted by that success, issued a 2,000 copy reprint. Carter's love affair with Browne, begun at Eton when he was eighteen, not only endured for over thirty years, but flowered in a series of well received scholarly publications.[46]

During his early years at Scribner's, Carter spent much of his free time writing book reviews. For a young man getting started in the trade, it was one more way to establish a reputation. The majority of his reviews appeared in *Publishers' Weekly*. They were characteristically forthright and opinionated. Quality was recommended, and incompetence condemned. At the end of one of his reviews, the editor inserted an appreciation, "He is an established authority on binding variants, and his reviews are scholarly and informed and his standards very high."[47] Carter was no less forthright on his own behalf saying, "It is my duty to apply the strictest bibliographical standards to book reviews in this column."[48] Geoffrey Keynes' *A Bibliography of Dr. John Donne*, second edition, 1932, won his approval as "an excellent piece of work" exhibiting a "high level of scholarship,"[49] while Andrew Block's *The Book Collector's Vade Mecum*, with its dogmatic pronouncements and flagrant inaccuracies, struck Carter as "a rather indigestible pudding in spite of its agreeable sauce."[50] Gilbert Fabes and William Foyle's *Modern First Editions, Points and Values* Second Series, 1932, suffered a similar blunt indictment. The authors failed to discriminate between a state and an issue and furnished price estimates that were, according to Carter, completely inaccurate. He concluded his review saying bibliography must be judged by the highest standards and that "a slovenly book of this kind may do a great deal of damage."[51]

By 1935, at the age of thirty, Carter was firmly established as an authority - although he would have objected to the label - in several areas of bibliophily. His independent voice and stylish prose won him a following among both advanced and beginning collectors. He was an author who was read for both pleasure and enlightenment. His best-known work of the 1930s, *An Enquiry Into the Nature of Certain Nineteenth Century Pamphlets*, deserves separate consideration.

CHAPTER FOUR
The *Enquiry*

There was no irony intended when in 1945 Carter described the Thomas J. Wise forgeries as "the most ingeniously conceived, the best executed, and the most successful fraud in the history of book collecting."[1] He was simply paying tribute to the man whose bibliographic forgeries surpassed anything that had gone before. By extension, he was perhaps paying tribute to the ingenuity of the investigators who unraveled the clever frauds.

Conversation around the Biblios table often turned on the gossip of the moment. Who had been forced to close up shop for lack of business? Why had no one bid on the Audubon prints at the last Sotheby sale? When was the American collector Wilmarth S. Lewis expected to arrive in town? Had anyone heard T. Sturge Moore's talk on Charles Ricketts at the last Double Crown dinner? The most compelling topic, and the one that engaged the group's closest attention during the early thirties, was the appearance on the market of a number of hitherto unknown first editions of works by notable nineteenth century authors. The pamphlets, taken at face value, pre-dated the accepted first publication of poems, stories, and essays by such luminaries as Dickens, the Brownings, Hardy, Swinburne, Ruskin, Thackeray, Matthew Arnold, and Robert Louis Stevenson. Often identified on the title page as "Printed for the Author,"

"Trial Edition," or "For Private Circulation Only," these pamphlets attracted wealthy collectors both in England and America.

There were several things about the pamphlets that caused the Biblios, especially Carter and Graham Pollard, to take a closer look. It was curious, they thought, that although dated back into the 1840s and 1850s, the pamphlets uniformly appeared in pristine condition - none were inscribed to the author's family or friends, as might be expected from such special issues, nor were any mentioned in the author's letters or memoirs. Library catalogs and published bibliographies, with one or two exceptions - of which more later- failed to provide any verification.

The Biblios were not the first to question the authenticity of these pamphlets. In 1897, Sidney Cockerell and F. S. Ellis, both executors of the William Morris estate, published a notice in *The Athenaeum* concerning several suspicious Morris reprints. Under the title "A Warning to Collectors," Cockerell and Ellis came right to the point, "We think it right to warn collectors that unauthorized reprints of some of his contributions to the weekly and monthly press are being offered for sale at high prices. It would be well for those concerned in the manufacture of such 'rarities' to remember that they are engaged in an act of piracy and that they lay themselves open to proceedings under the copyright law."[2] Apparently the warning failed to deter the pirates. In his examination of E. T. Cook and Alexander Wedderburn's thirty-nine volume edition of Ruskin's *Collected Works* (1903-1912), Pollard noticed a statement that *The Queen's Garden* (1864) and *The National Gallery* (1852) were fakes, and *The Scythian Guest* (1849) and *Leoni* (1868) highly suspicious. In 1898 two New York bookdealers, George D. Smith and Alfred J. Bowden, raised similar concerns:

There is an uneasy feeling among collectors on this side
regarding the numerous little privately printed pamphlets
by celebrated modern authors which are being offered
from England. Grave suspicions are entertained that some
of these are being manufactured - but that these suspicions
are well-grounded cannot be said. One thing is certain,
however, the rarity of these ephemera has been much exag-
gerated. Maybe "Last Tournament" by Tennyson is worth
$300, but it is curious that every Tennyson collector of
note has been supplied with one lately.[3]

Three years later, Smith and Bowden took an even
stronger stand:

Does the reader remember a period about two years ago
when "rare" privately printed little pamphlets by
Tennyson and Swinburne were being "boomed"? At least
one inexperienced collector in New York was misled by a
perfectly reputable firm into buying thousands of dollars
worth of these things. The firm had taken the word of the
London "shark" for gospel and themselves paid high
prices. . . . Such items as "The Window," "Laus Veneris,"
"Gold Hair," and a dozen other small books of this ilk
cropped up with distressing frequency. . . . It is significant
that all these high-priced and "rare" privately printed items
are of the pamphlet variety and of modern date - few being
over 20p and of an earlier date than 1865. They are easy of
fabrication and we believe they have been fabricated.[4]

Although some collectors and dealers may have been put
on alert by these turn-of-the-century alarms, questions
about the validity of the pamphlets remained unanswered
until 1931, when Carter and Pollard began to probe into
the history and distribution of a rare edition of Elizabeth
Barrett Browning's *Sonnets from the Portuguese*, printed,
according to the title page, at Reading in 1847. It took

three years of intense investigation before the true identity of the *Sonnets* could be established.

Before the 1847 pamphlet had started to appear at auctions and in dealers' catalogs, it was generally accepted that the first publication of the *Sonnets* occurred in 1850 in the Chapman & Hall edition of the author's *Poems*. The 1847

SONNETS.

BY

E. B. B.

READING:

[NOT FOR PUBLICATION.]

———

1847.

16a. Title page from the forged edition of Browning's 'Sonnets,' the centerpiece in Carter and Pollard's investigation that eventually led to the publication of 'An Enquiry Into the Nature of Certain Nineteenth Century Pamphlets.'

date tempted collectors to pay as much as $1,200 for a copy in the heady rare book market of the mid-1920s. It was not only the date that appealed to collectors, but the romantic story attached to the printing of the pamphlet itself. According to the literary critic Edmund Gosse - relating a story he had heard from an unnamed individual - while the Brownings were living in Italy during the first year of their marriage, Mrs. Browning presented the sonnets to her husband by slipping them under his plate at the breakfast table. In spite of his wife's wish for anonymity, Browning insisted that the poems be published, and sent them back to England, to Mary Russell Mitford, one of Mrs. Browning's close friends. With the manuscript in hand, so the story went, Mitford arranged for a limited number of copies to be run off for the Brownings and their friends. Harry Buxton Forman, an editor and literary figure, repeated the Gosse story in *Elizabeth Barrett Browning and Her Scarcer Books,* (1896) as did the bibliographer Thomas J. Wise, first in his *Bibliography of Elizabeth Barrett Browning* (1918) and then in *A Browning Library* (1929). As for his own part in the story, Wise explained, with some delight, how he purchased two copies of the 1847 printing after enjoying tea and toast and sausages with a Dr. W. C. Bennett, a friend of Miss Mitford. Bennett also supplied copies to a number of Wise's collector friends. This story was to be changed considerably as Carter and Pollard continued to work on their investigation.

The Gosse/Buxton Forman/Wise account troubled Carter and Pollard for a number of reasons. Why had Browning sent the manuscript back to England when printing in Italy would have been a more reasonable approach? Why was there no mention of the publication in the Mitford or Browning correspondence? Why were

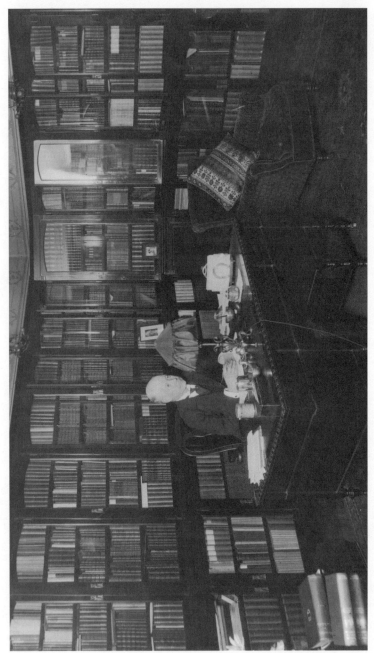

16b. *Thomas J. Wise, book collector, bibliographer, and forger in his library at 25 Heath Drive, Hampstead, London - c. 1927.*

none of the copies inscribed by the author or her husband? Why were no copies present in the 1913 sale of Browning's library? Why had no copies appeared on the market between the publication date and 1885? How had Dr. Bennett come to own a dozen or more copies of the rarity? There was also a discrepancy in the date of the wonderfully romantic incident at the breakfast table. Gosse said it was in 1847, but in a letter to Leigh Hunt, Browning remembered it as 1849. These and other questions prompted Carter to write to Wise for further information. He came right to the point: "In making some notes on the history of the privately printed edition of Mrs. Browning's Sonnets From the Portuguese 1847 we find on page 72 of your bibliography, 'The history of the volume has already been so fully told etc.' Would you be kind enough to let us know where the story can be found? With apologies for troubling you."[5] At the top of his carbon, Carter wrote a note to himself identifying the letter as "The First Gun." Wise answered immediately, "You will find all about the 1847 edition of Mrs. Browning's Sonnets in the H. B. Forman 'Elizabeth Barrett Browning and her Scarcer Books' pp 17-29. Also T. J. Wise 'A Browning Library' pp 83-88. Gosse also has a chapter devoted to the subject in one of his volumes of collected essays."[6] Carter's attempt to elicit information failed, as he no doubt expected it might. Wise simply repeated the titles of standard sources known to anyone who had an interest in the *Sonnets*.

Wise's unhelpful reply may have been triggered by an earlier incident. In September 1932 the *Times Literary Supplement* published a letter from Carter questioning the accuracy of some of the conclusions in Wise's recently published bibliography of Byron. "In the absence of supporting evidence," Carter wrote, "some of the rulings seem

The first gun.

T.J.Wise Esq.,
25 Heath Drive.
Hampstead.   19th December 1932.
N.W.3.

Dear Sir,

        In making some notes on the history of the privately
printed edition of Mrs Browning's Sonnets from the Portuguese
1847 we find on page 72 of your bibliography "the history of
the volume has already been so fully told etc."   Would you
be kind enough to let us know where the story can be found?

        With apologies for troubling you,

                We are,

                    Yours truly,
                Charles Scribner's Sons.

*The original of this letter
is in the collection of
Maurice Pariser, of
Manchester*

---

17. Carter's letter to Wise asking for more information on the history of the infamous 1847 edition of Browning's 'Sonnets.' His handwritten note in the upper-righthand corner, "the first gun," is suggestive of the intensive bibliographic detective work to follow.

dogmatic and arbitrary."[7] Wise had little patience with criticism, but didn't rise to Carter's bait until the following April when Carter's long review of the Byron bibliography appeared in the *Times Literary Supplement*. He began his ten page handwritten reply in a most conciliatory tone, thanking Carter for his comments. He had been ill, he said, or would have replied sooner. The letter included a declaration of friendship of sorts, and an invitation - "I would never dream of contradicting <u>you in public</u> but should and shall write to you personally. I wonder if you would come here one afternoon, after my return and have a chat over the questions you have raised?"[8] The chat never took place, but the debate continued. Carter's extended review of the Byron bibliography added more heat to the exchange. He claimed many of Wise's points were misleading and others lacked proper backing. Carter argued, for example, that Wise had overlooked evidence on the priority of printing in Isaac Nathan's 1815 folio edition of *Hebrew Melodies*.[9] In a testy reply Wise asked, "By the way, have you ever <u>seen</u> the folio with music? I think not."[10] Carter stood his ground, "I am not in the habit of describing in print books which I have not examined. My original notes were taken from a copy which I collated about a year ago." He concluded his four page letter with some vigor. "You have obviously not taken the trouble to read with any care the notes which I contributed, with (I thought) due diffidence, to 'The Times.' This is a pity, because there were a number of points brought up there on which fuller information from you would have been of interest and value to students at large and I must confess that your letter to me has done little to clarify them."[11] The flurry of charges and counter charges ended on a rather ironic note. On September 21 1933 the *Times*

Literary Supplement published a highly critical review of the second volume of the Byron bibliography. Wise assumed it was Carter's work, and dashed off a two-page handwritten defense. "I welcome criticism!" he wrote, "I don't like my boots licked: I long only for real criticism that my sins should be brought before me, and I am enabled to repent and correct."[12] The sentence must have amused Carter since he felt sure the opportunity to fulfill Wise's wish would soon be at hand. He replied in a strictly businesslike manner, "Thank you for your interesting letter. You are mistaken, however, in supposing that I wrote the review of your second volume in the Literary Supplement, so that I am afraid many of the strictures are misdirected. Would you care to have a copy of it forwarded to the Editor for transmission to the reviewer? This would save you the trouble of writing again, and it would be no trouble to have it copied here."[13]

Carter's first hint that something was not as it should be with the 1847 *Sonnets* came through the trade. In 1929 Mrs. J. Insley Blair, a wealthy American collector, asked the staff of Scribner's New York office to find her a copy of the *Sonnets*. Coming from one of the firm's best customers, this had the force of a royal command, and sent Carter hustling around the London shops. When he asked Mr. Mudie, Quaritch's rare book specialist, about the chances of securing a copy, he was told simply and without further explanation, "It's a book we don't much care for."[14] That comment, coming as it did from a discriminating specialist in one of London's most important rare book houses, carried considerable weight.

By the end of 1931, with their suspicions growing about the Reading *Sonnets* and other similar publications, Carter and Pollard decided to approach the question of authenticity from a technical point of view. A careful analysis of paper and type, they reasoned, might well provide accurate dating. Type analysis had already been used by bibliographers such as Robert Proctor to date early printed books, but no one had tried that approach on nineteenth century publications. Pollard labored through specimen books at the St. Bride Printing Library in an attempt to trace the history of the type faces found in the suspect pamphlets, and both investigators worked on sales records and bibliographies at the British Museum. Years later Carter reminisced, ". . . our joint investigation of the nineteenth century pamphlets brought us much more closely together from 1931 onwards, with lunch once or twice a week at Brice's restaurant in Wardour Street and a solid day on Saturdays at the British Museum (with a tea break at the Express Dairy among the other bibliographers)."[15]

An important part of the investigation involved the collation of copies of the suspected forgeries. Various libraries and collectors in London supplied most of the questionable pamphlets, but a difficulty arose when a copy of the *Sonnets*, the centerpiece of the investigation, could not be found in England. It was fortunate at that point that Pollard and Carter could rely on help from noted type historian Stanley Morison. He was not a regular member of the Biblios, and probably viewed the group with some amusement, but enjoyed working with the investigators on questions related to typography. On a trip to the United States in January 1933, Morison examined the copy of the *Sonnets* in the Pierpont Morgan Library in New York. In a letter to Pollard he reported that the Morgan copy included lower-case kernless, "broken backed" letters f and j, and, curiously, a tilted question mark that didn't match the rest of the font. Kerned letters, which had been used since the fifteenth century, extended beyond the body of the type and broke easily under the pressure of high-speed presses. Toward the end of the nineteenth century printing firms began to correct this wasteful process by using fonts that eliminated kerned letters. Morison felt sure the kernless letters as seen in the 1847 *Sonnets* could not have been in common use at that time. "Had you asked me before this enquiry," he wrote, "I would have given you a guess that it first appeared during the 90s."[16] He advised Pollard to find out exactly when kernless letters came into use in English printing shops. It was a stroke of good fortune when, during an examination of Matthew Arnold's *Alaric at Rome* (1840), a type facsimile reprint edited by Wise and produced for private circulation in 1893, Pollard recognized a familiar type configuration: the same kernless f and j, and tilted question mark used in the printing of the *Sonnets*. The pamphlet's colophon identified the printer as the well known firm of Richard Clay and Sons, of Bread Street Hill in London. Further investigation showed the type face, designated as Number 3 Long Primer, was used for the first time by Clay between 1880 and 1883. The investigators identified sixteen pamphlets, including Swinburne's *Dolores* (1867), Tennyson's *Morte d'Arthur* (1842), Ruskin's *The Queen's Gardens* (1864), Browning's *Sonnets* (1847), and Stevenson's *On the Thermal Influence of Forests* (1873) as having been printed with the kernless font, therefore produced after 1880, and therefore forgeries. The officers at the printing firm were unable to provide any information on the person who had commissioned the work since all of their pre-World War I records had been destroyed. Further, the investigators found no evidence that the employees of Clay and Company were involved in any act of deception. It was standard practice for them to print facsimile editions for the Browning and the Shelley Societies, and for private collectors like Wise, with dates that had no relation to the year in which the printing was completed. If a customer in 1905, for example, ordered a pamphlet printed with the date 1847, the job would have been completed without question.

Another approach taken by Carter and Pollard to determine the validity of the 1847 *Sonnets* and the other publications under scrutiny called for chemical analysis of the paper on which they were printed. Again, the evidence on the *Sonnets* had to come from the United States. Flora Livingston, the rare book specialist at Harvard's H. E. Widener Memorial Library (already at odds with Wise over disputed Kipling and Swinburne printings), with what must have been some considerable trepidation, took a small clipping from a page of a copy of the Reading *Sonnets* from the library's collection and sent it to Carter. "I have had the courage," she reported," to trim off a little slip of paper from the bottom of a badly folded leaf of the Sonnets. It will never show and if it does, no will know the who or why."[17] Working with the knowledge that esparto grass came into general use as an ingredient in the manufacture of paper sometime between 1861 and 1865, and that chemical wood was not introduced until the late 1870s, the investigators had clippings from the suspected forgeries analyzed by paper chemists at the well-known firm of Cross & Bevan. As with the typographical tests, the results were conclusive. The clipping from the Harvard copy of the *Sonnets* contained traces of chemical wood fibers, and therefore, in spite of the 1847 date, could not have been manufactured before 1874 and perhaps, as Carter and Pollard suggested, not before 1883.[18]

Continued analysis showed twelve pamphlets containing chemical wood but dated years before the introduction of that substance, and ten, including Tennyson's *Morte d'Arthur* (1842) and Morris's *Sir Galahad*, (1858) with traces of esparto grass. These were indisputable forgeries. In addition, the investigators found probable cause to indict, as highly suspicious, thirty additional pamphlets based on type, paper, or textual irregularities.

As the physical evidence mounted the investigation began to take on all the ingredients of a good detective story. Carter and Pollard began to examine auction records and dealers' catalogs for clues to the identity the person or persons responsible for the creation and distribution of the spurious pamphlets. In January 1933, Flora Livingston, now actively engaged in the investigation, wrote Carter that the Amy Lowell copy of the *Sonnets* held by Harvard, and copies owned by private collectors Edwin N. Lapham, Edwin B. Holden, and John Henry Wrenn "all came from the bookseller who at one time was private-secretary to T. J. Wise."[19] Earlier, one of the Biblios had called Carter and Pollard's attention to the large number of nineteenth century pamphlets listed in a catalog issued by Herbert E. Gorfin, a South London dealer known to specialize in literary ephemera and private printings. In the summer of 1933, Carter and Pollard showed Gorfin the evidence they had gathered and asked him to explain his part in the distribution of the pamphlets. Gorfin was entirely cooperative once his own perilous situation was made clear. Trade in fraudulent goods was a crime, and, if proven, as seemed certain in this case, court proceedings and jail would follow. He told Carter and Pollard that between 1892 and 1912 he had been employed as an office boy for H. Rubeck, a merchant in essential oils. During that time, Wise, the firm's manager and cashier, offered him a chance to act as a commission agent in the sale of pamphlets and books. In 1912, based on early success, and working with an expanded stock purchased from Wise, Gorfin went into business for himself. His carefully preserved records showed that between 1909 and 1912, he paid Wise £400 for some nine hundred pamphlets and books, some legitimate, but many on Carter and Pollard's list of forgeries. Along with the Ruskins, Stevensons, Rossettis, Kiplings, Swinburnes, and Tennysons, he had sold or placed at auction as many as a dozen copies of the 1847 Reading *Sonnets*. Where had Wise obtained such a cache of rarities? As far as Gorfin knew, and he had no reason to ask for more specific details, Wise had secured them through a third party, unnamed, who had found them among publisher's wastes. At that point Carter and Pollard's excitement must have been hard to conceal. The paper trail they had been following seemed now to have both a beginning and an end. Gorfin's assistance had been crucial. In a letter of August 29, 1933, Carter acknowledged the help and enclosed a check for £3/3. "Please do not regard this as a payment for the information which I know you gave without any such idea," he wrote, "but accept it as something towards the expenses which you have incurred in our behalf."[20]

From the beginning of the investigation, several pieces of circumstantial evidence pointed to Wise, but to assume his direct responsibility for the forgeries seemed almost beyond belief. In 1933, at age 74, Wise was not only *a* prominent English collector/bibliographer but perhaps *the* prominent English collector/bibliographer. He had accumulated a highly acclaimed private library - the Ashley Library - of modern English literature, and between 1922 and 1936, published an elaborate eleven volume catalog of its holdings. Over the course of twenty years, he had compiled detailed bibliographies of such important literary figures as Ruskin, Tennyson, Wordsworth, Landor, Swinburne, the Brownings, Coleridge, Conrad, and Dryden. In these reference works he gave prominent place to the very pamphlet publications that Carter and Pollard later identified as forgeries. He served as President of the Bibliographical Society in 1922, and two years later was named an Honorary Fellow at Worcester College, Oxford. In 1927, he was elected to membership in the Roxburghe Club, the pinnacle of exclusiveness in book-collecting circles. He served as honorary secretary of the Browning and Shelley Societies, and in that capacity, during the 1880s, oversaw the publication of a number of facsimile reprints. Beginning in 1893 Wise edited a regular column in *The Bookman*, a position that gave him an opportunity to defend many of the pamphlets later condemned in the *Enquiry*. In print, and in person, he had little patience with anyone who had the temerity to disagree with his pronouncements. The younger members of the trade, such as Carter and his friends, considered Wise something of a self-righteous bully. An incident from Pollard's time at Oxford illustrates the point. Pollard had gathered some important first editions including George Crabbe's *Inebriety* (1775), one of three known copies, and with notes in Crabbe's hand, but lacking the title page. On being shown the book during a visit to Pollard's rooms, Wise commented that one should never invest in imperfect goods.

Once Carter and Pollard had Gorfin's records in hand, the investigation moved forward like an end-game in chess, with Wise pinned into one untenable position after another. On October 14, 1933 after writing for an appointment, Pollard called on Wise at his home at 25 Heath Drive, and laid out the findings of the investigation up to that point. There were irregularities concerning the dates of certain type faces and paper used in the pamphlets sold to Gorfin. Where had Wise obtained such a large stock? Had he any idea about their true nature? Wise said he had no knowledge of any problems; as far as he knew, all the pamphlets were genuine. Pollard's visit had one immediate result. Wise hurriedly called Gorfin, whom he had not seen in ten years, and invited him to lunch. Wise offered to pay £25. for any remaining pamphlets in the dealer's possession, saying they were now merely waste paper with no market value. He also asked Gorfin to say that they came from H. Buxton Forman, not Wise himself, a lie the dealer refused to support. Gorfin had intended to tell Wise about his conversations with Carter and Pollard, but face to face with his former employer, he was unable to do so. In order to move the negotiation forward, Carter advised Gorfin to write to Wise, saying there could be no confusion about the source of the pamphlets, since he had already made his receipt books available to the investigators, a message that brought Gorfin a second hurried invitation to Heath Drive. Wise at first assumed a conciliatory attitude, and told Gorfin he would now pay £400 to have the pamphlets destroyed. This, on condition that Gorfin name Buxton Forman, who had died in 1917, as the person responsible. Gorfin again refused to involve a man whose name had never come up during the negotiation. Furthermore, he found the offer of £400 insulting. If the pamphlets had been legitimate, as he thought they were, they should have been worth, at his estimate,

£2000. Wise made a remark about blackmail and as Gorfin got up to leave, asked him it he was going to "stir up further mud."[21] After talking with Carter and Pollard, and securing legal advice, Gorfin agreed to accept Wise's offer, but with reservations. His letter of acceptance, certainly done under the watchful eye of Carter and Pollard, was a masterpiece:

> Dear Mr. Wise, Anent our conversation of last Friday week, the 20th inst., and your proposal that, in consideration of my destroying the whole of the forged pamphlets remaining in my possession, you would compensate me in the sum of £400. I have carefully considered the matter and am prepared to accept your proposal. It would of course be understood that I am not expected to state that I purchased the pamphlets from Mr. H. B. Forman and that you undertake, as you agreed to do, to accept responsibility for any claim that may be brought against me by former purchasers. Although such a settlement as this takes no account of the serious damage to my reputation that must result and has indeed already shown itself, I am anxious to be clear of the whole very unpleasant business.[22]

Early in November, Gorfin received his payment, and delivered the pamphlets to the offices of Messrs. Gedge, Fiske & Company, Wise's lawyers, where all were destroyed. At least it seemed at the time all were destroyed. In 1950, Carter wrote to Gorfin's sister about a number of forgeries she had placed on the market through Maggs Brothers. "I was somewhat surprised," he wrote, "to note that Mr. Gorfin had not only kept copies of a number of the forgeries, but even three or four copies of some of them: for you may not be aware that in 1933 Mr. Gorfin, in consideration of the payment of £400 which Mr. Wise made him, undertook to 'destroy the whole of the forged pamphlets remaining in my possession.' This undertaking, together with a statement that the pamphlets were delivered to Mr. Wise's solicitor, and confirmation by the solicitor that these had been destroyed, were contained in a statutory declaration."[23] Part of Carter's objective in pursuing this matter with such force was to try to secure letters and papers that still might be in the family hands. That hope vanished when Miss Gorfin told him she had burned all her brother's papers. Carter could not disguise his anger. "Dear Miss Gorfin, The greatest possible disservice you could have done to your brother's memory was to destroy the letters and documents which he supplied to Mr. Pollard and myself in 1933 and 1934. It was the evidence which enabled us to defend him from the charges of conspiracy with Wise in the forgeries: and we were the only people who did defend him. Those charges are still made, and your action has gravely weakened any future defence against them."[24]

When Carter and Pollard first began to dig into the mystery of the nineteenth century pamphlets, they discussed publication of the results with fellow Biblio member Michael Sadleir, a partner of the Constable publishing firm. Sadleir was encouraging but cautious. Publishers do not like to be drawn into expensive court battles based on charges of criminal libel and many of the passages in Carter and Pollard's draft text, as presented to the Constable directors, seemed libelous. It didn't help that the preliminary outline carried the playful title "Wisecracking, or Have With You to Heath Drive." Carter and Pollard then suggested, "The '1847' Edition of Mrs. Browning's Sonnets: An Exposure." Finally, they chose *An Enquiry Into the Nature of Certain Nineteenth Century Pamphlets,* an insider's reference to Edmond

Malone's study of the William Henry Ireland forgeries, *An Inquiry Into the Authenticity of Certain Miscellaneous Papers . . . Attributed to Shakspeare, Queen Elizabeth and Henry, Earl of Southampton* (1796).

Sadleir and his fellow directors continued to debate the wisdom of publication through the fall and winter of 1933. In order to avoid any legal entanglement, they asked the distinguished lawyer and book collector J.P.R. Lyell to read the text and offer an opinion. In his lengthy report, Lyell refused either to support or to discourage the publication of the book, but warned that it was potentially libelous, since it contained "a veiled attack upon the honesty and bona fides of Mr. Thomas J. Wise in his capacity of a bibliographer and author." Further, the book provided an "abundant opportunity for Mr. Wise to take proceeding for defamation."[25] Would Wise sue? In view of the accumulated evidence, Lyell thought not. Even with that legal opinion in hand, some of Constable's directors wanted to get a second opinion. In a diplomatic letter, Carter argued that Lyell's word should be good enough since "Wise will see that it will pay him best to keep absolutely quiet, since whatever the event, any such publicity as a law suit would entail would bring such a hornet's nest about his ears as no verdict or damages (in the highly unlikely case of his getting either) could compensate him for."[26] On the basis of Carter's argument, Sadleir and his fellow directors agreed to proceed.

In one final step to protect themselves, the directors insisted that Gorfin submit a sworn statement covering all the details of his negotiations with Wise. One month before the *Enquiry* came out, he signed two affidavits before a commissioner of oaths. The first described his experience working in the Rubeck firm, outlined his role as Wise's commission agent, and included a complete list of pamphlets purchased from Wise between 1909 and 1912. The second affidavit outlined the events of October 1933, when Wise had tried to induce Gorfin to commit perjury on his behalf. [27]

Within the circle of London bookdealers and collectors, word of the investigation slowly leaked out. It became known that Wise would be identified, if not as the source of the forged pamphlets, at least as one heavily involved in establishing their credibility and directing their distribution. Wise's powerful friends in the academic and literary world began to put pressure on Sadleir and his colleagues to abandon their plan to publish what they deemed to be a rash and irresponsible book. After all, they argued, Carter and Pollard were mere tradesmen. Why should a dignified publishing firm encourage such troublemakers? Negative reaction to the book also came from America. Collectors such as A. Edward Newton and W. T. H. Howe and the bookdealer Gabriel Wells complained that in attacking Wise, Carter and Pollard were in effect trespassing on hallowed ground. Without mentioning names, Wells published a bitter personal attack on the investigators. "During my last stay in England," Wells wrote, "I found that those who were unsparing in their pronouncements were often persons who cannot be considered irreproachable in their own conduct." And again, "Experience shows that people of indifferent character are led to think that by lowering the reputation of others they are raising their own."[28] Wells's pamphlet was of no service to Wise or, for that matter, to himself. As a last ditch effort to protect himself, Wise wrote a rambling letter to the *Times Literary Supplement* two months before the *Enquiry* came out. Beginning with a reference to the

AN ENQUIRY
INTO THE NATURE OF CERTAIN
NINETEENTH CENTURY
PAMPHLETS

by

JOHN CARTER

&

GRAHAM POLLARD

With four plates

London

CONSTABLE & CO LTD

New York

CHARLES SCRIBNER'S SONS

1934

18a. Title page of 'An Enquiry into the Nature of Certain Nineteenth Century Pamphlets.'

Sonnets, he wrote, "The suggestion has been pressed upon me that this book with an imprint Reading (Not for Publication) is an impostor not printed until many years after 1847." After repeating

" The whole thing proves once more that, easy as it appears to be to fabricate reprints of rare books, it is in actual practice absolutely impossible to do so in such a manner that detection cannot follow the result."

THOMAS J. WISE,
Bibliography of Swinburne, I. 93.

18b. The quotation from Wise's 'Bibliography of Swinburne.' Used, with a touch of venom, on the dedication page.

the Gosse account of how the poems were sent to Miss Mitford, he retreated somewhat from his early defense of the publication and admitted, "I may be driven to the conclusion that the 1847 book is not authentic."[29] He also remembered that his own two copies came from Buxton Forman and not, as he reported in the Ashley catalog, from the hospitable Dr. Bennett. Finally, he brushed aside the arguments based on the irregularities of paper and type as insubstantial and misleading. If the intent of the letter was to draw support, it failed completely.

Once the Constable officers had satisfied themselves that placing their colophon on the *Enquiry* would not involve them in a legal battle, the publication process moved forward rapidly. From the original print run of two thousand copies, Scribner's agreed, although somewhat reluctantly, as Carter remembered, to take seven hundred. The official date for publication on both sides of the Atlantic was Monday July 2, but, based on the sensational nature of the revelations, several papers rushed ahead and printed editorial comments before that date. A note in *The Sunday Times* headed "Famous First Editions Challenged," announced that the *Enquiry*, which had "already caused considerable controversy behind the scenes . . . casts doubt on the authenticity of about 50 first

109

editions. . . ."[30] Five days later, an article in *The Times* reviewed the history of literary forgeries, then went on to describe how suspect publications could now be analyzed by close examination of paper and type. The article supported Carter and Pollard's findings, but put in a word of defense for Wise, who, they claimed, in a line somewhat reminiscent of Gilbert and Sullivan, was "well equipped for controversy in matters bibliographical."[31] The banner headline on the front page of the London *Daily Herald* for June 30 read "50 FAMOUS BOOKS DENOUNCED AS FORGED." The subhead, in only a slightly smaller type face, declared, "British Museum Deceived, Declare Experts, Fraud Unsuspected for a Generation." The *Herald* scooped the other London papers by publishing a lengthy interview with Wise, whom they found recovering from an illness in Hastings. In defending himself, Wise maintained a lofty position as far as the pamphlets were concerned. Yes, he may have been taken in but he was not alone. Prominent figures such as Edmund Gosse, Harry Buxton Forman, and William Michael Rossetti had also accepted the pamphlets as genuine. Why should he have questioned their validity? Further, he told the interviewer, most of the pamphlets had come to him directly from Buxton Forman "in exchange for manuscripts and letters of the Brontes, Swinburne, Rossetti, Borrow, and George Eliot." He had simply passed them along to Gorfin. "I was," he said, "only the vehicle. I was the messenger lad who took the goods for delivery."[32] In another part of the interview he made an attempt to place the blame for the production of the forgeries on the nineteenth century literary renegade Richard Herne Shepherd. That argument held no validity, since Shepherd died in 1895, several years before the last of the fakes was completed. As to why

18c. *Biblios at ease - left to right, Percy Muir, Carter, Graham Pollard lounging outside Michael Sadleir's house in the Cotswolds - c. 1934.*

Carter and Pollard should have cast doubt on his reputation, Wise replied, "All my life I have been preaching against bad copies of books and teaching people to leave bad copies alone. That has done small booksellers a lot of harm and so they curse and hate me."[33]

No one could control informal newspaper articles, but Carter had definite ideas about who should write the formal reviews. It would be best to have reliable people, Viscount Esher for the *Observer*, John Sparrow in the *Spectator*, and John Hayward in the *New Statesman and Nation*. "I do hope," he wrote Sadleir, " we shall get Sayers for the Sunday Times."[34] It all happened as he wished - with reviewers expressing universal delight and approval for what many of them referred to as a carefully designed bibliographical detective story. Sparrow said, "The authors . . . reconstruct the conception and execution of the fraud so lucidly and excitedly that even those who know nothing of book auctions and bibliography will ask, 'Who was the forger?'" [35] Dorothy Sayers, the well-known author of detective fiction, suggested the book might well have been titled The Catalogue Crimes or The Case of the Crookbacked F. "Connoisseurs of detective method," she claimed, "will find it more fascinating than any fiction, while for the book-collecting world it is obviously of urgent importance."[36] According to Hayward, the *Enquiry* was "a model of careful scholarship and skillful reconstruction." [37] American reviewers were no less impressed. Carter's friend David Randall, writing under the heading, "A Bibliographical Sensation," declared, " the general manner in which the authors . . . have handled the investigation reflects nothing but credit upon themselves, the trade, and bibliography itself."[38] Philip Brooks concurred, "What they have done here is just what they had to do, and they have accomplished their purposes in brilliant fashion. The result is an admirable volume, a pitiless, inexorable exposure, remarkably fair and restrained in its charges."[39]

R. B. McKerrow, writing for *The Library*, the official journal of the Bibliographical Society, where Wise had many friends, took a somewhat more conservative approach. After describing the *Enquiry* as "a brilliant demonstration of the fraudulent character of a number of pamphlets purporting to be first or separate editions of works by such famous Victorians as Tennyson, the Brownings, Swinburne, Ruskin and others," he said, "it is perhaps of no great importance, now that the deception has been so completely exposed, that we should know the name of the villain." Was it a unconscious play on words that caused him to continue, "It is easy to be wise after the event, but I think that few will read Messrs. Carter and Pollard's book without feeling that what happened shows a singular lack of mental alertness - to say the least - among collectors of nineteenth century books and the dealers who supplied their wants."[40] McKerrow's only conscious reference to Wise, and this obliquely, came at the end of his circumspect review: "If the eminent bibliographer whose name is most frequently mentioned in the volume under discussion had any more intimate connection with these pamphlets than that of being deceived by them, he must have acted in a manner strangely inconsistent with the character of his bibliographical work as a whole."[41] Those words, coming as they did from a revered bibliographic scholar, may well have caused Wise more pain than any of the more strident attacks from the popular press.

Viewed from the outside in its typographically conservative, light maroon colored dust jacket, the *Enquiry* looked harmless enough, but inside, the first sentence hinted at the lethal nature of what was to come -"During the past few years a vague rumour has been circulating, with gradually increasing frequency and volume, that the privately printed first edition of Mrs. Browning's "Sonnets from the Portuguese" (*Sonnets by E. B. B.*, Reading, 1847) was not all that it pretended to be."[42] The early chapters outlined the story of the Reading *Sonnets,* and the techniques used by the investigators to determine its authenticity. A second narrative section examined the forger's methods and marketing techniques, while a third presented a dossier for each of forty pamphlets, including a printing history, collation, provenance, bibliographic citations, auction records, and a statement of conclusions based on the examination of paper and type. The pamphlets were clearly not all they pretended to be. Who was responsible? Wise was the person best able to answer that question. In one of the book's concluding sentences, saturated with irony, the investigators wrote, "We find it difficult to believe that Mr. Wise cannot now guess the identity of the forger; but, as long as it remains a guess, he has followed a very proper course in making no suggestion; and unfortunately the state of his health has prevented him from giving us the information, which he was good enough to promise, about the source of the "remainders."[43] Appropriately, the *Enquiry* began with a another ironic note. On what would ordinarily have been the dedication page, the investigators printed a note from Wise's *Bibliography of Swinburne* - "The whole thing proves once more that, easy as it appears to be to fabricate reprints of rare books, it is in actual practice absolutely impossible to do so in such a manner that detection cannot follow the result."[44] It was a tease, of course - one that Carter and Pollard couldn't resist.

Letters of appreciation came from such disparate individuals as the eminent bibliographer/literary scholar/surgeon Geoffrey Keynes: "bound to be a bibliographic classic,"[45] and the rambunctious American bookdealer Max Harzof, "A shipload of praise to you and Mr. Pollard for the greatest work in Bibliography ever produced. . . . The old faker had it coming to him. Now it's the duty of Oxford University to cancel the degree of M.A. bestowed on Mr. Wise. I should like to see him get the degree of M.F. (master forger) from Bow Street Police Court with the term of seven years at Reading Gaol."[46] Holbrook Jackson, the author of *Anatomy of Bibliomania*, called the book a "distinguished contribution to bibliographical research."[47] A few people were unconvinced. The American collector W.T.H. Howe, who owned most of the forgeries, wrote, "I still have very definite faith in the authenticity of the Browning "47" sonnets."[48] Wise responded to friends and foes with an inconclusive letter to the *Times Literary Supplement*, once more pleading his innocence and placing the blame on Buxton Forman. He tried to back his claim by inserting a letter sent to him from Buxton Forman's son who recalled his father's buying and selling remainders of books and pamphlets. Beyond that, the evidence was vague. Maurice Buxton Forman admitted he had spent most of his adult life in Africa and had no positive knowledge of his father's transactions. Wise repeated a story that by now had a certain familiar ring: "I never held stock of any one of the condemned or questioned pamphlets. . . . The proposal to have all "remainders" in his own hands pleased Mr. Gorfin; and in consequence I obtained the pamphlets from Forman in batches as he found time to make them up and sold them to Mr. Gorfin.[49] Gorfin's letter of reply was brief and to the point. " In all our many transactions this connection of the pamphlets with H. Buxton Forman was never mentioned, even by implication; and the suggestion that he was the source from which they came was only made to me by Mr. Wise himself, on October 14, 1933 - two days after Mr. Pollard had visited him and explained that they were forgeries. Mr. Wise had previously given me a totally different account of their origin."[50]

In spite of a promise to have something to say about the *Enquiry*, after he had read it carefully, Wise remained silent. It was time to apply more pressure. Carter and Pollard wanted the appeal for information to come from someone of stature in the bibliographic community. For that purpose they asked Viscount Esher, a distinguished bibliophile and member of the Roxburghe Club, to write a letter to *The Times*. Again, Carter wanted to control the timing. "We are anxious," he wrote, " that the authoritative request for further information should come from you, and in the Times, well ahead of a similar request from Symons [A.J.A. Symons, Editor of *The Book Collector's Quarterly*], and if possible want to secure the interval of a week or two between the two publications in order to allow anyone else who can throw light on the matter (such as, we very much hope, Clay) time to reply in the Times before the Book Collector's Quarterly comes out."[51] Esher was happy to oblige. The tone of his letter was polite but determined. "Book collectors throughout the world are still waiting to hear from Mr. Wise an explanation of the forgeries. . . . Those of us who have bought the forged pamphlets for large sums of money cannot consent to leave the matter where it is." Was Buxton Forman the forger? If not, who planted the forgeries on him? "Some evidence of these prolonged transactions must exist and should be produced. We collectors have been accustomed to look upon Mr. Wise as an expert bibliographer. . . . He has stated that on a more careful reading of Mr. Carter and Mr. Pollard's book, he will have something further to say. A considerable time has elapsed, and the collectors who have followed Mr. Wise have a right to know how they stand in the matter."[52] In reply, Mrs. Wise wrote a brief note to the editor saying her husband had been ill and with his doctor's advice was withdrawing from any further public correspondence.

In spite of positive reviews and the intense interest shown by collectors, dealers, librarians, and bibliographers, sales of the *Enquiry* were disappointing. With the world still in the grip of the Depression, the reading public was not inclined to buy a book in a plain dust jacket with a daunting academic title written by two unknown London bookdealers. The original press run was two thousand copies, with seven hundred designated for sale by Scribner's in the United States. Ten years after the book came out, copies were still available from the publisher.

Carter and Pollard always considered the *Enquiry* a work in progress. Even while the book was in press they began to plan a supplement. As new facts came into their hands from librarians and collectors in the United States and England, they drafted notes to expand and correct their original findings. Over time, these comments, corrections and additions turned into a sizable archive. During the war, with shortages of paper and manpower, Sadleir wasn't able to publish a revision, but even without that delaying factor, there was little enthusiasm within the Constable firm to reinvest in a book that had essentially failed to attract an audience. In 1939, Carter approached Rupert Hart-Davis, then a director with

Jonathan Cape, with the suggestion that his firm use the original Constable plates for a revision. A contract was drawn up, but ten years later, with no text in hand, Carter admitted defeat. As a compromise, and in answer to the urging of friends, the investigators decided to publish some of their current findings in abbreviated form. In 1948, Hart-Davis, now established with a firm of his own, brought out their first effort, *The Firm of Charles Ottley, Landon & Co.*, subtitled "a footnote to the *Enquiry.*" The ninety page text condemned four Swinburne pamphlets, considered suspicious in the original *Enquiry*, but now, with further study, proven to be forgeries. The pamphlets purported to be published by Charles Ottley, Landon & Co. of London and printed by T. Rignall of Whitefriars. As it turned out, there was no such publisher and no such printing firm. Philip Brooks praised the authors - "They deliver a round unvarnished tale with dignity, restraint and fairness."[53] As their research continued into the 1960s, the investigators issued four Working Papers designated to supplement the text of the original *Enquiry.* "In the course of preparing supplementary material for a second volume," the authors explained, "we have written several memoranda on related topics. Some of these are too long and too detailed for inclusion in their present form, but they contain evidence and conclusions to which we may need to refer later."[54] The Working Papers; "Precis of Paden or the Sources of the New Timon" (1967), "The Forgeries of Tennyson's Plays" (1967),"The Mystery of the Death of Balder" (1969) and "Gorfin's Stock" (1970) came out in limited editions of from two to four hundred copies. This hardly satisfied the interested public who had by this time waited for over thirty years for the promised revision.

Early in 1964, the University of Chicago Press expressed an interest in doing a reprint of the *Enquiry* with a supplementary volume to follow. This seemed promising. A contract was written, and the investigators set to work. There were long delays as Carter and Pollard drafted and redrafted their original text and the dossiers. Part of the problem arose from Pollard's deliberate working style, and part from the difficulty of coordinating efforts between London and Chicago. It sometimes took Carter six months to a year to obtain corrected drafts from Pollard. Finally, as Carter admitted to Professor William Todd, his loyal supporter at the University of Texas, "after so long an interval and so many interruptions, I have (as I write you) gone stale on the whole subject."[55] In February 1972, the press and the investigators released each other from any further obligation.

In many ways Carter and Pollard were an ideal team - Pollard the meticulous technical expert, Carter the graceful writer and careful organizer. It was Carter, with his experience in the Scribner's office and his close friendship with Sadleir, who negotiated the contract, saw the book through the press, and managed the publicity. With his circle of friends in London and New York, he knew whom to call on for support and advice. The early chapters and the author dossiers were done cooperatively - drafts went back and forth for months. Carter's lively style can be read in the chapters on "The Modern First Edition Market 1885-1895," and "Marketing the Forgeries," and Pollard's handiwork can be identified in the chapters dealing with the analysis of paper and type. With his contacts in the publishing and rare book trade, Carter became the book's spokesman. He gave talks at meetings of bibliographic societies and book clubs in England and the United States, defended the book's findings in the *Times Literary Supplement* and elsewhere, assisted in the production of several radio and television programs devoted to the forgeries, and wrote dozens of articles on Wise and the forgeries for popular and scholarly periodicals.[56]

Along with the public acclaim there were occasional complications. Less than a year after the *Enquiry's* publication, Carter found himself in the middle of a frustrating confrontation with a prominent American book collector. Although the *Enquiry* pointed directly to Wise as the person responsible for the manufacture, sponsorship, and distribution of the "first editions," the investigators possessed only circumstantial evidence against him. In March 1935, William A. Jackson, the scholarly librarian for Carl Pforzheimer, a wealthy collector of English literature, came upon a note in Wise's handwriting not only admitting to the forgeries, but identifying Buxton Forman as a co-conspiritor. Wise and Buxton Forman had cooperated on a number of literary projects. In one exchange of letters Buxton Forman complained that Wise was hoodwinking the public by saying in his bibliographies only a few copies had been printed instead of mentioning an actual number. Writing between the lines of Buxton Forman's letter Wise responded "Quite so. And we print "Last Tournament" in 1896, & want someone to think it was printed in 1871 ! - The moral position is exactly the same."[57] This was the proof Carter and Pollard had been waiting for to complete the story of the *Enquiry*. For reasons of his own, and in the face of repeated requests from Carter, Pforzheimer refused to allow the incriminating information to be published. In February 1936, Carter wrote to Pforzheimer about rumors he said were circulating around the British Museum Reading Room about a document that would for once and for all convict Wise of the forgeries. "I am afraid," he wrote, "that this so far underground rumor cannot fail before long to come to the surface; and it would probably do so in such a way as to nullify your own efforts, with which we have every sympathy, to handle the matter with the utmost possible consideration for those concerned." Pleading his own case, Carter continued "I think the "Enquiry" is an adequate guarantee that in our hands the inclusion of this crucial piece of evidence among other supplementary matter, now awaiting publication, would be handled with all the restraint and sobriety you could wish. . . . Let a newspaper man run across the tail end of this story, and you can imagine what an elegant lot of headlines would result."[58] Pforzheimer didn't answer. Before writing directly to Pforzheimer, Carter had asked Jackson to intercede. The prospects, Jackson answered, were not encouraging - "Unless you can show that someone actually is injured by the withholding of the publication of the document, I don't believe he will budge from his stand."[59] Shortly after Wise's death in May 1937, Carter wrote again asking if now, in the best interests of all concerned, the evidence of Wise's guilt might now be released. Pforzheimer replied that everyone now knew Wise was the forger so the release of any documents would be beside the point. Carter's desperation grew. At one point he considered identifying the document in a journal article in spite of Pforzheimer's wish to keep it secret. That brash scheme never materialized. Finally, in 1945 Pforzheimer allowed Fannie E. Ratchford, the rare book librarian at the University of Texas, to publish the document along with a commentary in *Between the Lines, Letters and Memoranda Interchanged by H. Buxton Forman and Thomas J. Wise.*

19. *Fannie Ratchford, rare book librarian, University of Texas, Austin, c. 1940. She challenged some of Carter and Pollard's conclusions and was instrumental in identifying Harry Buxton Forman as a co-conspirator with T. J. Wise in the creation of the forgeries.*

If Pforzheimer was a major stumbling block to Carter and Pollard's plans for a supplement, Ratchford was another. In 1920, the University of Texas had purchased the six thousand volume library of Chicago businessman John Henry Wrenn, Wise's favorite American customer. A frequently told story had it that Wise claimed Wrenn was worth £1000 a year to him. Salted away among many authentic rarities Wise sold his friend - the two men and their wives took long European vacation trips together and were on the most cordial terms - were all of the forgeries backed by letters promoting their importance and authenticity. Working with those promotional letters and other documents, Ratchford published her own views on

122

the forgeries. In articles published in *The Southwest Review,* *The Papers of the Bibliographical Society of America,* and *The Library Chronicle of the University of Texas,* she praised Carter and Pollard for some of their findings, but claimed they had overlooked certain important facts. Ratchford countered the investigators' belief that the forgeries were the work of one man, by suggesting likely co-conspirators, prominent among them Harry Buxton Forman, Herbert Gorfin, William Michael Rossetti, Richard Clay, of the printing firm of Clay and Taylor, and the literary critic Edmund Gosse. Carter and Pollard considered her claims unfounded. In 1938, Ratchford secured a Guggenheim Foundation grant to prepare a book based on the Wise/Wrenn letters. The news of the grant set off a London vs. Austin fencing match. Each party had information needed by the other, but both were wary of giving up what they held without a guarantee of some quid pro quo. In October Carter wrote to Pollard, "She is prepared, even (I gather) anxious to "cooperate" with us to the extent of letting me see the letters; on condition that she okays our use of them for quotation, and in exchange, no doubt, for any help she can get out of us. That is, we can have access to the evidence, but we must not steal any of her thunder." The situation, as Carter pointed out, was delicate. "Does it pay us," he asked, "to play ball with her? On the one hand, the letters are obviously full of interest, and a knowledge of their contents might, if nothing else, keep us from putting our feet in any holes, even if we did not make much actual use of them. On the other, we might run into a Pforzheimer situation, finding out something and being prevented by Fannie from noting the evidence to support it."[60] Pollard favored a diplomatic approach. "I should be friendly with the Ratchford, if you can, but use your own judgment in estimating what her position will be. If you think I am correct, I should not be too forthcoming. But by all means get as full and precise an idea as possible of her evidence."[61]

Carter and Pollard eventually saw the letters, but it was Ratchford who managed to get them into print. In 1944, Knopf published *Letters of Thomas J. Wise to John Henry Wrenn, a Further Inquiry into the Guilt of Certain Nineteenth-Century Forgers,* with Ratchford's lengthy introductory essay. The next year she followed with *Between the Lines.* In both books she continued to press her theories concerning co-conspirators. The publication of *Between the Lines* was particularly galling to Carter since after erecting a stone wall around the document which proved Wise to be a forger, Pforzheimer turned it over to Ratchford. Understandably peeved Carter struck back with a lengthy article in *The Atlantic Monthly.* The case against Gorfin, Clay and Gosse, he argued, had no merit.[62] The critic Edmund Blunden sided with Carter:

> What was first and foremost a scientific and practical purge of the literary history of the nineteenth century, which had been infected by a species of black-market concoctions, has been confused by an increasing mixture of personalities. Miss Ratchford's readers might well think now and then that the Enquirers were the real suspects, or at least as worthy of her indignation as the fabricators of the fifty or more forged editions."[63]

It was the publication of *Between the Lines* that brought Carter and Ratchford into serious conflict. The sequence of events is somewhat jumbled, but in January 1944, according to Carter's account, Pforzheimer asked him to edit the text of *Between the Lines.* Carter declined on the basis of an over-crowded schedule at the British Information Service. A few months later however, he agreed to provide a postscript and, if Pforzheimer wished, to supervise the printing and marketing of the book. Scribner's, he suggested, might handle part of the printing for fifty percent of the retail sales.[64] By the time Pforzheimer received Carter's letter he had already signed a contract with the University of Texas Press. Would Carter write a postscript? Exasperated with the whole affair, Carter sent back a draft loaded with provocative phrases such as "withholding of evidence," "handicapped the progress of scholarship," and "obscured the face of truth." This was hardly what Pforzheimer had in mind. Furious, he returned the text with a check for fifty dollars - a dismissive tip for a somewhat untrustworthy servant. Carter knew how to play that game. Back went the check with a note saying he was happy not to be included in the publication since it would enable him to comment freely as a reviewer. In a stinging attack on *Between the Lines,* Carter and Pollard claimed that in Ratchford's lopsided view Wise emerged not as a criminal, but as a "rather plaintive figure."[65] Randall followed up in *Publishers' Weekly* berating Ratchford for her careless editing of what he called a pretentious and "ridiculously expensive" book.[66] Ratchford, never one to hide from controversy, fought back with two accusations of her own. In a letter to the editor of *Publishers' Weekley* she claimed that the *Enquiry* itself suffered from careless editing, and then, on a truly discordant note, accused Carter of trying to profit from an arrangement he proposed to Pforzheimer that would have included Scribner's in the marketing of *Between the Lines.*[67] Carter replied icily that it was unfortunate Ratchford had seen fit to publicize a private matter. Although nothing was settled, it must have been a satisfaction for Carter, four years later, to be invited to deliver the main address, "Thomas J. Wise in Perspective," at a symposium on Wise held at the University of Texas on All Fools Day, April 1, 1959. Carter paid a passing tribute to Ratchford, now curator emerita, for her contributions to the study of the forgeries, but made no mention of Pforzheimer. In addition to bringing the story of the forgeries up to date Carter challenged his listeners to continue to dig into the archives held in the University of Texas Library. There were still questions to be answered. Carter had a knack for ending an article or talk with a resounding turn of phrase, and this was no exception. Considering the forger and his work, Carter concluded, "The nineteenth-century pamphlet forgeries were ethically reprehensible, bibliographically scandalous, bibliophilically deplorable, and economically distressing. But their maker was an artist."[68]

The words scandalous and deplorable have a special weight when applied to one particular facet of Wise's bibliographical career. Clearing her husband's estate, Mrs. Wise sold the Ashley Library to the British Museum for sixty-six thousand pounds, a total, according to experts, far below what it might have realized before the publication of the *Enquiry*. In 1956, in the process of cataloging the Ashley books, D. F. Foxon, one of the Museum staff, discovered that Wise had stolen over two hundred leaves from the Museum's collection of early English plays in order to "improve" his own copies.[69] It was, as John Collins and Nicolas Barker wrote, a demonstration of wanton ruthlessness, "arguably in moral terms the most damaging of all the forgers' doings."[70]

Carter was always candid about his working relationship with Pollard. "People link our names," he wrote his collaborator, "as if we were a pantomine horse, but, they know as well as I do, and so do you, which were the front legs in that particular variety turn; it was a good turn too. It was my good luck that brought us together thirty - no nearer forty years ago, and I only hope we shall both survive the effort of cleaning things up in the Supplement."[71] That hope was never realized. After Carter died in the spring of 1975 and Pollard the following year, John Collins and Nicolas Barker took up the project. The result of their efforts, published in two volumes in 1983, consisted of an annotated reprint of the 1934 edition and *A Sequel to An Enquiry . . . The Forgeries of H. Buxton Forman & T. J. Wise Re-Examined*. Collins and Barker added their extensive findings to notes and drafts written by the original investigators. The *Sequel* offers an extended account of the typographical evidence and proves for once and for all that Buxton Forman was an equal partner in the fraud.

Carter would always be identified with the Wise forgeries. The *Enquiry*, with additions and corrections, remains a classic - a tribute to the creative energy and determination of the two young bibliographers who decided to take a close look at the 1847 Reading edition of Mrs. Browning's *Sonnets*.

CHAPTER FIVE

Continuing with Scribner's

By the end of 1935, there were encouraging signs that the economic depression had run its course. In both England and the United States employment levels regained some of the strength lost during the previous six years; production figures were up, housing construction boomed, and there was increased demand for consumer goods. In the United States, President Franklin D. Roosevelt's New Deal had started to create a feeling of optimism. After years of simply holding the line, publishers began to expand their lists, and book dealers started to issue more catalogs in the firm expectation that old customers would return, and that new customers could be lured into buying. Yet against these signs of recovery, and in spite of the efforts of the League of Nations, there was growing political unrest in Europe. The Spanish Civil War gave the Germans and Italians an opportunity to test their military strength. In 1936, German troops invaded the demilitarized zone in the Rhineland, a clear violation of the Treaty of Versailles. It was the first in a series of ruthless takeovers that led to the outbreak of the Second World War.

In London, between 1938 and 1939, as the threat of war grew stronger, gas masks, rationing, blackout alerts, and bomb shelters became everyday realities. At 23 Bedford Square, the Scribner's office took on wartime dress, with sandbags in the basement and blackout curtains over the skylights. Overseas shipping lines could no longer promise delivery, and every transaction had to be completed under strict, ever-changing regulations from the Board of Trade. Viewing the situation from New York, Scribner considered closing the London office, but after discussion with Kingsley decided to keep it open with limited services and a skeleton staff. By the end of September 1939, two of the packers, the chief accountant, and the building caretaker had been called to military service. Two years later, the staff consisted of Arthur Dust, the office manager, Miss Hale, a long-time secretary, and, on a part-time basis, Carter.[1] In a "Memorandum on Plans for the Conduct of the Rare Book Department During the War," dated September 13, 1939, Carter announced his appointment as a press censor in the Ministry of Information. Since the Ministry's office was just around the corner from Bedford Square, he was able to put in a few hours a day attending to Scribner's business. In a letter to Randall's secretary, he described his work as "fighting rearguard actions on behalf of press and public against the obscurantists of the fighting services; and on the other hand, keeping a sharp eye open for the ingenious gentlemen of the press who are always busy trying to evade the Defence Regulations and to catch some pore bloody censor napping."[2] According to Carter, the atmosphere at the Ministry office was chaotic. In a small smoke-filled room messenger boys rushed from desk to desk, while phones rang constantly and a giant duplicating machine thudded away in the background. The job did have its rewards, however, and as Carter, somewhat primly, reported to Scribner, "It is, I think, a good thing for the prestige of the firm that I should be doing some government work, and since, as far as can be seen at present, this will be compatible with carrying on the work of the department, public duty and the good of the firm can be satisfactorily combined."[3]

Since Carter now drew £395 annually from the government it seemed only fair to all parties concerned that his Scribner's salary be reduced. As with all matters connected with money, Carter handled the details with infinite care. " So long as I can continue to conduct the main business of the rare book department, on however restricted a scale," he wrote Kingsley, "I conceive that I am worth £400 a year to Scribner's. Consequently it seems to me reasonable that any increase in my government salary should not be offset by further reductions in my salary from the firm."[4] In the midst of these negotiations an uncomfortable diversion occurred. Randall, in a gesture of support, went directly to Scribner and asked that Carter's full-time salary be extended to the end of the year, a small acknowledgment of continued excellent work in the face of wartime dislocations. What followed was a classic case of office communications gone awry. Scribner passed along the good news to Carter who immediately wrote back: "What with everything going up and this crashing raise of the income tax and the extra liquor tax and all, I didn't see how I could possibly make out."[5] Unfortunately, Kingsley had not been notified and when he heard about the arrangement, blamed Carter for tampering with the usual lines of authority. Scribner apologized to Kingsley, and followed with a long letter to Carter; "Randall and I seem to have gotten our wires crossed with Mr. Kingsley and yourself. . . . I told Kingsley that I would straighten the matter out with you by sending this draft (for £98-15-0) which I would charge against the rare book department in

New York. . . . I also assured him that the suggestion of maintaining your salary came entirely from the New York end and that you had nothing to do with it. I realize that it must be difficult for you to be doing two jobs at the same time and we wish to show our appreciation of your zeal in helping Randall at this time when it may be possible to make some valuable purchases and arrange to have books sent to us on consignment."[6]

This petty flare-up hinted at a serious underlying problem. From the time Randall joined the Scribner firm in March 1935, Kingsley had become increasingly uneasy about plans being hatched, as he imagined, between the two rare book men. Early in 1936, he heard about a scheme that would take Carter out of the office for several months, with a stop in New York, followed by a trip to Cleveland, Ohio to examine the distinguished collection formed by Paul Lemperly. From Kingsley's point of view, as he constantly reminded Scribner, Carter's chief responsibility was in London. Spring was a busy time, and he did not want to be without Carter's services. "I had an experience of what it meant last year, when he was away from December to May," Kingsley wrote, "and I am physically unable to stand another experience of that kind. . . . Carter's time is fully occupied here with this end of the business."[7]

Instead of inviting Carter to New York, Scribner decided to send Randall to London. It was an opportunity for Randall to get acquainted with the members of the London trade and see their stock firsthand. The trip was a success, but once back in the States, Randall reopened the question of a trip to the Midwest, where he felt Carter's influence would help swing some important sales. This time Carter appealed directly to Scribner. Leaving the office again would not please Kingsley, he admitted, but "any time is as bad as another from the point of view of the routine of this office and it does seem to be the only way of handling what's got to be done."[8] Carter sailed on the *Berengaria* and arrived in New York during the first week in December 1936. He didn't return to London until the middle of March, much to Kingsley's dismay. It may have softened the blow slightly when Kingsley learned that, on December 26, Carter had married Ernestine Fantl, an assistant curator of architecture and industrial design at the newly established Museum of Modern Art in New York.[9] She was a southerner, born in 1908 and raised in comfortable affluence in Savannah, Georgia where her father, Sigfried Fantl, was a member of the Cotton Exchange. After attending a private school in Savannah, she went on to graduate from Wellesley College in Wellesley, Massachusettts in 1927. The marriage took many of Carter's friends by surprise. Philip Hofer, the curator of prints at Harvard University Library, sent a handwritten note to Percy Muir, "I forgot to say a word of John Carter's wife. Bunnie [Wilmarth S. Lewis] and I have met her, like her. She is young, small, dark, <u>rather</u> pretty, <u>very</u> bright, self-possessed, capable, quite liberal politically, or do I exaggerate, being rather a conservative as you know. They seem blissfully happy and act as if they had been married for years. It was a surprise here as in England."[10] Charles Scribner chose a wedding gift for Carter with affection and wit, the infamous 1847 Reading edition of the Browning *Sonnets*, boxed and in an elaborate Zaehnsdorf blue levant morocco binding.[11]

Carter returned to London after a honeymoon in Nassau but was immediately laid low with a bout of tonsillitis that kept him out of the office for seven weeks. On

20a. *Carter and Ernestine Fantl on their wedding day,*

top of that, Kingsley heard, again quite by chance, that Randall wanted Carter to come to New York for several months in the spring. Kingsley expressed some of his concerns in a long, handwritten letter to Scribner - "It may be imagination on my part, but he seems a very different sort of person since his marriage. It is not easy to put one's finger on anything definite, but he seems to have adopted a very independent attitude toward me and gives the impression of thinking he is quite indispensable to the business and behind it all I can discern the influence of his ambitious wife. I've been wondering if by any chance there might not be some unfortunate plan for Carter and Randall to step off some day on their own. . . . Don't get the idea that there has been any friction between John and me. We are, as far as I know, on the best of terms, but I don't know just what Ernestine may be cooking up, though to me she is sweet as honey."[12] Scribner's reply was conciliatory. "I appreciate how much added work you have had put on you. Randall is in my opinion comparatively safe and sane and more to be counted on than John, now that he has a wife who may have decided ideas of her own. I do not think he would count John as a sufficient asset to join him in partnership in setting up a business of his own."[13]

The alarms of 1937 seem to have blown over by the spring of the following year. In April, Carter prepared a

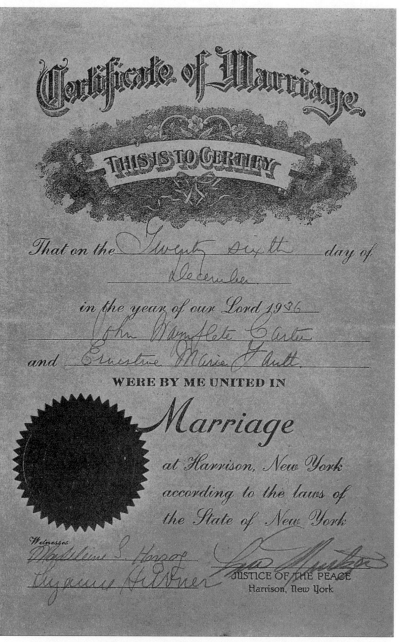

20b. Carter and Ernestine Fantl were married by the Justice of Peace in Harrison, New York on December 26, 1936.

lengthy analysis of the problems faced by the firm's wholesale department. For one thing, he argued, it was a waste of time and money to try to produce a line of fiction in competition with English firms. "Publishing novels," he wrote, "is the easiest kind of publishing, but it is not the easiest kind of publishing with which to make money. Unless Scribner's are prepared to develop London as a separate and individual publishing house, which will eventually develop a policy of its own, they will be best advised, in my opinion, to keep to the quieter line of importing publishing, rather than to get into the speculative fields of popular publishing where they are likely to be at a disadvantage in competition with the Houses which are already well established."[14] This confidently worded memorandum, certainly written with an eye on his future position within the firm, helped Carter regain some of his lost credibility with Kingsley. His plans for a fall trip to New York met with approval, especially as he had recently secured two large collections for the American market. First in importance was the Diaghileff archive. This was an impressive collection of scores and manuscripts, once the personal property of the Russian ballet impresario Sergei Diaghileff. There were full orchestral scores covering performances of the Ballets Russes from 1909 to 1929, along with letters and unpublished manuscripts annotated by Igor Stravinsky and Sergei Prokofieff. In spite of the richness of the holding, and what seemed a reasonable enough price, $7,500, no buyer came forward. Eventually, Randall split up the collection and sold scores and letters piece by piece. The second collection, made up of books and pamphlets covering the early years of the Russian Revolution, went into the library of the Cincinnati, Ohio businessman Bayard L. Kilgour.

If Scribner's London office was to continue with any success during the war, Carter knew he had to have the support of the members of the book trade. In this case, as he explained in a letter distributed to the London dealers, support meant an ongoing supply of quality rare books for the American market.

> We are of the opinion that the market for rare books in America will remain satisfactory throughout the war, and we shall therefore endeavour to continue supplying our New York house with suitable material, so long as we have a roof to work under.
>
> Our address remains the same, and all correspondence and books sent on approval will be punctually dealt with. But we would ask the London trade to note that our rare book department will be compelled to keep somewhat irregular hours, owing to Mr. Carter having been called up for service in one of His Majesty's Ministries. Mr. Carter will, however, be in this office for some hours every day: appointments for the inspection of likely items can be made by telephone at any time: and we feel confident that, if his rounds of the book shops are inevitably curtailed, the trade will appreciate the reason and by their co-operation help us to keep business moving.
>
> England needs American currency. The trade needs the American market. We need good books. *Verb. sap.*[15]

There were, of course, old friends who could be depended upon, war or no war. After thanking Percy Muir for sending several Oscar Wilde books, Carter wrote, "I promise to go on buying good books at the right prices until further notice. I am grateful to you for letting me have a shot at these, and I hope you will let me know if anything else turns up."[16] The close relationship between Carter (Scribner's) and Muir (Elkin Mathews) worked to the benefit of both men and both firms. Muir needed Scribner's support and was willing to extend a number of privileges in order to maintain that support. "Apart from special purchases for individual customers," Muir declared, "your firm has first run of anything I buy. . . . I not only send you proofs of catalogues, which I do to no one else, but I give you 10% off the prices, which I don't suppose anyone else would do. . . . It's policy to do all one can to please one's best customer."[17] Carter replied in kind, "I want you to feel in fact that if we are your best customer, this position is one which we value highly - and will endeavour to cement by trying also to be your promptest."[18] Through the war years, Carter and Muir kept up a steady correspondence - a mixture of business and social chat. Carter had a Rupert Brooke customer: could Muir put his hands on any of Brooke's manuscripts? What did Muir know about the binding of *The Misfortunes of Elphin*? Carter thought it was in a remainder binding, although, as he pointed out with his typical command of the facts, "The first and the last pages of the book itself have those brown stains (of which there is no sign on the end papers), which always appear in the remainder copies, and which I suppose to be due to the sheets having lain in bundles for a long time. Anyway I don't much like the look of it."[19] Could Muir furnish some authentication for a set of Lear drawings? What did he think of sending the drawings to Randall, asking him to do the authentication with an agreement that Scribner's would take half the profits from a sale? Muir politely declined: "To be quite frank without being greedy, I hardly feel inclined to part with a half interest in the transaction."[20] For a time, it seemed almost like business as usual - the byplay of buying and selling, customers' demands, bargains to be found, and, as usual, a healthy ingredient of insiders' gossip.

As 1939 merged into 1940, Carter had less time and less incentive to work on Scribner's business. The war had taken over every aspect of daily life. There were fines for blackout violations, food rationing, shortages of oil and gas, and cellars lined with sand bags. During one period in the fall and winter of 1940, bombs fell on London for fifty-seven consecutive nights. Carter reported the conditions at Bedford Square to Muir, who had moved to the country - "We've lost all our back windows again and I'm sick of it. And it always pours with rain immediately afterward."[21] As Carter explained to American readers, the book business was in ruins. "The shortage of fresh, saleable stock is the salient feature common to the whole rare book trade in London at the moment. Dealers all around report that they have had virtually no opportunity, even had they had the inclination, to recruit their stock by fresh purchases from private sources. In bad times, books simply do not come into the market, because potential sellers need at least a few good prices to persuade them that this is not a suicidal time to sell."[22] Carter's days were controlled by his schedule at the Ministry of Information. On the four-to-midnight shift he found it possible to work at Bedford Square for an hour or so in the morning or visit a few bookshops, before joining Ernestine for a late lunch at the Ivy. If, on the other hand, he worked the midnight-to-eight shift, he would often return to Scribner's and, as he put it, "doss down behind D.N.B. and the Encyclopaedia Britannica and a large stack of electro-plates for "The Post-Nicene Fathers" which have long cumbered our basement only to come at last into their own as bomb proofing."[23] He bicycled from his home in Kensington to Bedford Square wrapped in his grandfather's Inverness shooting cape - "a noble if somewhat eccentric sight," as he reported to Randall's secretary.[24]

In the midst of the wartime crisis the Library of Congress in Washington, D. C., offered Carter the post of Curator of Rare Books. His impressive publication record, backed by the support of influential American friends, like Wilmarth S. Lewis, made him the selection committee's first choice. Carter turned down the invitation for the same reasons he would use ten years later when he declined to enter his name as an applicant for the post of Librarian at Cambridge University - he wanted and needed a considerable freedom of manoeuvre, a quality he felt sure would be lacking in an institution like the Library of Congress. For the record, he gave Kingsley a somewhat different explanation - "I think it right that you and Mr. Scribner should know that I have been offered the post of Curator of Rare Books in the Library of Congress in Washington. I have declined this invitation, for reasons into which I need not proceed here, except to remark that my ambition for the continued progress of the Rare Book Department was not the least of them. But it seems to me that so signal an honour reflects credit on the Department as a whole; and the firm may like to take unofficial note of it on that account."[25] Part of Carter's decision was certainly based on his understanding that Kingsley's retirement was imminent. In response to Carter's note, Kingsley wrote a "what's this all about" letter to Scribner: "It is not quite clear to me just what the purpose of this memorandum is. You will note that he has turned the proposition down, and I am glad that he did so, for the Rare Book Department at least appears to be on a sound basis, and should continue on a profitable one unless the whole world goes smash, and I can see no reason why he should not continue his work here no matter what may happen to the rest of the organization."[26]

By January 1940, with both import and export transactions tied up by Board of Trade regulations, with a severely reduced supply of rare books, and no hope of expanding the publishing department, the flow of business in the London office all but ceased. Kingsley, who had recently turned sixty-six, told Scribner he was tired of fighting the government bureaucracy and wanted to return to the United States. In reply, Scribner promised him a position in the home office if he wanted to continue with the firm. It took several months to work out the details, but by mid-June Carter found himself in charge of the office aided by a secretary, an accountant, and a part-time packer. Before he left, Kingsley asked Scribner to increase Carter's salary from £400 to £700 in recognition of the added responsibilities that would be placed on his shoulders. In a note of appreciation Carter's offered to return part of the salary if circumstances prevented him from doing an adequate job. At the end of the letter he gave Scribner an intimate look at wartime life. "Thank goodness," he wrote, "there is apparently enough claret in the country to last some time. But my wife is worried about lemons and olive oil, which are going up fast. I look very odd with a rifle, on guard duty with our local Defence Volunteers."[27]

Carter's assignments at the Ministry changed as the war progressed, making it more difficult for him to give time to Scribner's. Summarizing some of the problems, he wrote, "Business is now so slack that any flow of stock from London of a volume approaching that of 1939 or 1940 would be embarrassingly uneconomic. Generally speaking, therefore, the volume of work which there is for me to do has shrunk to a point roughly comparable with the decreased time and addition available for it."[28] A complete break came in the fall of 1943 when Carter was assigned to New York as Head of the General Division of the British Information Services. His chief responsibility was to supervise the production of books and pamphlets of a popular nature such as *Victory in Burma,* a general description of the British war effort in the Far East, *Churchill's Speeches,* and *Miracle Harbor,* a tribute to the forces involved in the D-Day invasion.

Back in New York for the first time in four and a half years, Carter was able to renew his acquaintance with Scribner, John Hall Wheelock, George McKay Schieffelin, and other officers of the firm. He needed to clarify his post-war position now that Kingsley had resigned. Scribner asked him to supervise the export and import end of the business, the publishing program, and of course, continue to run the rare book department. Carter reminded Scribner that they had spoken of a salary increase up to $10,000 or $12,000 a year. Beyond money, Carter wanted assurance that the office would receive support from New York and that he would be given freedom of action in London. Getting these things settled, as he explained to Scribner, was simply a matter of good business practice:

> I know you will understand why I am asking you for these things to be formally set down at this particular time. I am now 40 years of age, and the approaching end of the war's six or seven years interruption of my normal work is the logical moment to take stock of my future. I have, of course, received offers of postwar jobs in other fields, and I have turned them down. I shall very likely receive others during what will probably be my last visit to London before the end of my term of duty here. I shall continue to turn them down in favour of the kind of

work I like, if I can be reasonably sure that the circumstances of that work and its financial prospects are such as I think I have a right to expect.[29]

After several months of negotiation, Carter and Scribner came to a compromise agreement on salary. Carter would be paid $7,000 annually, with an expense account of $750 and the opportunity to share in any profits earned by the Rare Book Department. Although the terms were considerably below his optimistic expectations, Carter accepted. The ever faithful Arthur Dust, who had been with the firm since the early 1920s, would be in charge of imports and building management. Following up on a suggestion from Carter, Scribner agreed to pay John Hayward, Peter Quenell, and John Summerson £100 a year for advice on English authors that might be drawn into the Scribner camp. He made the promise somewhat reluctantly because, as he wrote Carter, "They have not yet had the opportunity of showing whether they can find books which we might publish. I only fear that their tastes are apt to be on the precious and scholarly side and that it will not be until Gilman or I can go over and talk with the publishers and agents that a great deal can be done in the way of securing new British authors."[30] Scribner was never convinced the consulting arrangement would work, and, probably for that reason, it never did.

Carter was named Managing Director in January 1946 and continued until the firm officially closed its London editorial and Rare Book Department in November 1953. During those seven and a half years his letters to the New York office, sometimes two or three a week, necessarily reflected concerns with royalties, reprint rights, stock levels, import and export regulations, contract agreements, and publication deadlines. In addition to the everyday correspondence, there was a never-ending incoming flow of manuscripts forwarded to his attention. While he encouraged authors like Roald Dahl, Ruthven Todd, Fitzroy Maclean, and Kenneth Clark, he dismissed manuscripts from Herbert Grenfell and Desmond Young as being too specialized for the Scribner's imprint. Carter's administrative duties, along with his responsibilities for the bibliographical and sales articles for the back page of the *Times Literary Supplement* and his own writing projects kept him extremely busy. His schedule also called for occasional trips to New York to coordinate his efforts with those of the home office. After working as Managing Director for four years he asked for a raise from £1,750 to £2,250. "If you and the others are satisfied with my work," he wrote to Scribner, "I hope you will agree that a raise is in order. I had intended, before the devaluation of sterling, to suggest an increase from £1750 to £2250: and I can now do so with the comforting support of the fact that this increase (to me) will effect a saving (to CSS) for £250 a year."[31] Convinced of Carter's special talents, Scribner was glad to meet the request.

During the early 1950s, Carter negotiated three important sales for the firm, all involving American customers. In 1952 Sir William Stirling of Keir sold William Blake's masterpiece of illuminated printing, *Jerusalem: The Emanation of the Giant Albion* (1804), through Scribner's to the American collector Paul Mellon. The price, £30,000, was the second largest amount ever paid in England for a printed book. As the transaction drew to a close, the Board of Trade took notice, referring the matter to their Reviewing Committee on the Export of Art. After six months of deliberation, the Committee recommended that Scribner's be granted the required export license. The decision was a satisfying personal victory for Carter, who had invested a great deal of time representing Mellon's interests.[32]

A year before the Blake acquisition, Carter located an unrecorded copy of the Gutenberg Bible in a private library in England. His part in securing the Bible, thought to be the earliest example of printing from movable type, started with a complicated chain of events. Estelle Doheny, the founder of one of the great rare book libraries in the United States, had for many years wanted to obtain the Bible to go with her impressive collection of illuminated manuscripts, early European printing, fore-edge paintings, and fine bindings. In 1947 she was the under-bidder on the Old Testament volume offered at the Dyson Perrins sale. Two years later, Randall, acting for Scribner's, brought a copy owned by the General Theological Seminary of New York out to Los Angeles for her examination. The Seminary officers wanted $150,000 for the Bible, an amount they planned to deposit in a scholarship program. Doheny was pleased with the book, and the sale appeared to be final. At the last minute, the trustees changed their mind, and voted against the transfer. Randall had to explain the unexplainable to Mrs. Doheny.

A year after the Seminary fiasco, Doheny received an inquiry from Maggs asking if she was still interested in the Dyson Perrins Old Testament volume, now priced at $70,000, a figure substantially under her bid three years earlier. The transaction was completed by return wire, and on October 14, 1950, Doheny, now nearly blind, pulled the mailing wrappers away from the precious volume. She detested publicity, and following her usual custom, asked that all the participants keep the details of the purchase confidential.

While Doheny was rejoicing over her good fortune, Randall was still smarting over the loss of what would have been a very profitable sale. He asked Carter to keep his eyes open. It was a long shot to be sure, but Carter passed the inquiry along to Edmund Dring, Quaritch's rare books chief, and was astounded to hear that a copy of the Bible had recently come to Dring's attention. The owner had wisely asked Sir Sydney Cockerell, eminent bibliographer and Director of Cambridge's Fitzwilliam Museum, to act as intermediary. He identified the Bible as the one purchased in the eighteenth century by Sir George Shuckburgh, and quietly passed down through several generations of the family. With Cockerell's advice, the owner set the price at $116,000.

As soon as Carter told Randall that he had located a copy of "The Book," the cable and telephone lines between London and New York began to hum. On January 15, 1951, Cockerell brought the Bible to London for inspection. Carter gave Randall an enthusiastic report and added, "Whichever way we play this there will be no question that you can take it out to California with full rights to sell it to her on the spot." In a handwritten note at the bottom of the page he asked Randall to be discreet: "I trust you have not mentioned the Gutenberg deal to a soul outside the 2 or 3 concerned. There are special angles on this end which would take too long to go into now, but which make it imperative to keep things absolutely dark, 'till we get our hands on The Book."[33]

Still unaware of Doheny's purchase of the Dyson Perrins Old Testament, Randall plunged ahead - this time going directly to the source:

> Dear Mrs. Doheny: I assume Miss Miller [Doheny's librarian] has told you of Scribner's acquisition of a newly discovered Gutenberg Bible. This is now in a London

office and our English director Mr. John Carter is flying to New York with it this weekend. I have not yet, of course, seen the book, but I have a full description. It is much larger than the Theological Seminary copy measuring sixteen by eleven inches with many uncut leaves.

Furthermore, had it not been for your interest in the Bible, it is extremely unlikely that this would ever have been uncovered. You were so generous and so gracious to me last fall that I was even more disappointed than you were when the Seminary decided not to sell. I feel morally committed therefore to give you the first refusal of this copy.

I don't feel you should make any decision without seeing the book, and with your permission, I would like to bring it to California for your, Miss Miller's and Dr. Schad's [Curator of Rare Books at the Henry E. Huntington Library in Pasadena] inspection at, of course, no expense or obligation on your part. I could come out next week perhaps, if that suits your convenience.[34]

Randall was less confident in a cable sent to Carter the following day, "Doheny lukewarm but not completely out."[35] By the end of the following week, Doheny had decided against the purchase. Neither Randall or Carter knew why. Carter transmitted the unhappy news to a Quaritch representative.

We are cabling the news that the Princess has declined the book. A decision was made known to us yesterday that she is definitely not interested in buying the book, so definitely in fact that she was not even interested in seeing it.

We don't know, of course, what lies behind her decision, but it appears that her keenness last autumn was connected with the fact that 1950 was a Holy Year and she wanted to make some special gesture during that time. She is also a very old lady and almost blind, so she may have realized that the book could not give her much pleasure any longer. Anyway, there it is.[36]

Later, in a light-hearted article in *The Bookseller* Carter described the Bible's discovery and journey to the United States. In the clipped, military report style Carter began:

Intelligence reports received late in December 1950 indicated the possible presence of a hitherto unlocated copy of the Gutenberg Bible in a private library "somewhere in England." M.I.47 (Muniments and Black Letter Section) were naturally sceptical, since such reports (usually second or third hand) are commonly found on investigation to refer to any Bible printed in gothic type and/or in a foreign language and more than a hundred years old, but otherwise of no interest and often lacking the title-page. . . .

January 20th. 1200 hours; Gutenberg Bible arrives under escort at 11 Grafton Street. Found to be a magnificently large copy (16 ½ X 11 inches) substantially complete (lacking 5 of the 643 leaves), crisp and unmarked . . . .

January 26th. 1630 hours: Carter packs the two volumes (weight 36 lbs.) into somewhat disreputable suitcase. 1700 hours: B.O.A.C. officials at first decline to regard suitcase as "hand baggage" permissible to accompany passenger. Passenger declines board plane if suitcase detached from hand. Customer always right. 1800 hours: First aircraft ever to carry a *Gutenberg Bible* takes off from London Airport.

January 31st: Mr. Scribner, after asking if there were not something rather cheaper he could buy for Randall and still make him happy, confirms purchase of the Bible. Carter and Randall, now at last able to admit publicly that this long-lost copy even so much as existed, emit studiously modulated cries of pleasure.[37]

On February 4, Carter returned to London leaving the Bible in a bank vault in Rockefeller Center. Immediately, he and Randall started looking for a new customer. Josiah K. Lilly and Louis H. Silver turned it down, as did the Pierpont Morgan Library and, after prolonged consideration, the Chicago Bible Society. Charles Scribner Jr., the firm's new director, grew impatient. The Bible needed to move from the debit to the credit side of the ledger. In the spring of 1952, he gave Randall an ultimatum - find a customer or cut it up and sell it page by page. With that unhappy possibility looming, Randall finally came to an agreement with Arthur A. Houghton, Jr., a prominent collector, and President of Corning Glass Works. Houghton already owned an imperfect copy of the Old Testament volume, which he proceeded to trade to Randall in part-payment for the Shuckburgh copy. Randall then broke up Houghton's copy and, since it was imperfect, sold individual pages with no regret. In the end the firm realized a satisfying $70,000 profit.

Carter and Randall refused to dwell on their failure to sell the Gutenberg Bible to Mrs. Doheny. As shrewd business professionals, they preferred to look ahead. The disposal of Michael Sadleir's Victorian fiction collection gave them an opportunity to do just that. Sadleir had recently published a catalog of his Victorian titles and was ready to move on to other things. He approached several British libraries but none of them had $65,000 to spend on Victorian fiction. The focus then shifted to the United States, where the collection was well known to nineteenth century specialists such as Bradford Booth, professor of English at the University of California, Los Angeles (UCLA), and Professor Gordon N. Ray, a senior member of the English Department at the University of Illinois. In the quest to secure the Sadleir books, the outcome, as is often the case with special purchases, depended on the speed with which an institution could come up with a large amount of money Although Illinois, with a long history of notable acquisitions, probably had the greater potential, UCLA had Lawrence Clark Powell. Appointed Library Director in 1944, Powell, known to his friends as "the Grand Acquisitor" or "Lorenzo the Great" had built a reputation based on his canny ability to come up with funds when they were most needed. Booth and Powell were a formidable team, but securing $65,000 outside the regular library budget was no mean task. To make matters more complicated, UCLA administrators wanted unbiased outside confirmation that the collection was as important as Powell and Booth said it was. When Powell wrote Randall for help, the dealer replied somewhat petulantly - "Adams of the Morgan, Babb of Yale and Jackson of Harvard all expressed informal approval of your prospective purchase of the Sadleir collection for $65,000. If Scribner's reputation and guarantee of value plus my and Carter's endorsement is not sufficient for your purposes just forget the whole deal. The University of Illinois is very interested in acquiring it and a decision is to be made by them after the first of the year." Randall's final sentence carried some encouragement: "Dr. Gordon Ray examined the books last summer and is writing you his opinion which may help."[38] Ever the gentleman scholar, Ray supported the purchase. "Illinois wants this, of course, but we are unable to close now so let's by all means get it to America and specifically to UCLA."[39] With that letter in hand, Powell and Booth made their case to President Robert Gordon Sproul. Several days later, Sproul cornered Booth and Powell at a cocktail party and told them he was giving them a Christmas present - the money from a special appropriation for the Sadleir books. The following year, Carter, serving a temporary appointment as personal assistant to Sir Roger Makins, the British Ambassador in the United States, had the pleasure of escorting the ambassador and his wife through the Sadleir collection shelved in all its dazzling glory in the special collections area of the UCLA Library.[40]

Charles Scribner III had always been an enthusiastic supporter of the London office. A month after his unexpected death on February 11, 1952 his son Charles Scribner, Jr. took over the presidency. With the change in administration, Carter felt it was the expedient moment to set down some long-simmering concerns related to his salary and work load. In a five-page, single-spaced memorandum addressed to Schieffelin, with a copy to Scribner, he described the responsibilities involved in his position, with emphasis on the difficulty of maintaining high standards while doing both administrative work and running the rare book department. "Under the mounting pressure of inflation here," he wrote, "I cannot hold things together any longer without some such reinforcement as I think is due to me. . . . I am now nearing 50 years of age [he was 47 at the time] and my whole working life has been spent in the service of the House. But I have never received sufficient salary to enjoy a solvent year since I can remember, though we live on a very modest scale. . . . I submit that if I am to continue to do two men's jobs and am expected to do them at Scribner standards, I should be paid one full man's salary." He concluded with what the Scribner officers must have thought was an outlandish proposal. If funds were not readily available for a raise, he asked, would the New York office be willing to pay off his £3,000 mortgage? The payment would be a "bonus for the five years 1950-1954, in consideration of which I should reckon my salary as frozen at its present level till 1955."[41] Carter's timing could hardly have been worse. After spending several months familiarizing himself with his new responsibilities, Scribner decided on an ambitious reorganization plan. The school text division in New York would be phased out, several publishing lines reduced, and, to Carter's dismay, the functions of the London office reduced to a bare minimum. The Rare Book Department would be shut down, and there would be no further export/import activity. Scribner said the decisions had been made for economic reasons and in order to resolve what he called complex relations between New York and London. To help ease the dislocation, he promised Carter a generous severance bonus equivalent to two years' salary. Although the decision to close the Rare Book Department had not come as a complete surprise - Carter had heard rumors of such an event - the immediacy of it was unexpected. Carter was understandably angry and depressed. He felt his twenty-five years spent building the good name of Scribner's London office had been wiped out. The fact that he had not been consulted at any point in the decision-making process was particularly painful. The situation took its toll. After working under high pressure in his new position in the Washington embassy for four months, he was admitted to a hospital in late August with what he later called a nervous breakdown. To help the recovery process, Ernestine asked Scribner to postpone any announcement concerning the London office. "John is home from the hospital now and the doctors are optimistic that two or three weeks absolute rest will put him back on his feet. What I am principally concerned with at the moment is to ask you if you will postpone the announcement of your plans for Scribner's London until John is a little more recovered. It is all very worrying for him and I feel that he would get better more quickly if this particular problem were removed until he is more fit to cope with the repercussions."[42] By the end of the month, Ernestine reported good progress, but asked again that the announcement be delayed - "as the speed of his recovery depends a great deal on his not being upset, I should like, if you agree to postpone bringing up the announcement problem a bit longer. Perhaps I shouldn't say this, but I wonder if you have quite realized the extent to which John feels the severing of his ties with Scribner's. After twenty-five years of identifying himself with CSS, he feels as badly as if I had left him: more so, perhaps, as he was married to the House eight years longer than to me. I know that the reasons for your decisions are good and cogent and I would not dream of questioning them but as John has been so ill, I wish to protect him, if possible from further pain until he is well."[43] Scribner honored the request. The official press release, issued November 2, simply stated that Carter would be on leave of absence for a year in order to act as a personal assistant to Sir Roger Makins, the newly appointed British Ambassador in Washington, D.C.

Earlier in the year, with the knowledge that his position in the London office might be in some danger, Carter allowed his name to be put forward as an applicant for a position in the Foreign Service. His chief support came from Aubrey Morgan, who himself had served as personal assistant to the British ambassador to the United States, and who knew Carter from the early 1940s when they had worked together in the British Information Service in New York. Carter's credentials for the post were impressive - an extensive knowledge of the American way of life, a fluent, effective writing style, the old school tie, an urbane manner, and a determined work ethic. The appointment went through, and Carter began work at the Embassy in April 1953. His position was pleasant enough, but as he explained to Munby, "I have no ambition or aspiration toward the official life. The bookish world, indeed, the old-book world, seems my natural habitat, and I have every expectation of returning to it again, in what capacity however remains to be seen."[44] When Munby suggested the possibility of a fellowship at King's College, Carter demurred:

> I am not a scholar in the proper sense of the word and I can't think of any subject into which I am halfway equipped to research which would hold my attention for four years.
>
> I had, perhaps still have, some aptitude for expressing bits of other people's research in persuasive forms, to give me an edge on most of my colleagues in the trade, but that's a very different thing.[45]

Carter worked at the British Embassy in Washington, D.C., from April 1953 to October 1955. His duties combined the political with the social. He handled protocol, managed the ambassador's calendar, drafted his speeches, and accompanied him on trips around the United States. A typical tour might include talks to members of the English Speaking Union in Louisville, Kentucky, representatives of the National Farm Institute in Des Moines, Iowa, students and faculty of the University of Southern Mississippi in Hattiesburg, and members of the Philadelphia Press Club. During a two-week trip in 1955, the ambassador, with Carter at his side, visited five states, called on three

*21. Carter and Sir Roger Makins, British Ambassador to the United States,
in Carter's office at the Embassy in Washington D.C. - c. 1954.*

governors, delivered four television interviews, gave eight
informal talks, and visited five universities. The speeches
were characteristically on standard topics such as "World
Leadership," "Education and World Affairs," "The Sinews
of Peace," "From a British Window in Washington," and
"Britain and the United States." Whether in Des Moines or
Louisville, the content of individual speeches remained
much the same, with a few local references inserted to
please the home town audience.

Sometimes Carter's social responsibilities outweighed
all else. Receptions at the embassy were often followed by
cocktail parties, formal dinners, and trips to the theater or

ballet. Carter was entirely comfortable in the midst of Washington society. He looked good in a tuxedo, knew how to make a perfect martini, - "A dry martini should be very dry, very strong and very cold. All you need is lots of ice, enough gin, a little vermouth, a lemon and an attitude of scrupulous respect"[46] and was adept at applying flattery where it would do the most good. At Scribner's there had been dealers to cajole, customers to please, and the New York accountants to satisfy. At the embassy, he was more or less free to exert his considerable personal charm without outside restraint.

Ernestine referred to the time spent in Washington as the golden years, and there is no reason to think Carter would have disagreed. They enjoyed the museums and galleries, and were regularly in attendance at opening night concert and ballet performances. During their second year in Washington, they rented a spacious house at 2808 N Street in Georgetown. Its large rooms and well-tended gardens made it an ideal setting for receptions and parties. They even had the right kind of automobile, a black 1947 Lincoln Continental convertible, on loan from David Randall. These were the Eisenhower years and, as Ernestine pointed out in her autobiography, the Democrats had more time to socialize. There were lunches and dinners with former Secretary of State Dean Acheson, and weekends with friends in Virginia, where Senator Lyndon Baines Johnson entertained the guests with his insider accounts of the Joseph McCarthy hearings.

Carter viewed his two years in Washington as a success; he admired Makins, "the best and most stimulating of masters and one of the most effective Ambassadors we have ever had in Washington," and enjoyed his colleagues "as brilliant (and congenial) a crew as perhaps any embassy has enjoyed anywhere."[47] His last day in office closed with a lavish social occasion. The embassy gave a party for the members of the the Sadler's Wells Ballet Company to celebrate their recently completed successful season in New York. Carter had the privilege that evening of escorting the company's principal ballerina, Margot Fonteyn, from the receiving line in to dinner. It was a splendid way to conclude his Washington tour of duty.

The two years Carter spent in Washington should not be viewed as simply an interlude. With his knowledge of America and his circle of influential friends, he was valuable to the embassy on many levels. He fitted into the Washington scene with the ease of a trained diplomat. Those who worked with him and those he met socially were impressed with his charm and intelligence. The government honored his service naming him a Commander of the Order of the British Empire.

CHAPTER SIX

Building a Reputation -
Beyond the *Enquiry*

Between 1927 and 1955 Carter's duties at Scribner's, then with the Ministry of Information and finally at the embassy in Washington dominated his daily life. In spite of those assignments, his typewriter was rarely silent. During that period he produced a stream of reviews, essays, journal articles, surveys, and bibliographies. The words that seemed to flow so easily on the page were the product of intense effort. Drafts were edited and reedited for accuracy and style. The word *style*, often applied to Carter's dress, manner, and conversation, was nowhere more appropriately employed than when used to describe his writing. He was the master of the well turned sentence - "The Roxburghe-Spencer-Dibdin type of bibliophily, with its concentration on early printing and early illustration, threw off as by-products the indiscriminate craze for Aldines, the elevation of a tall Elzevir (most of the Elzevirs being dumpy little books) to a pinnacle of esteem, and all other fashions of a century or so ago which now seem to us fads and fetishes."[1] - the apposite comparison "Rarity is as it were of two kinds - absolute rarity, and market, or temporary, rarity, and it is usually easier to determine the basis of the former than of the latter,"[2] the vivid description - "a dapper lawyer, with a sharp but twinkling blue eye and a genial sense of standing no nonsense,"[3] and the bite of wry humor - "Rarity is the salt in book-collecting. But if you take too much salt, the flavour of the dish in spoiled; and if you take it neat it will make you sick."[4] The result was a readable, jargon free, sophisticated prose, appealing to both the amateur and specialist. According to the sketch in *The Dictionary of National Biography*, "Carter's fame rests principally on his writing."[5]

At first it might seem strange that this quintessential Englishman found the best outlet for his early writing in New York rather than in London. There was a straight-forward explanation. Although a few collecting journals appeared in England between 1920 and 1940, notably *The Book Collector's Quarterly* and *Bibliographical Notes and Queries,* none of them survived for more than a few years. The reason, Carter said, was that "they were cold-shouldered by the 80 percent of the book trade which has as profound suspicion and instinctive dislike of bib-liographic and bibliophilic journalism as it has of bibli-ographies themselves."[6] The record was only slightly better in the United States, but at least *Publishers' Weekly*, in its rare book section, and *The Colophon*, that handsomely designed product of Elmer Adler's Pynson Press, served those interested in collecting, bibliography, printing, and the book trade.

When Carter's name appeared on the table of con-tents of *The Colophon* for the first time in 1931, he joined a veritable Who's Who of bibliographers, type designers, and artists - among them Frederick B. Adams, W. A. Dwiggins, Frederic W. Goudy, Dard Hunter, Rockwell Kent, and Carl Purlington Rollins. It is not clear how Carter first became acquainted with Adler and his "Quarterly for Bookmen" but it may have been through Michael Sadleir, who had published an article in one of the early issues, or more likely through John T. Winterich, who knew Carter's writing from working with him on *Publishers' Weekly*. In any case, Adler saw Carter as a rising star.

Carter's contributions to *The Colophon* included a study of Victorian binding styles - "The Origins of Publishers' Cloth Binding," - an evaluation of six author-corrected copies of Sir Thomas Browne's *Urne Buriall* - "The Iniquity of Oblivion Foil'd," - an examination of several private libraries - "The Library of Frank Hogan," - and "The Library at Dormy House," - to a consideration of the nature of rarity - "Reflections on Rarity." The list is incomplete, but suggests the lines of Carter's chief interests - bibliography and collecting. He fashioned his approach to match the goal of the journal itself where, according to Winterich, "the flag of bibliography flew at the masthead."[7] In this case, Carter followed the flag.

In spite of his talent for interpreting bibliography in accessible language, Carter never claimed the title of bibliographer for himself. In May 1954, in an address given at the 50th anniversary meeting of the Bibliographical Society of America, he admitted publishing what he called "contributions to the bibliographic literature" but said he preferred to be known simply as a professional rare book dealer. The term bibliographer, he said, "always sounded rather pretentious for an occasional compiler of technical memoranda and commentary. . . ."[8] In spite of this disclaimer, his active participation in bibliographic studies was regularly on display in publications of the various bibliographic societies in England and the United States. After serving as a member of the Council of the Bibliographical Society (London) for a number of years he was elected President in 1968.

Publication of the *Enquiry* in 1934 brought Carter a considerable amount of acclaim. Based on that success, he had little trouble placing his articles and reviews in a variety of popular and scholarly journals. His graceful and sometimes provocative prose appealed to editors and readers alike, whether he was clarifying a bibliographic point or explaining the joys and sorrows of collecting. In addition to compiling checklists and bibliographies, he wrote about topics he knew firsthand, the history and techniques of the rare book trade, Victorian binding, the international rare book market, detective fiction, and book production.

One of Carter's continuing interests focused on the writing of the poet A. E. Housman. He began to collect Housman's works, starting with the various editions of *A Shropshire Lad,* while he was a student at Cambridge. Housman's collected poetry and the classical studies on Manilius, Juvenal, and Lucan were relatively easy to obtain, but difficulties arose when he tried to obtain copies of poems published in obscure journals and ephemeral pieces such as Housman's "Introductory Lecture" delivered at University College London in 1892. Beyond the published works, and essential for the determined collector, lay the daunting territory of letters and association materials. On behalf of Scribner's customers but also to improve his own collection, he read dealers' catalogs, attended auctions, visited family members, and scanned the shelves in rare books shops from Liverpool to Chicago.[9] Early in the fall of 1936 Carter heard that Blackwell's of Oxford was scheduled to sell the bulk of Housman's personal library on a designated Saturday morning. He made the trip up from London in his battered Chrysler, arriving fifteen minutes before the sale began. As he watched, assistants dumped armfuls of books on long tables - literary histories, criticism, poetry, guide books, and Victorian novels - all jumbled together. Soon, a few other buyers began to circle the tables. Were they experts looking for rarities, or merely curious undergraduates? Anyone who has hunted through sales tables in similar circumstances will appreciate the tension in the room:

> One needed to be both lynx-eyed and swiveleyed to pick the grain from the chaff and to make sure that no bit of special knowledge was wasted. One needed to be quick-fingered without the impoliteness of grabbing (this was Oxford, remember, not the Charing Cross Road.) One needed to watch not only the incoming books but also the eyes and hands of the competitors. By 9:30 or 10: o'clock there were a dozen people picking the books over, and a desultory finger could fall on a prize just as fatally as a knowledgeable one. . . .
>
> It took a couple of minutes to scan any but the most obviously attractive title . . . in case there should be worthwhile annotations or some obscure association.
>
> By midmorning the back room was full of people. And though the armfulls kept coming, the gamesmanship got progressively trickier. By noon everything was out in the open and we were reduced to gleaning over reaped stubble. At 12:15, in a hurry and a fluster, the first London bookseller appeared (his car had broken down, I learned later). He sized the situation up in one minute flat. He gave me a look of such concentrated venom that I can feel it now. It had been a wearing morning, but a rewarding one.[10]

Although Carter was able to buy a substantial number of attractive titles, the sale ended on a somewhat discordant note. As he was paying for his purchases he noticed several assistants sitting off to the side erasing notes from a large stack of volumes. When Carter asked what was going on, the chief salesman told him that according to Housman's stipulations, all marginal notes were to be erased from the classical texts before they could be sold. If the writing was in ink, the volumes had to be destroyed. Agreeing never to divulge any part of the transaction, Carter rescued a Plautus and a Sophocles before the assistants did their deadly work.

By the beginning of the decade of the 1960s, Carter's personal collection included 43 first and significant later editions of works by or edited by Housman, 15 books with contributions by him, 20 articles published in non-classical periodicals, 93 in learned journals, 24 biographies, 8 manuscripts, and 10 books from Housman's personal library. Carter's copy of the first edition of *A Shropshire Lad* had Hugh Walpole's bookplate, and was one of only four known with the original dust jacket. Early in 1961, somewhat pressed for funds and after considering a variety of options, Carter decided to sell his collection to the Lilly Library at Indiana University. The choice was deliberate. His old friend David Randall was now the Lilly Librarian, and, of even more importance, the library had recently acquired H. Bacon Collamore's collection of Housman's books and papers. Bringing the two collections together made perfect sense. It was a step Carter took with regret but, as he wrote to Randall, "I can't afford either to give it or to bequeath it . . . let us have a quiet word about this when we meet."[11] After several years of negotiations, Randall agreed to pay Carter $19,600, and in the spring of 1965 the books and papers moved to Bloomington. In announcing the acquisition, Randall praised Carter for his "fastidious attention to condition" and his "concentration on the significant and the associative."[12]

Carter's first attempt to bring Housman's scholarly work to the attention of a wider audience had come in 1933. He and John Sparrow, then a Fellow at All Souls, Oxford, commissioned the printing of one hundred copies of the poet's "Introductory Lecture" delivered at University College, London in 1892. The lecture had never been published, and constituted a *rarissima* in the Housman cannon. Housman regarded the whole enterprise with disdain, saying he only consented "because it seemed churlish to refuse."[13] In 1940 Carter and Sparrow published "A. E. Housman: An Annotated Check List," as a supplement to A. S. F. Gow's *A. E. Housman, A Sketch, Together with a List of his Writings and Indexes to His Classical Papers*. Their goal was to provide a "compilation . . . for the convenience of collectors and amateurs rather than for the instruction of literary critics or scholiasts." The compilers eliminated formal collation and title page transcription, leaving entries that were "stripped bibliographically to the barest essentials."[14] In several instances however, Carter and Sparrow found it impossible to resist brief flights of bibliographic virtuosity. Their description of *A Shropshire Lad*, for example, included a lengthy note comparing the variant spine labels found on the 1896 edition. It was the kind of devotion to minutia that was on Housman's mind when in 1922 he wrote his publisher Grant Richards concerning a misprint in the forthcoming volume of *Last Poems*. When Richards asked if an erratum should be inserted calling attention to a punctuation error, Housman replied, "No, don't put in an errata slip. The blunder will probably enhance the value of the 1st edition in the eyes of bibliophiles, an idiotic class."[15] There is every reason to believe he would have regarded the compilation of a check-list a foolish waste of time. In 1952

Rupert Hart-Davis published Carter and Sparrow's revised version as part of the Soho Bibliography series. Aside from its appearance as a monograph, reviewers claimed there were few changes from the original journal article. The compilers defended the lack of revision saying a scholar in the United States was preparing a full-length bibliography. Had they known that William White's second and enlarged edition, *A. E. Housman: A Bibliography*, would not appear for thirty years, they might have spent more time on their own revision.

Carter's enthusiasm for Housman's writing went far beyond bibliographic compilation. After the poet's death in 1936, his brother Laurence took charge of the remaining manuscripts. According to Housman's careful instructions, drafts of certain poems and all the prose drafts were to be destroyed. The task of sorting through the poetry manuscripts was far from easy. The drafts and notes were in complete disarray, most lacked dates, and all were in the author's nearly illegible handwriting. The archive needed to be organized. With his long-standing interest in Housman and his bibliographic reputation, Carter seemed to be the ideal person to do the job. In addition, his position at Scribner's would be useful when it came time to place the manuscripts on the market. As the sorting and organizing proceeded, Laurence gave Carter the right to edit and publish the results of his findings. Although he had no experience as a literary editor, Carter believed he could produce a creditable volume. In 1939, Jonathan Cape in London, and Holt, Rinehart, Winston in New York brought out *The Collected Poetry of A. E. Housman* with Carter's editorial notes. The book was popular with the reading public, going through fourteen impressions in as many years, but drew a barrage of negative criticism from Housman scholars in the United States. William White and Tom Burns Haber, two professors of English literature, were particularly unhappy with Carter's editorial efforts. In letters to the *Times Literary Supplement,* both men claimed Carter had failed to carry out his editorial responsibilities.[16] Carter responded that neither he nor the publisher thought the book was free from error, yet felt it supplied a better text than had been previously available. With a sly reference to a work in progress, he went on to say, "Mr. White's reference to the number of faults in the text . . . shows how much we are about to owe to American research." Warming to the topic, he continued, "Yet it may be permissible to remind the correctors that in the 55 cases where Housman's unfinished drafts show alternative readings, someone had to decide which reading was to be "preferred;" and that the person authorized to perform this, by far the most important editorial duty, in respect of the posthumous poems was the author's brother, whose judgment they are not entitled to challenge."[17] The claims and counterclaims continued for several years. In an evaluation of Carter's editorial efforts Haber wrote, "The necessary documents were at the new editor's hand, but time and ability to use them were unfortunately lacking. Since *Collected Poems* appeared before the end of 1939, it is evident that Mr. Carter could not have spent more than a few months doing what should have absorbed his undivided energies over as many years."[18] Finally, Carter politely bowed out, saying the controversy, into which he had been drawn against his will, had gone on much too long. Earlier, with the battle still in progress, he published an article in *The Colophon* attacking Haber's book, *The Manuscript Poems of A. E. Housman: Eight Hundred Lines of Hitherto Uncollected Verse from the Author's Notebooks.*

Carter claimed Haber had violated copyright since the manuscripts, housed in the Library of Congress, remained legally under the control of Laurence Housman's estate.[19] The story of how the Housman manuscripts got to the Library of Congress in the first place is a prime example of book trade high jinks. In 1938, Laurence Housman sold the manuscripts to Scribner's for approximately $10,000. Barnet J. Beyer, an opportunistic New York dealer, obtained them from Scribner's on consignment for $15,000, then asked Randall to reduce the price to $13,500, since, as he explained, his customer was a philanthropist who planned to give the manuscripts to the Library of Congress. In a departure from his usual hard-headed bargaining style, Randall agreed. Beyer's philanthropist, Mrs. Gertrude Clarke Whittall, gave the manuscripts to the Library of Congress after writing Beyer a check for $40,000, a mark up to warm the heart of even the most pernicious entrepreneur.[20]

Although the fires of the Haber/White/Carter controversy burned low after 1960, Carter never forgot the heat produced. In March 1961 he wrote to Randall, who had asked him to attend a ceremony at Indiana in honor of the Housman collector H. Bacon Collamore. "If you are thinking of inviting HABER," he wrote, "let me know, so I can carry side arms."[21]

In 1961, putting aside the criticism surrounding his work on the poetry, Carter edited a volume of Housman's prose. The collection included Housman's lesser known contributions on classical scholarship - prefaces, articles, biographical tributes, reviews, and letters to the press. With the exception of a caustic review by M. I. Finley, in the *New Statesman*: "To plunder 50 years of scholarship for the sake of an anthology of invective and abuse is unpardonable,"[22] the critics accepted the volume as a useful contribution to Housman scholarship.

From the early 1920's, when as a student at Eton, he first read Housman's lyric poetry, Carter's enthusiasm never faltered. He admired the poet's uncompromising intellect and caustic wit as well as his devotion to excellence. These were qualities not only to be admired but emulated. When Carter wanted to stress the importance of scholarship, he often quoted Housman's pronouncement, "Knowledge is good, method is good, but one thing beyond all others is necessary; and that is to have a head, not a pumpkin, on your shoulders, and brains, not pudding, in your head."[23]

In one instance Housman gave rather poor return for Carter's devotion. The year after he graduated from Cambridge, with his Catullus collection growing in size and importance, Carter decided to edit a translation of the poet's work. The Secretary of the Cambridge University Press, S.C. Roberts, sent Carter's proposal to Housman, the person on the faculty most likely to have an informed opinion on the subject. The poet's reply was not encouraging,

Dear Roberts,

I do not think that at present there is room for a new edition of Catullus even from the most competent hand. New MSS must be forthcoming, or Latin scholarship must make great advances, before it will be worth while. Kroll's handy Teubner edition of 1923, though far enough from perfection, is better than any Englishman is likely to do. Moreover I gather that Mr. Carter proposes to rearrange the poems in what he thinks their chronological order; that this is to be the chief novelty; yet not so novel neither, for he holds that the order has already for the most part been established by others. I should regard such a rearrangement as a definite evil, if [deleted] even if the chronology were more certain than it is. And I get the impression that he wants to cater for dilettanti, which, as a pedant, I cannot approve. But many people do not approve of pedants, and we must live and let live. Yours sincerely A. E. Housman[24]

Six years later, Carter tried again. This time he had the help of Robert Gathorne-Hardy, a fellow classicist and a partner in the Elkin Mathews firm. In a letter to Carter, Gathorne-Hardy asked about Sadleir's possible interest in publishing a new translation. If that didn't work, and it didn't, Gathorne-Hardy said he would take on the job himself at the Mill House Press, his own private printing enterprise. In 1934, after two parts of a projected six part series came off the press, the project died. The end came, as Carter pointed out, due to a lack of subscribers and "unflattering comments from better Latinists."[25] Although Carter never got a publication of any substance from his collection, it did eventually achieve a scholarly status. In 1960 he sold his various Catullus editions, along with detailed notes for a bibliography and a chronological index, to the University of Texas Humanities Research Center. William B. Todd of the English Department placed the acquisition in context in a memorandum to Chancellor Harry B. Ransom: "Word just received that we have the Catullus collection, some 130 editions, among them 7 incunabula and 30 from the 16th century, a brave show I think for the Academic Center. With a few exceptions, all in best condition, contemporary bindings, assembled over 35 years by a distinguished English bibliographer."[26]

During the war years Carter's published output slowed. His demanding government assignments left little time or energy for writing. It was difficult enough to carry on basic daily activities as the bombs fell. Lack of opportunities for publication also entered the picture as both *The Colophon* and *Bibliographic Notes and Queries* became wartime casualties. The Biblios dinners became another casualty after several members joined the armed services, and Percy Muir and John Hayward moved to the country. Repeating Lord Beaverbrook's dismal analysis, Carter said he was coming to believe, reluctantly, that, "there is no room for culture in war time."[27]

The two journals that continued to print Carter's articles and reviews were *Publishers' Weekly* and the *Times Literary Supplement*. Under the pseudonym "Waynflete," Carter published half a dozen articles in *Publishers' Weekly* describing the London rare book trade and the English wartime spirit of courage and determination. Many book shops continued to do business with boarded up windows and basements converted into air-raid shelters. "Sotheby's originally reckoned, as did most people, that conditions in London might be impossible," Waynflete reported. "Now, however, on the principle that anything which can be kept going, should be, they have just put on a sale and hope to follow it with others if conditions are encouraging."[28] Carter's sense of humor never completely deserted him. According to one of his reports, a number of visiting Republicans had to be revived with a free copy of Herbert Hoover's *The Challenge of Liberty* when they noticed the bright red paint on the boards covering Scribner's broken windows. The best approach, Carter concluded, was to "doff your hat to misfortune and go quickly about your business."[29] The tone was distinctly Churchillian.

The summer of 1941 brought Carter into direct contact with the Prime Minister. Earlier that year, Churchill had delivered a radio address to the American people in which he quoted the two concluding stanzas of Arthur Hugh Clough's stirring poem, "Say Not the Struggle Nought Availeth." The Scribner's firm happened to own Clough's manuscript of the poem, and, at Charles Scribner's request, Carter delivered it in person to 10 Downing Street. Handing the manuscript to Churchill and hearing him read a few lines from the poem was a memorable experience, and not one easily relayed in dry text: "It is not easy for an Englishman, proverbially awkward at expressing his feelings, to put down in words for American readers what it means to spend ten minutes talking to Mr. Churchill, in this year of crisis 1941. I shall not attempt it."[30] The meeting also gave Carter an opportunity to give Churchill a copy of *Grim Glory,* (published in the United States under the title *Bloody but Unbowed*) a book of wartime photographs taken by Lee Miller, edited by Ernestine Carter and with a preface by the American radio commentator Edward R. Murrow. Carter wrote the graceful dedication, "To the Right Honourable Mr. Winston Churchill Prime Minister of Great Britain the embodiment and the inspiration of that indomitable spirit of the common people to which this book pays tribute." In return Churchill presented Carter with one of his huge trademark cigars.

Although the war years limited publication opportunities, Carter found ways to keep involved. In addition to writing reviews for *Publishers' Weekly* and the *Times Literary Supplement,* and doing occasional theater reviews for *The Spectator,* he edited a collection of light verse and co-edited a history of printing.

In the fall of 1938, with the help of his younger brother Will, the proprietor of the Rampant Lions Press, Carter edited a collection of four-line rhyming verses called Clerihews, named for the originator of the form, Edmund Clerihew Bentley. Carter and his friends composed the satiric couplets as a kind of parlor game. It is easy to imagine Michael Sadleir, Brooke Crutchley, John Sparrow, and other friends sitting around the Carters' living room after dinner with a drink in hand, enjoying each other's origi-

22. Carter and his brother Will (left), proprietor of the Rampant Lions Press, on the veranda of Will's house at 12 Chesterton Road in Cambridge - c. 1939.

nality and wit. Sadleir's contribution was typical - "Mrs. Henry Wood/ Took no interest in food/Even after the success of 'East Lynne'/She remained painfully thin." An anonymous contributor provided a bit of Hollywood humor: "Miss Mae West/ Is one of the best:/ I would rather not/ Say the best what."[31] Attractively printed in a limited edition of five hundred copies, *Clerihews* was one of the earliest productions of the Rampant Lions Press. In a second edition, published in 1946, Carter presented himself as "John Waynflete, B. A.," a pseudonym with an undertone of humor but little credibility as a disguise. John and Ernestine Carter collaborated on several of the verses, including Cleopatra - "The Egyptian Queen/Thought a laurel wreath dreadfully mean./'I only wear it to tease her', Said Caesar."[32] These frivolities, as Carter might have called them, were simply amusing diversions, nothing more, nothing less. Both editions have become highly collectable.

Early in 1941, Carter and his friend Brooke Crutchley, then assistant to the printer of the Cambridge University Press, brought out a second edition of Harry G. Aldis' *The Printed Book,* a manual originally issued in 1916. The first five chapters, covering events from the introduction of printing in the fifteenth century up to the contributions of John Baskerville and William Bulmer at the end of the eighteenth century, needed little revision. Instead, the editors devoted their attention to the chapters on nineteenth century developments, book construction, illustration, and binding. Critics praised the revision saying the changes had been woven so cleverly into the text as to be almost indistinguishable from the original. The popularity of the book was such that Cambridge brought out a revised second edition in 1947, and a third edition in 1951. Based on steady sales, Crutchley urged Carter to do a completely revised fourth revision. The proposal brought a negative reply:

> At least half my spare time that is, steady desk work all Saturday or all Sunday, week in and week out - is mortaged to TLS; and the other half is seriously cut into by reading potential Scribner MSS."
> All right, say I dedicated a year or a year and a half to the job. Is it worth it? I am too old to care any more about advertising myself (fame, they call it), even if CUP would allow the new book to be called Carter instead of Aldis, which they won't, for it would damage the sales. I am too tired to profit by the education I could undoubtedly gain from the extensive reading involved. And finally, I am too

broke to consider the project a paying proposition. A steady 1,000 copies a year, if maintained, even at 10/6, if the price were raised again (as it ought not to be) means, at 10%, £50 a year gross for the author, which is £25 a year net, or thereabouts. I ask you.[33]

Time and money were not the only factors involved in Carter's decision on the Aldis book. In March 1952 when Charles Scribner, Jr.decided to shut down the major functions of the London branch, the implications were obvious. The disheartened tone of Carter's letter to Crutchley - too old, too tired and too broke - reflected the depth of his depression.

If it had not been for the upheaval at Scribner's, Carter would have been justified in viewing his career up to that point with satisfaction. The post-war economic recovery stimulated a broadening interest in collecting, which in turn encouraged editors and publishers to seek out authors who could illuminate the subject for the novice as well as the seasoned practitioner. Carter had a proven track record. It was satisfying, of course, when *Publishers' Weekly* and the *Times Literary Supplement* continued to accept his articles and reviews, but it was a cause for special celebration when, in 1948, *The Atlantic Monthly,* a highly regarded American journal of literature and opinion, published "Bookseller and Auctioneer," a survey of trade practices taken from his 1947 Sandars Lectures at Cambridge. As a barometer of the rising interest in collecting, the officers of the R. R. Bowker Company of New York lifted the Rare Book Section from *Publishers' Weekly,* and used it as a base for a new journal focused on the antiquarian book trade. Under the lively editorial direction of Sol Malkin, the first issue of *Antiquarian Bookman, (AB)* a weekly for dealers, librarians, and collectors, appeared on

March 1, 1948. Over a period of twenty-five years Carter contributed dozens of articles, reviews, letters to the editor, and notes. When *Taste and Technique in Book Collecting* came out in the fall of 1948, Malkin used Carter's photograph on *AB*'s cover. It was a solemn likeness with the subject, elegantly dressed, looking off in the distance with a slightly bemused expression. The caption identified him as "John "T N T" Carter, book-collector, bibliographer, and rare-book dealer," and explained he had just made "another most welcome contribution to the book field with his latest work *Taste and Technique in Book Collecting*."[34]

In the winter of 1947, in acknowledgment of Carter's growing reputation, the Syndics of Cambridge University Library invited him to give the prestigious Sandars Lectures in Bibliography. The honor was significant since it was the first time a member of the trade had been so nominated. From 1895, when Sir Edward Maunde Thompson, Principle Librarian of the British Museum, delivered his lecture, "Greek and Latin Palaeography," the post of Sandars Reader had been filled by distinguished bibliographers, librarians, and historians, among them W. W. Greg, R. B. McKerrow, Seymour de Ricci, Geoffrey Keynes, Michael Sadleir, Stanley Morison, and Julius Victor Scholderer. Carter refused to be intimidated by the scholarly weight of his predecessors. He had served nearly twenty years in the trade, made substantial contributions to bibliographic literature, and was supported at Cambridge by a host of friends, including S. C. Roberts, the Secretary of the University Press and A.N.L. Munby, the Librarian at King's College. His only concern, as he reported to the members of the Bibliographical Society in 1969, was that the Syndics might consider his topic on book collecting unworthy of serious consideration. That worry proved groundless.

In the first of three lectures Carter presented himself to the audience of students and dons, gathered in a drab lecture hall in the Arts School, not as a bibliographer, a book collector, or a man of letters but as a professional book dealer. His comments, he warned, would not constitute propaganda for book collecting, nor would they serve the beginner who required explanation for terms such as incunabula, cancel, or extra-illustrated. Instead, he promised to examine a number of topics he felt had been neglected in the past. He wanted to consider "the essential nature of book-collecting, the play of cause and effect in its development, the evolution and also the rationale of our present technical approach to it." His remarks, he said, would be "aimed at a thoughtful and moderately knowledgeable audience."[35]

Carter was hardly the first to examine book collecting. In the early nineteenth century, Thomas Frognall Dibdin roamed from one country house to another and produced a series of books in praise of the elaborate collections formed by the gentry. During the so-called "Golden Age of Book Collecting," 1910-1930, John T. Winterich and Iola A. Williams wrote basic "how to" manuals while A. E. Newton, Holbrook Jackson, and A.S.W. Rosenbach romanticized the topic in books that echoed Dibdin.[36]

Carter's approach was different. He divided the topic into two parts. In the first, "Evolution," he traced the history of collecting in England and America from the middle of the nineteenth century to the Jerome Kern sale in 1929, and in the second, "Method," dealt with specifics of the collecting process. As a starting point, Carter provided his listeners with his definition of a book collector:

The book-collector, then, is not just an eccentric who prefers one edition to another for some ritually compulsive reason. He is not a man who says simply "the old is better" or who thinks that rarity is an objective in itself. He is rather a man (or of course a woman, though bibliophily, like dandyism, is less common among women) who has a reverence for, and a desire to possess, the original or some other specifically admirable, curious or interesting edition of a book he loves or respects or one which has a special place among his intellectual interests. Furthermore, he enjoys, with a degree of intensity which will vary according to his temperament, his training, and the standards of his fellow-bibliophiles, that exercise of his natural and intellectual facilities which is involved in the application of knowledge, observation, ingenuity, foresight, enterprise and persistence to the pursuit of his quarry, its scrutiny and appraisal when found, its use and perhaps formal description when secured.[37]

The lectures and the book produced from them, *Taste & Technique in Book Collecting*, covered the changing tastes and methods of collectors over a period of one hundred years, a description of the environment in which they worked, and a consideration of the qualities of condition and rarity. Carter described how social and economic factors influenced changes in taste and supported his arguments with frequent reference to collectors such as William Beckford, Robert Hoe, W. H. "Measure" Miller, Henry Huth, Henry E. Huntington, Michael Sadleir, and Frederick Locker-Lampson, and to the dealers who worked with them, men like George D. Smith, A.S.W. Rosenbach, A.W. Evans, E. P. Goldschmidt, and James F. Drake.

The three chapters in *Taste & Technique in Book Collecting* that discuss technique, "Education of a Collector," "Tools and Terminology," and "Bookshop and Auction Room," while useful, seem somewhat out of place in what Carter referred to as a "ruminative treatise." Presumably, most readers would be aware of the importance of visiting good book shops, reading catalogs, and consulting standard bibliographies. Far more important were his discussion of rarity and condition. Taking up arguments that he had pursued fifteen years earlier in *Publishers' Weekly*, Carter called for a common sense approach to evaluating condition. Why should a collector pay a high price and attribute superior status to eighteenth century books in boards or wrappers, when those cov-

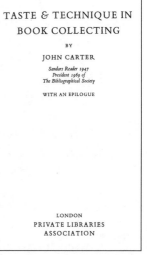

TASTE & TECHNIQUE IN
BOOK COLLECTING

BY

JOHN CARTER

Sandars Reader 1947
President 1969 of
The Bibliographical Society

WITH AN EPILOGUE

LONDON
PRIVATE LIBRARIES
ASSOCIATION

23. Title page from 'Taste & Technique in Book Collecting,' the second impression, 1970.

erings were never meant to be permanent? And what of collectors who insisted, unreasonably, on uncut edges? These were old arguments and ones he didn't expect to win since, as he noted, "There is no aspect of collecting technique on which the connoisseurs are so variously opinionated, so vocal and so intolerant of heterodox opinions: no area in which dictated criteria have been more ruthlessly applied, in which tastes have more often become fetiches, in which reason has more repeatedly been stifled by rules."[38]

Carter was well served by his years in the trade when it came to a discussion of rarity. He identified four types - absolute, relative, localized, and temporary - and went on to analyze the variables that effect those categories - criteria such as the number of copies printed, reputation of the publisher, the books' reputation, and the position of the book in the author's career. In his entirely positive review, Winterich wrote, "The chapter on rarity is a careful, sound, lucid analysis" and supplies "a yardstick that can be applied, at least roughly, on sight."[39] Frank C. Francis agreed, "Each of the topics is treated with a wealth of detail presented with the confidence which comes from knowledge and experience and brilliantly illuminated by innumerable telling examples."[40] The American bibliographer Donald Wing characterized the book as "A genial, informative discussion of the interrelationships of taste and technique,"[41] while the anonymous reviewer (Carter was correct in thinking it was John Hayward) in the *Times Literary Supplement* said Carter "proved himself to be a first-class tutor: wearing his learning easily and often with a pleasing air of dandyism; very apt in his examples and allusions; and refreshingly dogmatic on the subject of untrimmed edges, boards and other irrational fetishes of those who blindly worship the mystery of "original condition."[42] In a handwritten note to the author Geoffrey Keynes wrote, "Very tasty and technical. . . . I enjoyed it very much and compliment you on its elegance and comprehensiveness."[43] The virtues of *Taste & Technique of Book Collecting* continued to be recognized. The novelist and book dealer Larry McMurtry gave it high praise in a long review written in 2001. "I don't think there is a better book about book collecting;" he declared, "the prose is splendid, the judgments accurate , the suggestions reasonable." [44]

In spite of favorable reviews, *Taste & Technique in Book Collecting* failed to attract buyers. Perhaps, as the reviewer in *Library Journal* suggested, it was too specialized for the casual collector. In any case, by 1960, with sales at less than one hundred copies a year, Cambridge University Press reduced the price by half and turned over all remaining copies to the National Book Sale. The following year, both Cambridge and Bowker, the American publisher, declared the book out of print.[45] There was a satisfying resurrection however in 1970, when the Private Libraries Association brought out a reprint accompanied by an epilogue, Carter's November 1969 presidential address to the Bibliographical Society. The reprint included a special note of appreciation to S. C. Roberts of Cambridge, "who got me appointed Sandars Reader," and Frederic G. Melcher of New York, "who commissioned my first article on book-collecting." The publication of *Taste & Technique in Book Collecting* was as important to the advance of Carter's career as the *Enquiry* had been fourteen years earlier and as *ABC for Book Collectors* would be in the decade of the fifties.

As Carter had taken pains to explain, *Taste & Technique in Book Collecting* was not intended as a manual for beginners. He advised those who wanted basic definitions to look elsewhere. Unfortunately, no dictionary of that kind existed. Aware of the gap, Carter offered Rupert Hart-Davis in London and Alfred A. Knopf in New York an outline for an annotated dictionary of terms commonly used by bibliographers and dealers. This time the book would be aimed at the beginning collector. To get the project started, Carter asked a select group of friends to help draw together a list of entries:

> I have undertaken to produce, for publication next year, an ABC FOR BOOK COLLECTORS. This is intended as an annotated glossary for explaining to the novice collector or the layman, the variegated jargon used in the descriptions and notes in antiquarian booksellers' catalogues. Many of these terms are borrowed from bibliography,

sometimes with special glosses or commercialized connotations. Others are native to the book market. The collector needs to be familiar with both.

I enclose herewith a provisional list of entries, compiled without much system in the course of a month's preparatory thought. I should be greatly obliged by the addition to this list of any similar terms which, in the course of the next six weeks, strike you as needing explanation.[46]

Contract negotiations took time and patience. When Carter originally discussed the book with Knopf in September 1950, the scope appeared modest; a dictionary format with approximately two hundred entries. When Knopf saw the first draft the following spring, he was astonished to see the number of entries had doubled. It had become, he said "a veritable monster." That didn't mean he had reservations about the book's success. He thought it would enjoy good sales, but doubted if it would bring in a profit. In a three-page letter he explained the firm's position on royalties:

> We simply cannot pay more than 10% retail on a book of this kind unless it should have a sale within a given twelve-month period far in excess of what either of us probably contemplate. There simply are no longer economies of manufacture in reprints which warrant an American publisher raising the royalty to any point so modest as 3,000, i.e., probably fewer than half as many copies as he would have to sell to get back his investment. . . . American printers and binders simply do not like to handle small runs and they are gradually pricing them out of the market. We have therefore come regretfully to the conclusion that we can only afford 15% for books which we can start off with a printing of at least 15,000 copies. 25,000 would probably be better.

A B C

F O R

Book-Collectors

B Y

John Carter

A unique and uniquely useful book by the author of
Taste and Technique in Book-Collecting, co-author
(with Graham Pollard) of *An Enquiry into the Nature
of Certain Nineteenth Century Pamphlets*

 ALFRED A. KNOPF, *Publisher, New York*

*24. Dust jacket design for first American edition (1952),
of Carter's popular 'ABC for Book-Collectors.'*

I think 10% straight a reasonable royalty for your book, but if you think it is not, I am perfectly willing to raise it after 5,000 copies have been sold, provided x number of copies are sold in any royalty year.

I can only hope that the point of view I have set forth, however unwelcome –and it is unwelcome to me, I assure you - will seem reasonable to you. I quite agree that this book should have a long and steady sale, but I do not honestly believe that either of us are likely to make much of a profit out of it - I feel quite sure its publisher won't and I speak of you in the same connection bearing in mind the immense amount of labor that you have had to put into it.[47]

Carter accepted the offer as reasonable, but couldn't resist adding, "As an author, of course, I shall continue to consider 10% a very modest remuneration."[48] He expressed himself with considerably more force when he wrote to Hart-Davis about the control of the American royalties:

I think a substantial proportion of the total number of copies which this book might sell over the years would be sold in America. I have thought it and still think it - reasonable to reserve control of the American arrangements, or rather in particular, the royalty arrangements; and although I have urged Knopf on the advisability of buying sheets from you in the hope that it would be of service to you and to the English edition if he did, I cannot see my way to doing more, and certainly not to accepting a royalty of 10% on price received for such a sheet sale. I hope you don't think this attitude unreasonable, for I am not to be moved from it.[49]

Carter organized his dictionary in the manner of Henry W. Fowler's *Modern English Usage*, with definitions ranging from one or two lines to page-length articles. Using another Fowler technique, Carter often included personal comments. He explained the approach in the preface:

Although, as a professional, I can hardly be expected to avoid some bias, I have tried to be impartial in those matters where buyer and seller do not always see eye to eye. It would be too much to hope that I have succeeded, in a book from which I have not attempted to exclude my own opinion.[50]

His opinions were generously spread throughout the book's 190 pages. Many entries such as CHAIN LINES, CHAPBOOKS, OCTAVO, and SIGNATURE called for and received straightforward definitions, while others like ELSE FINE - "Favorite phrase with the never-say-die type of cataloguer; used in such contexts as 'somewhat wormed and age-stained, piece torn from title, headlines cut into, joints repaired, new lettering-piece, else fine,'" received the caustic, yet witty treatment they deserved. BIBLIOMANIA, according to Carter, was "Literally, a madness for books. A *bibliomaniac* is a book-collector with a slightly wild look in his eye." ROAN was, "A thin, soft kind of sheepskin used by binders as a cheap substitute for MOROCCO from about 1790 onwards. Not at all desirable, and seldom elegant even when well preserved." POINT MANIACS were collectors "who do not merely love POINTS but love them to excess." Terms that describe the physical parts of a book were illustrated graphically within the book itself. The end papers in *ABC for Book Collectors,* for example, were used to demonstrate the positions of FORE-EDGE, HEAD, and PASTE-DOWN ENDPAPER. Terms such as SIGNATURE, DROPPED LETTER, and SHOULDER-NOTES were illustrated at appropriate intervals.

The book was deliberately titled ABC, instead of encyclopedia or glossary, because Carter wanted to imply a text for beginners. His audience was to be made up of "novices, would-be-collectors and that section of the literate public which takes an interest in our pursuit without necessarily wishing to share it."[51] That shrewd market analysis paid big dividends. The book sold remarkably well, as edition followed edition, and carried Carter's reputation to new heights. Knopf's prediction that the book would have a long and steady sale proved to be true beyond his imagination. A second edition came out in 1953, a third, completely reset, and in paperback in 1961, and a fourth edition in 1966. The last edition to be edited by Carter came out in 1972, and was followed by a sixth, 1980, and seventh, 1995, both edited by Nicolas Barker. Oak Knoll Press, the American publisher, reports sales of some 3,000 copies annually.

ABC for Book Collectors was an unqualified critical success. Sadleir was lavish in his praise: "This book is more than just the latest specimen of Carterism. Indeed, I incline to regard it as the best Carter hitherto, because it most fully displays his varied qualities as an educator and as a writer on bibliographic themes."[52] Wilmarth S. Lewis called it "a delight - clear, accurate and witty."[53] Carter's favorite comment came from another old friend, the eminent type-historian Stanley Morison. In Morison's sardonic view the book "ought to be a serviceable thing by the time it reached its fifth edition."[54] Most users, unwilling to wait that long - the fifth edition didn't appear until 1972 - found the book immediately serviceable. The most entertaining analysis came from Carter's own hand. In September 1952, Edmond Segrave, the editor of *The Bookseller*, commissioned a spoof that might be called Carter on Carter. The review was signed, but the authorship was not given. He began the review by saying the author must be either "a fool or a knave" to think he could attract the attention of serious collectors or offer useful advice to the novice. That opening was a mere warm up to the next rhetorical flourish:

> If . . . he has conceived the base notion that beginners are humble enough to believe any claptrap about the bibliophile mystery that they read in print, just because an otherwise reputable publisher has been bamboozled into undertaking a book like this, then he is a cynical ruffian: far more of a menace than the issue-mongers, mint-condition fetishists, point-maniacs and other strange fry whom he holds up to disapproval in the course of his 190-odd pages.

In spite of these difficulties, Carter continued, people would buy the book, but for the wrong reasons:

> Antiquarian booksellers, of course, will buy it to foist on their unsuspecting customers as propaganda. People interested in outlandish cults and esoteric rituals will buy it out of curiosity. People wanting a Christmas present for an uncle who is "a great reader" will succumb to the fallacy that book-collecting is connected in some way with literature, and the old boy won't like to send it back. People who hate book-collecting and despise collectors will buy it out of malice, as ammunition for ridiculing their bibliophile friends and catching them out on some technical point.
>
> Novice book collectors (the poor, credulous creatures) will fall on it with grateful cries, in thousands, under the fond impression that here, at last, is someone able and willing to tell them in plain language the meaning of all those weird terms which clutter up booksellers' and auctioneers' catalogues; . . . Finally, the experienced collector will buy it - not, of course, because he expects to find anything useful or informative in it, but on the contrary because he happily (and quite correctly) assumes that it will be full of idiotic mistakes which he will then be able to impale, with a withering comment, on a postcard to the author.[55]

It is impossible to say whether the withering review tempted anyone to buy the book, but that, of course, was not its purpose.

Carter regarded the dictionary as a work in progress and solicited comments and corrections from a wide range of readers in England and the United States. The 1953 second edition carried his acknowledgment for help received. "Thanks to the kindness of observant friends and acquaintances, and the stimulus to further research applied by one more than avuncular reviewer, some of the *bêtises* which disfigured the first edition of this book have been corrected. Notice of surviving errors, whether of fact or judgment, would be warmly welcomed."[56] Among the terms added to the second edition were CHRONOLOGICAL OBSESSION and BOOKSELLERS' CATALOGUES. The completely reset third edition introduced CALLIGRAPHY and SILKED, and substituted BINDING for a somewhat rambling description of BINDING MYTHS printed in the earlier editions. The fifth edition, the one Morison predicted would be a serviceable tool, was heavily revised. Among the additions were BLANCK, HAYWARD, GASKELL, GOFF, and SADLEIR in recognition of those distinguished bibliographers and their guides.

For over fifty years *ABC for Book Collectors* has continued to charm and instruct. Praised as a classic, an indispensable *vade mecum*, and the answer to a book-collector's prayer, it is recognized as a unique guide to the vocabulary of book collecting. As a result of the book's success, Carter's name, well established in bibliographic circles, for his *Enquiry* and *Taste and Technique in Book Collecting*, became known to a broader readership.

After the success of *ABC for Book Collectors*, Carter found it easy to convince Hart-Davis to publish *Books and Book Collectors*, a selection of essays, reviews, and short articles, but Knopf, who had done well with the American edition of the dictionary, was unenthusiastic. He called the book a scissors-and-paste job and criticized what he saw as an overemphasis on bibliographic technicality. Carter replied saying if a reader found himself "in danger of being knocked cold" after reading one page of the essay,"Nineteenth Century English Books: Some Bibliographic Agenda," he could quickly move on to "Operation Shuckburgh" or the review of *ABC for Book Collectors*.[57] After Knopf turned down the manuscript, Hart-Davis sold the American rights to William Targ, director of The World Publishing Company in Cleveland, Ohio. Targ had been a rare book dealer at one time and appreciated the book's focus on collecting and bibliography He promised Carter the usual ten percent royalty on the first two thousand copies sold and a $500 advance.

The selections in *Books and Book Collecting*, as Knopf had noted, varied in tone from the technical to the light-hearted. There was an essay on collecting detective fiction, originally written in 1934, two pieces on Wise, eight biographical sketches devoted to collectors and typographers, and five short essays on bibliophily. The critics agreed that the book proved again, if any such proof was needed, that Carter could write with style and insight. He compiled the book, he said, in order to mark a milestone in his career; his return to the rare book business as Sotheby's American agent. In essence, it was a gentlemanly tip-of-the-hat, intended to honor old friends and underscore continuing interests.

CHAPTER SEVEN

Early Days with Sotheby's

D uring the spring of 1953, before taking up his position at the embassy in Washington, Carter had time
to think about his future. It would, of course,
involve rare books, but where and on what basis? He knew
and was known by the officers of the leading London auction houses and by the proprietors of many of the rare book
firms in London and New York. With his reputation as a
bibliographer, and his connections in the trade, he felt reasonably confident that after a year or two in Washington, he
would be able to locate a satisfying permanent position. Still,
at age forty-eight and married, it couldn't be just *any* job. He
began to test the rare book market for suitable openings. In
the spring of 1954 he wrote at length to Frederick B. Adams,
the Director of the Pierpont Morgan Library:

> The matter on which I sh' value yr advice is this (strict-
> ly confidential at present). Goldschmidt's young partner-
> assistant, Jacques Vellekoop, whom you have doubtless
> met, having inherited the business, has asked me to join
> him. He realizes, better perhaps than any of us, that EPG
> is an irreplaceable loss; but he has been in effect running
> the firm for the past two years, wants to keep it going, per-
> ceives the need for some addition of people and authority
> to any successor to such a one-man business, is anxious to
> widen its scope as well as maintaining if possible, its flour-
> ishing connections in the learned world and the fraternity
> of scholarly collectors and has proposed to me terms

which are within negotiable distance of being satisfactory. It is, of course, for me to decide whether, in principle, I should find the most useful employment of my rather miscellaneous abilities in the rare book business. But assuming that the answer was yes, are you disposed to agree with Stanley Morison, Tim Munby, Graham Pollard and John Hayward (all of whom Vellekoop has consulted privately as being known friends of mine, the first two of whom I have myself consulted as valued counsellors) that this is probably the most advantageous opening I could hope for in the antiquarian trade?[1]

After commenting on his rather limited, but positive, experience with Vellekoop, Adams replied:

I should think he would make a very satisfactory partner to work with. I can't believe that the stock amounts to too much as far as value goes. As you know, E.P. really preferred buying books to selling them and sold them mainly to finance his buying. . . . On the other hand, everything he bought had an unusual interest of some kind attached to it, provided the right person could be found to appreciate that unusual significance.

It takes more courage but it is also more fun to run your own shop and from this point of view the Goldschmidt proposition looks more satisfactory over the long term than a connection with Sotheby's, which already has a good many cooks in the kitchen.

The gist of all this is that I would be in favor of your joining Vellekoop. The prospects offered by the association are on the highest level and I think with your many devoted friends in this country, you can surely make a go of it.[2]

While these negotiations were still in progress, Carter turned to Sotheby's. With its established international reputation and a sophisticated, highly professional staff, many of whom Carter knew intimately, Sotheby's held a special appeal.

The practice of offering goods for sale by open bidding began on a modest scale in England in the middle of the sixteenth century, modeled on similar trade practices on the Continent. As a growing business and banking center, London offered the ideal environment for the exchange of goods. Auctions ranged from the opulent to the shabby, with one dealer offering important paintings and another chipped china tea cups. Book auctions began in London in 1676 with the dispersal of the library of Dr. Lazarus Seaman, a Puritan divine, and former master of Peterhouse College, Cambridge. During the early decades of the eighteenth-century, book auctions grew in popularity. In 1744, after selling old books in the conventional way for several years, Samuel Baker, an energetic young Londoner, issued a catalog of books to be sold at auction from the library of the Rt. Hon. Sir John Stanley. The sales took place over a period of ten nights in the Great Room over the Exeter Exchange in the Strand. For Baker, success followed success. As his business prospered, he took on several assistants, among them his nephew, John Sotheby. After Baker's death in 1778, Sotheby became a partner and in so doing set the firm's name permanently in place.

Sotheby's went through many changes during the nineteenth and early twentieth century, but remained essentially a hierarchy, with partners and art specialists at the top of the organization chart and accountants, clerks, and porters at the base. In 1924, the firm changed from a partnership into a private unlimited company. Partners became directors. To be considered for a directorship, a candidate had to evince a proper social background, professional expertise, and, probably most important of all, a substantial bank account. In the 1950s, it would have been expected that a newly-appointed director would invest something between £10,000 to £50,000 in the firm. It was this array of considerations, and the fact that no director-ships were immediately available, that C. Vere Pilkington, Sotheby's chairman, and a friend from Eton days, placed before Carter in December 1953. As an alternative, Pilkington suggested an arrangement under which Sotheby's would pay Carter a commission on profits from sales of books or manuscripts. He would find his own customers and make all the financial arrangements on his own. It was not what Carter had in mind. In a four page, single-spaced letter marked "Personal and Confidential" he outlined his thoughts. First, there was the matter of his own credentials:

> Since my twenty five years in the rare book business have been mainly devoted to the servicing of the American market, I can see that you and your colleagues will be thinking of me - since you are good enough to be thinking of me - mainly in connection with that market. And it is true that my connections among the collectors and private libraries of England and the Continent, as distinct from the antiquarian booksellers, are not as extensive as they would be if Scribner's had been sellers as well as buyers in the home market. Yet, apart from such reputation as one may acquire, outside the circle of personal acquaintance, by writing books and articles and other similar means, my name has inevitably been con-nected with Scribners' purchasing operations, at least during the eighteen years since I reorganized the rare book department in New York and became responsible, with David Randall, for the firm's policy in that field as well as for its European representation.

Before anything could be put in motion, however, England's prohibitive Board of Trade and Treasury

Department regulations would need to be changed. Carter presented the case:

> If you and I are right in agreeing that a fruitful source of future supply lies in American libraries, cut off for nearly fifteen years from the London market by the exchange control, one of your main problems is to break down the Treasury's and the Board of Trade's reluctance to let you make a bid for the sale of books and MSS from across the Atlantic, as well as from across the Channel. Apart from any assistance which someone like myself might be able to give towards formulating and putting over a persuasive case to the authorities, one of your prime needs is hard evidence that a rewarding proportion of material sold under the hammer at Sotheby's is sold, whether directly or indirectly, for dollars (as well as Swiss francs, escudos, etc.)

Carter was sure American collections could be acquired if the right person managed the negotiations. It would take "someone in whose judgement and taste, as well as knowledge and integrity, they [American collectors and librarians] had confidence: confidence based on personal or professional acquaintance as well as on public reputation." If there was any doubt as to who that someone might be, he continued:

> These same qualities, were they at your disposal, would, I should suppose, considerably enhance your chances of securing American libraries for sale, as and when the green light may be given for such operations. I am not suggesting that Sotheby's prestige will not in itself be a powerful magnet when that time comes; not to mention your own and Anthony's [Hobson] connections and standing here. But Parke-Bernet are pretty well entrenched: it is a long time since an important American library was consigned to London; and if the

habit of forty years is to be reversed, a representative with a fair number of long-standing American connections and (if I may say it without vanity) a substantial reputation in America, might contribute some effective leverage to the necessary reversal.

Finally, Carter rejected the idea of working as a commission agent:

> I cannot conceive of working at Sotheby's, . . . without taking an active interest, not merely though most obviously in the book and MS department, but in the business as a whole: after all, though ignorant, I have the ordinary educated man's interest in pictures, silver, furniture and china, even if not much in jewellery. And I am vain enough to suppose that I could be of some use - and fairly consistent use, too - to the book and MS department in matters of strategy and tactics, as well as, now and again, in the exploitation of material of which I had specialist knowledge.

Any potential risk in the appointment, he argued, would be his own rather than Sotheby's:

> I hope you and your colleagues will give this letter your careful consideration; and I hope that in so doing you will bear two general points in mind. The first is that in offering to throw in my lot with you, at the mature age of 48, I am taking a much more serious step than you - collectively or individually - would be taking in adding my name to your existing masthead: and this is not merely because I should have to borrow some of the money to do it. The second, which I submit with some diffidence, is that a firm whose historic name and handsome reputation are priceless assets in every week's business, not only can afford to, but positively cannot afford not to, take a long view of any

risk of a short-term discrepancy between a predictable accretion to its prestige and the inevitably unpredictable addition which might derive therefrom to the business of, say, the 1956/7 auction season.[3]

Carter apologized for the length of the letter but said he had been busy with no time to condense it.

In December 1954, the Board of Trade lifted exchange controls, and for the first time in fifteen years American goods could be sold in London for a return in dollars. This was what the Sotheby directors had been waiting for. Pilkington set down the terms under which Carter would be invited to join the firm. He would be paid an annual salary of £1,500 plus a percentage of gross commissions earned on any properties he brought in. He would act as Sotheby's representative in the United States, primarily to obtain collections to be sold in London, by making two six-week visits annually, with travel and living costs absorbed by the firm. While in London he would be expected to work in the book department on a part-time basis - perhaps ten to fifteen hours a week. Still pending was the question of Carter's position in the administrative hierarchy. Pilkington said the issue had been troubling some of the directors: "We are still not sure we have thought of a good title for you. If you don't like 'Representative' would some title like 'Associate' suit? We are so much looking forward to having you in the bosom of the Sotheby family."[4] Earlier, Carter asked to be allowed to resume his connection with the *Times Literary Supplement* and to take on independent bibliographic consulting opportunities as they might come to him from institutional libraries. The directors had no hesitation in agreeing to those requests.

Carter asked for advice from two American friends, Donald F. Hyde, a prominent New York attorney, and Frederick B. Adams, director of the Pierpont Morgan library. In explaining the position to Adams, he emphasized its half-time nature:

> The economic practicability of a part-time association with Sotheby's, as a sort of special consultant on American operations, depends on my being able to make such arrangements for the other half of my time and energy as would (a) make us respectable living and (b) allow me to develop the function of independent consultant/agent in London to the point where it could be expanded into a full-time job if, after 2 or 3 years, my Sotheby arrangement had served its purpose without encouraging me to want or expect the chance of moving in closer as a partner. You share my view, I think, that certain institutional libraries in this country, plus perhaps a selected very few private collectors, might have sufficiently frequent occasion to make use of such professional services as I could offer, to be ready to consider some such liaison on a regular basis.
>
> The question I am now considering is, how to mobilize enough support for the initial stages to make this double-barrelled project reasonably water proof. I think naturally of PML [Pierpont Morgan Library]. I have also thought of Larry Powell (UCLA), Gordon Ray (Illinois) and perhaps Jim Wells (Wing, Newberry) as regionally and by subject interest unlikely to clash.
>
> I should need to be able to rely on a select nucleus to begin with. Ideally, of course - and economically on both sides in terms of accounting and paper work, I should prefer to work on a retained basis rather than on commission.[5]

Although he could not promise direct support from the Morgan Library, Adams thought the Sotheby offer well worth considering. Hyde agreed and enumerated the positive aspects of the appointment - "(1) Live in London (2) Earn a living through books (3) Enjoy some comfort (4) Travel regularly to the United States. Your risk is greater than Sotheby's, at your age," he concluded, "BUT you could try it out for three years. I think you should do it."[6] In March 1955, with all the paperwork in place, Carter accepted Sotheby's offer. In a letter to Randall he explained the particulars of his post. "My arrangement as an 'associate' of Sotheby's is that I give them half my time (and my name on the masthead) to look after U.S. business and, of course, to procure any consignments I can. Thus, if I hear of a suitable collection (whether books, pictures or anything else) which is not bespoke or in negotiation, my first duty is to try and get it for Sotheby's. But I am certainly free, as far as they are concerned, to act as a consultant and negotiator for institutions and private collectors."[7] Once more, Carter had found a way to satisfy his need for freedom of movement.

One of Carter's first jobs, mundane but essential, was to attach Sotheby's name to a New York address and phone number. Hyde offered secretarial help and provisional office space at 61 Broadway in the midst of the Wall Street district. With the New York base established, Carter returned to London for a period of orientation. There was much to learn. He felt confident working with books and manuscripts but "hadn't the least idea of the going price of a Rubens oil-sketch, a T'ang horse, an Oeben commode, a Kaendler figure or a pair of George II candlesticks."[8] Several directors came to his aid. Carmen Gronau shared her knowledge of paintings and prints, and Cyril Butterwick, a former Eton master, helped with values of silver and jewelry. Carter understood the basic workings of the auction business - securing consignments,

preparing catalogs, and finally offering goods for sale, but
if he was to lure American customers into doing business
with Sotheby's he needed detailed knowledge of accounting practices, publicity, shipping and receiving, and all the
other departments that made the firm's day to day activities function smoothly. His ten years' experience managing similar complicated accounting and shipping details in
Scribner's London office was a considerable help. His chief
working associate at 34-35 New Bond Street was Anthony
Hobson, the thirty-five year old chief of the book and
manuscript department. By the time Carter arrived, the
Hobson name was deeply embedded in the firm's history.
When Geoffrey Hobson, Anthony's father, joined the
firm as a partner in 1909, Sotheby's was a successful and
reasonably well known London auction house. When he
left, forty years later, it had assumed an international reputation for quality based partly on Hobson's scholarly cataloging. Anthony joined the firm in 1949 as assistant head
of the book department under Charles des Graz and
became department head on his death in 1953. The relationship between Carter and Hobson, sixteen years apart
in age, was cordial but guarded - slightly better than an
armed truce. Carter, the associate, was the experienced bibliographer with an impressive array of publications, a wide
knowledge of the book trade, and an intimate understanding of the American market. Hobson, the director, was
linked to the firm by strong family ties. Carter had a small
office down the hall from Hobson's roomy suite. Some of
the directors found Carter's appointment perplexing.
How should they treat this new "associate"? What did the
title mean? Would he blend into Sotheby's complex hierarchy? Carter worried about many of the same questions.
Would the old guard consider his background in the book

trade somewhat beneath the standards of the auction house? The appointment was sure to be a balancing act with sensitivity required on both sides.

Carter's first priorities were to announce his presence representing the firm in New York, and to publicize the removal of the trade restrictions. He drafted an advertisement for the book trade journals:

> London has long been recognized as the world centre of the art market, where the greater stability of prices and the special facilities for both American and Continental buyers offer exceptional advantages to owners disposing of their collections.
>
> Sotheby's, the oldest established auctioneers of books and works of art in the world, can now again freely import collections for sale from the United States and the Continent and remit the proceeds, without difficulty or delay, *in dollars or the appropriate currency.* Libraries have been sent from abroad to Sotheby's for sale since the 18th century, and the Firm is currently disposing, in a series of sales, of the celebrated collection of autograph letters of André de Coppet of New York.
>
> Sotheby's Associate, Mr. John Carter, visits the United States regularly to maintain touch with American collectors, institutions and dealers.
>
> Sotheby's rates of commission are substantially lower than those obtaining in New York, Paris or Geneva: works of Art, Paintings, etc., 10 per cent on lots over £100; Books and Manuscripts, 15 percent.[9]

Another release for overseas dealers presented the specific financial advantages of trading with Sotheby's:

> There is NO import duty on antiques of any kind coming into Britain nor on pictures or books of any date.

There is NO government or any other tax (as in some Continental countries) on sales by auction.

There is NO export duty out of the United States.

Payment of the proceeds of sale in London can now be made, without formalities or delay, IN DOLLARS.

It is often supposed that because American buying is one of the strongest factors in the international market, auction prices will automatically be higher in New York than in London. Facts and figures prove that (except for material of exclusively American interest) this is not so. The London market is not only more stable than any other; its prices are not only more authoritative; they have also been, for the past decade or more steadily higher.[10]

Carter's major responsibility was to promote London as an inviting base for the sale of American libraries and art objects. This was not the first time Sotheby's had sent an agent to America. As a partner, Montague Barlow traveled to the United States regularly before World War I, promoting the firm's goods and services. He was followed by Charles des Graz, who had at one time worked for the British Library of Information in New York, and who knew his way around in the upper reaches of East Coast society. With a permanent office in New York, Carter had an obvious advantage over these early travelers. Did a collector in Cleveland want to talk about selling his library? If so, he didn't need to cable London or wait two weeks for his inquiry to go through by mail; he could simply call Sotheby's Bowling Green number for immediate help.

In New York Carter developed a schedule of visits to museum curators, librarians, collectors, and dealers. In addition to book dealers, he called on those who traded in paintings and drawings, china, silver, furniture, and jewelry, and other *objets d' art*. He also made appointments with trust officers, bankers, and lawyers - men who frequently made decisions or offered advice on the disposal of collections. This was ground-breaking for, as Carter discovered, "Not one of them, I found, had ever even thought of advising consignment from an art-rich estate to London, and hardly any of them had heard of Sotheby's. But they very quickly grasped the economic argument, they were impressed by the selection of catalogues, they welcomed my offer to put not only themselves but also their branch managers around the country on the list for our monthly Burlington Calendar and at least a half a dozen of them proved very useful connections."[11]

His message was invariably the same: consignment to Sotheby's, in contrast to the leading American house, Parke-Bernet, meant higher prices received and lower commissions charged. He spoke respectfully of Sotheby's long and distinguished history and its international standing. He also took pains to explain that the trade restrictions which had hampered any useful exchange of goods between 1939 and 1954 were a thing of the past. In the spring of 1956, after spending a short time in New York, he took Sotheby's message on the road. Over a three week period he spoke to dealers, curators, newspaper editors, and librarians from Philadelphia to Kansas City, with stops in between at Cleveland, St. Louis, Chicago, Boston, and Washington D. C. Along the way he attended lunches with members of the Caxton Club in Chicago, the Club of Odd Volumes in Boston, the Grolier Club in New York, and the Rowfant Club in Cleveland. He renewed friendships with dealers and librarians with whom he had done business during his years at Scribner's - George Goodspeed in Boston, Mabel Zahn of Sessler's in Philadelphia,

William A. Jackson and Philip Hofer at the Houghton Library at Harvard, and Frederick B. Adams at the Morgan Library in New York. Carter's years in Washington continued to pay dividends. He made it a point to visit the officers in charge of the various British Consulates, many of them known to him from his recent travels around the country with the ambassador. As Carter observed, "The British Consul normally enjoys a wide acquaintance among the notables in his area: and my ex-colleagues were invariably helpful - after all Anglo-American trade is an important component of their work - in arranging for me to meet over lunch or a drink people whom either I had marked down or they had suggested as useful connections for the firm's two-way business."[12]

Another opportunity to publicize his new position came from an unexpected source. The officers of the English Speaking Union (ESU) in London, aware of Carter's background at the embassy, invited him to con-duct, on their behalf, an expense-paid speaking tour in the United States. Instead of traditional topics like "Whither Africa?" and "Britain and the Commonwealth," Carter addressed members of the ESU on the international art market and particularly Sotheby's place in that market. It was almost too good to be true. For two weeks in the spring of 1961, then again in 1962 and 1963, Carter trav-eled through the Midwest and South and, as he reported, "preached the Sotheby's gospel from pulpits flanked by the Union Jack and the Stars and Stripes."[13] The first year, he made stops in Cleveland, Detroit, Chicago, Cincinnati, Toledo, Indianapolis, and Bloomington addressing dinner or luncheon meetings with audiences ranging in size from 120 to 200. With his patrician manner, Saville Row suits, monocle, and long-bowled pipe he was the picture of the sophisticated English gentlemen. The titles of his talks, "Going, Going, Gone," "Sold to the Highest Bidder," "Bull Market in Bond Street," "Behind the Scenes at Sotheby's," and "A Renoir is a Girl's Best Friend, or Is it?" left little doubt about the speaker's affiliation. The tone was light, and the content filled with anecdotes. Carter always concluded his Renoir talk with a tribute to a "young American painter" whose work he had seen and appreciated. He had purchased several of her pictures for reasonable prices and showed them back home to the admiration of his friends. (Then the punch line) She is seven years old; she lives in Cincinnati. Her name is "Beauty." She is a chimpanzee! (laughter all around).

Whatever the title of his talk, Carter's message was essentially the same: Sotheby's was the most important and successful auction house in the world. In a memorandum to the firm's directors, Carter summarized his ESU experience saying, "In addition to general propaganda, each meeting produced some useful local leads, all of which have been followed up. The volume of questions (15 or 20 minutes at the end) was encouraging evidence of the interest aroused over the past ten years by newspaper and word-of-mouth reports of high jinks in Bond Street. In Chicago, a trustee of the Art Institute admitted that she had with difficulty repressed the temptation to ask the chairman whether Christie's were going to be offered equal free time (I managed never to mention any other auction house by name)".[14]

In one further effort to attract attention, Carter sent letters to newspaper editors offering information on London fine art sales and exhibitions. "There is a growing interest everywhere," the letter began, "in antiques, works of art, pictures, rare books, fine furniture, etc. London is the centre of the international market in such things. The auction room has a fascination even for those who have never been to a sale, and Sotheby's (founded in 1744) is the oldest auction house in London. We suspect that American reader-interest in news stories of unusual happenings in the fine art market will be even keener now that Americans can again sell - as well as remaining extensive buyers - in London. We are accordingly inaugurating a service of news bulletins for distribution by airmail to a select list of U.S. periodicals and newspapers which devote some space to the world of connoisseurship. Would such bulletins interest you?"[15] This was less a publicity campaign than a publicity barrage.

A friend whose name always had a place on Carter's travel itinerary was David Randall. A few months before Carter completed his assignment at the British embassy, Randall had resigned his position as director of Scribner's rare book department in New York. On July 1, 1956 he moved to Indiana University in Bloomington as Lilly Librarian and Professor of Bibliography. In his autobiography, *Dukedom Large Enough*, Randall explained his decision saying:

> I had been in the business for over a quarter-century and thought that was enough. I had had some years of commuting (from New York to Cos Cob, Connecticut, then an hour and a half each way from door to door), apartment living, Long Island living, club living, a private home in the heart of New York - all of which made a beautiful university campus seem infinitely attractive. Besides, I had gone into my profession in the first place because I liked to be around books which, individually, I could never have aspired to. But the trouble was (or so I rationalized), someone was always buying them and taking them away just

25. *David Randall, Lilly Librarian, Indiana University, displaying treasures from the George A. Poole library acquired in 1958. He is holding a leaf from the Constance Missal (1472). The Gutenberg Bible, New Testament volume is lower right (1453-54). In the middle, is the first illustrated edition of Chaucer's Canterbury Tales (1543), and to the left, a 1330 Italian Bible.*

when we were becoming friends. Here I could get them
and keep them - and what a lot of old friends I had to begin
with. I never regretted my decision.[16]

It was an acceptable public statement, but there was
another side to the story. The same administrative agenda that eliminated Scribner's London office had also nar-
rowed the functions of the rare book department in New
York. Without a London base, Randall found himself
unable to satisfy customers in the manner to which they
had become accustomed. His relationship with Josiah K.
Lilly, the president of one of the country's largest pharmaceutical companies, went back to 1932, when, as an
agent for the New York dealer Max Harzof, he traveled
to Indianapolis with a suitcase full of early Americana - a
poor choice as it turned out, since at the time Lilly was
only interested in literature. In spite of this unpromising
start the men became friends, as Randall, with considerable help from Carter, supplied the wealthy collector
with the cream of the crop from Scribner's rare book
shelves. In 1954, with other interests absorbing his time,
Lilly decided to give up book collecting. What would
happen to the library he had built over the course of
three decades? Would Randall be willing to leave
Scribner's and go into business as an independent dealer
with the Lilly collection as his stock? It was a bookdealer's dream come true. Randall did a comprehensive
inventory, but after the lawyers and accountants completed their work, Lilly found it would be cheaper to give
the books away. Never a fan of the East Coast establishment, he decided to deposit his books sixty miles down
the road at the state university. Randall was the obvious
choice for the job of librarian, although Carter's name

was considered. "A fine bookman," Lilly was rumored to have said. "But so *very* British."

In July 1955, Carter and Randall congratulated each other on their new appointments. Carter looked forward to his return to London and Randall to his move to Bloomington. But what of the Scribner's stock, so carefully built over a period of twenty years by the Carter/Randall team? Carter advised Randall to buy anything he could,

26. *Josiah K. Lilly, President of the Lilly pharmaceutical company - c. 1950.*

even borrow money if he had to, and put the books up for sale at Sotheby's. "Think about this seriously, I beg," he wrote, "there are fine things there, and I would hate to see them jobbed off locally just because Charles Scribner wants to reduce the inventory."[17] And what about Carter and Randall's old customers? Could they be salvaged? Perhaps Barton Currie would be willing to have his books sold at auction in London where, Carter felt sure, they would do better than in New York. And what about Emmy Martin? "What are the chances," Carter wondered, "of prying loose her music collection? It is really a very fine lot, as you and I know, having sold her 90% of it, and she had some of our best things. It would make a sensation at Sotheby's; it's of manageable size; and it's very well catalogued, if I do say so myself. Let me know what you think."[18] Finally, Carter asked Randall to keep an eye on H. Bacon Collamore's collection of Housman books and manuscripts. When Carter found out in early 1956 that the Library of Congress had declined the Housmans, he urged Randall to buy them for Indiana or, if that didn't work, try to get Collamore to assign them to Sotheby's. "I am bound to say," he wrote, "that if I had the handling of them I should try, as you have been doing, for a bulk sale; but if this does not look like coming off I feel pretty sure that the material would do better here than it would in New York, so keep this in mind."[19] Although none of these schemes fell into place, Carter continued to press Sotheby's interests at every turn.

Shortly after he settled back in London, Carter wrote Randall about a projected trip to New York in the fall, and when that failed to materialize, a March-April visit. He planned to spend a few days in Chicago, then go down to Bloomington. Randall immediately set up a lecture for him but had to cancel. "Sad news, bad news!" he wrote, "The English Department has had scheduled, and for a long time, a lecture (by some Englishman) on April 4, so that date is out and there seems no point in having another on the 3rd."[20] The correspondence quickly picked up on more pressing questions. What did Carter think Mrs. Emerson's copy of Blake's *Songs of Innocence and Experience* would bring at auction? Would anyone in the States be interested in Michael Sadleir's books on London lowlife? Would Indiana like to bid on the Defoe items from Lord Haddington's library?

Carter's single minded interest in bringing American collections to Sotheby's auction rooms came to a head in 1959, when he learned that Randall had acquired George A. Poole's rare book library. For the next three years Carter followed every lead, wrote dozens of letters, and put his personal reputation on the line in pursuit of the

Poole collection. The fact that he lost the contest in the end did not seem to make him regret the chase. During a period of only a few years, Poole, a Chicago printing executive, gathered an impressive collection of early European printing, including the New Testament volume of the Gutenberg Bible, a 1460 *Catholican*, a leaf from the 1475 Constance Missal, and Caxton's 1478 printing of Chaucer's *Canterbury Tales*. The Chicago dealers, Frances Hamill and Marjorie Barker, known to their friends in the male-dominated rare book trade as "the girls," bought the collection with the idea of selling it to the University of Chicago. That plan fell through when university representatives failed to show the slightest interest in the books. Supported by President Herman B. Wells and the University librarians Robert Miller and Cecil Byrd, Randall bought the library for Indiana for $410,000, a price he considered a great bargain. Since Lilly had never been particularly interested in illustrated manuscripts,

27. *Herman B. Wells, left, and Josiah K. Lilly breaking ground for the Lilly Library, late 1959.*

incunabula, or medieval texts, the Poole purchase filled a gap and was one of Randall's most important achievements as the Lilly librarian.

When a university library purchases a collection *en bloc,* duplication is inevitable. Many of the Poole duplicates were extremely valuable. Managing such books in a state-supported institution can pose a number of problems quite unknown to private schools. If the decision is made to sell them, numerous approvals are required, since the funds for the original purchase came from a state-approved budget. Should the duplicates be offered to a trusted book dealer, turned over to an auction house, or simply sold locally in a fund-raising event? In order to answer these questions Carter drafted a lengthy memorandum summarizing the positive benefits of sale at auction:

1. First, and crudely, this method would produce more money, for the Library to spend on books it needs, than could be realized by any other.
2. Second, it is the only method by which, in respect of any one of a number of highly prized books involved, the Library can play absolutely fair with those other institutions, private collectors and dealers, who would be willing purchasers, whose collective goodwill is of practical value to the university, and whose individual chagrin (or even resentment, however unreasonable) if some desideratum were privately offered elsewhere, would inevitably be debited against the Library. It is hard enough for any rare book librarian to keep on equally good terms with all his professional colleagues, with the book sellers on whom he depends for supply, and with those temperamental creatures, the book-collectors, without putting him in a position where he cannot help being accused of playing favorites. Where the librarian is a graduate of the rare book business, the force of this factor may be squared, or even cubed.

3. Thirdly, Indiana has here the opportunity of setting an
example of public spirit which I consider would pay
excellent dividends in terms of public relations. The
sort of bulk-purchases which come naturally to any
fast-growing institutional library can never be exactly
popular elsewhere; and the current rate of institutional
absorption, right across the board, has private collectors and the book trade worried to death. Everything,
they say, is going behind the glass doors: nothing ever
comes out again, for us and our descendants. A pur-
poseful public demonstration that this is not always
true would, in my judgment, be very good politics. It
would also allow Indiana to give a clear and common-
sensical lead to the American Library world in a matter
where it is badly needed. The disposal of duplicates has
in the past often been handled "under the counter." It
has long been high time it was regarded rationally, as
something not merely necessary and natural but also
something friendly and salutary to the bibliophile community as a whole.

These observations are made in the perfectly disinterested spirit. If Indiana agrees with the conclusion to which
they lead, it will be for Indiana's consideration where the
books in question could be sold to the best advantage. But
I should be lacking in candor if I did not add that in my
opinion they would sell to the best advantage in the oldest
and the most expert, and today without question the fore-
most, book auction house in the world.[21]

Discounting Carter's characterization of himself as a
"disinterested spirit," it would be difficult to fault his carefully structured appeal. When Randall warned him that it
might be necessary to get an estimate from other auction
houses, Carter replied "I should think it quite likely that
Parke-Bernet might offer to cut their exorbitant rates to
get this sale, but even if they cut them right down to ours,

the point still is the University will get the best and most authoritative cataloguing and presentation at the hub of the international market."[22] All negotiations ceased at the end of the summer, when President Wells announced his forthcoming retirement. Carter still felt he had an inside track with Wells and decided to make one more appeal. This time, he based his argument on the weaknesses of the competition - "In addition to the already powerful arguments in favour of Sotheby's over New York as the venue for a sale, the Parke-Bernet Galleries have since had the misfortune to lose, one after another, both Arthur Swann and his successor so that their book department already in low water, cannot help being also in a state of serious disarray."[23] His best efforts were all in vain. In the spring of 1962, the trustees decided to sell the duplicates in New York. Randall delivered the verdict, "I am afraid I have some bad news for you, but there is nothing I can do about it. The decision has been made to sell our duplicates this fall at Parke-Bernet. There seems to be a very strong feeling that even though the cost would be higher and the net return less than at Sotheby's, the University might be subject to criticism for selling the books out of the country. This attitude represents Mid-West chauvinism but is an attitude that I cannot change along with other things in my current environment."[24] Was the decision absolutely final? Carter told Wells other institutions had sold duplicates in London with no apparent problem. He cited the Pierpont Morgan Library, Yale University, Harvard University, the Boston Museum of Fine Arts, and the Library Company of Philadelphia as satisfied customers. By that time, however, it was too late to make any changes, even if there had been a will to do so. The new president of the university, Elvis J. Stahr, Jr., felt obliged to defend the sale against those who might look askance at an institution of higher learning entering the book trade. In the foreword to the sale catalogue he wrote:

> Indiana University hopes to accomplish two things by offering duplicates books from the Lilly Library at public auction. Since the books herein described came to the University as unrestricted gifts, the sale will afford our other friends and patrons from the book world an opportunity to acquire titles that are increasingly difficult to obtain. Secondly. funds realized from this sale will be used to increase the resources of the Lilly Library, thus making it more useful both to the University and to the community of scholars.
>
> It is hoped that the action of Indiana University in disposing of these duplicate books will serve to advance the art of book collecting. Many college and university libraries count great resources today because of the generosity of the book collector and the labor of the bookseller. This sale is a slight gesture of recompense to that noble fraternity.[25]

The sale of the duplicates began on Thursday evening, November 8, 1962 when Parke-Bernet's chief auctioneer, Louis J. Marion, took the rostrum and offered Jose de Acosta's *Geographische und Historische Beschreibung der uberauss grosser Landtschafft America* (1598) to the assembled dealers and collectors. The atlas, bound in blue morocco with twenty double-page engraved maps, brought a satisfying $2,000 from the New York dealer Lew David Feldman. John Howell of San Francisco paid $7,500 for an illustrated Christopher Columbus letter while H. P. Kraus topped all other bidders, giving $47,500 for Caxton's 1478 printing of Chaucer's *Canterbury Tales* and $48,500 for two Colard Mansion imprints bound

Incunabula · Americana

Literary & Scientific Classics

DUPLICATES *from the* LILLY LIBRARY
INDIANA UNIVERSITY

And An Important Single Addition

A VOLUME IN CONTEMPORARY BINDING

Containing

TWO COLARD MANSION IMPRINTS

From a European Private Owner

Public Auction

Thursday Evening · November 8 at 8 o'clock

PARKE-BERNET GALLERIES·INC

980 Madison Avenue · New York · 1962

28. *Cover of the 1962 Parke-Bernet Galleries catalog listing the
duplicates from the George A. Poole library which Carter tried
so diligently to obtain for Sotheby's.*

together, the French version of Guillaume de Tignon-
ville's *Dicta Philosoporum* (1477) and Jean Le Fèvre's *Cato*
(1476). Prices may not have reached the level Carter promised they would have in London, but the officers of the
university were pleased with the $220,000 total. For
Carter, the loss of the sale was disappointing enough but,
as he explained to Randall, the subtle damage to Sotheby's

reputation - and to his own - was more upsetting. Over the years, book trade gossip had it that the Poole duplicates would go to Sotheby's. Carter said at least a dozen people had congratulated him on securing the books - to which his standard reply had been, "that I was delighted to be given a piece of such excellent news, that I had no idea any decision had been reached! and could Mr.X tell me when we were likely to hear from Indiana."[26] Now, with the books in the hands of Parke-Bernet, it was a defeat for Sotheby's. Carter implied that Randall, who had a hard time keeping a secret, discussed the sale with people in the trade and thereby created the embarrassing situation. Of course it was too late to do anything about it, but Carter had the satisfaction of registering a complaint.

In a continuing effort to wave Sotheby's flag, Carter wrote short promotional pieces for a number of journals and trade newsletters. His conversations with bankers and trust officers encouraged him to prepare several articles for their house organs, *The Trust Bulletin* and *Trusts and Estates*. It was straightforward publicity, and, as Carter admitted, the articles "did not detain the reader for more than a few paragraphs from the detailed reasons why, for anything fine, the obvious place to sell was Sotheby's."[27] Between July 1956 and September 1959, writing under the pseudonym John Waynflete, he published several short articles in *The* [London] *Financial Times*. With such titles as "Busy Market in Rare Books," (July 1956), "Investing in Rare Books," (December 1957) and "Rare Book Market Still Buoyant," (August 1958), he encouraged readers to consider the rare book market where, he claimed, substantial profits could be achieved. At the same time he kept reminding American collectors that the best place to dispose of rare books was London - "Many shrewd judges today would favour consigning to London rather than New York. Prices are more dependable, there is more buying for stock, continental dealers are only a couple of hours away, Americana and continental commissions are handled by the London trade with the efficiency born of long practice."[28] Shifting ground only slightly, Carter wrote an article for the *Atlantic Monthly* on the influence of taste on collecting paintings and drawings. He described how works of art considered florid and extravagant by one generation sometimes appealed to the next. That led him into a discussion of the monetary value of paintings and books, tax restrictions, limits on international trade, and export bans. He concluded with a low-key plug for the London auction establishments:

> Today, however, American owners are no longer penalized by British regulations in this particular respect (being unable to have the proceeds of sales remitted in their own currency). Although most of them do not realize it yet, and Europe has been so strictly cocooned in currency restrictions for so long the distrust of punctual dollar remittances is understandably widespread , they can now sell as well as buy in London if they wish. If they want to know *how* European collectors manage quite often to outbid the numerous Americans who habitually place commissions in the London auction rooms, they must ask an economist. If they merely want to know *whether* this is so, they need only look at the records of the past few years.[29]

William Jackson, director of the Houghton Library at Harvard, teased Carter for the obvious sales pitch. "I read 'Pendulum of Taste'in the Atlantic," he wrote, "and found it fascinating to see how much advertising you managed to get into the article. I was amused that it was possible in put over such a blurb in a magazine like the Atlantic"[30]

Without apology, Carter seized any and all opportunities. If he could insert "advertising" into one of America's leading literary journals, so much the better. In 1960, *Harpers* published "Playing the Rare Book Market," another discussion of changing tastes, this time focused on books instead of paintings. "Book collecting," Carter declared in one of his most colorful linguistic flourishes, "is the orchid in the hothouse of connoisseurship."[31]

It was important for Carter to be able to prove that Sotheby's could draw substantial amounts of money for American collections. Fortunately, an important historical archive had come to Sotheby's a few months before he joined the firm. In a series of sales beginning in 1954 and extending to 1959, Sotheby's dispersed a large collection of autographed letters and historical documents belonging to the New York broker André De Coppet. The ten De Coppet sales brought in $552,800, more than twice the estimate suggested earlier by the book experts at Parke-Bernet. The timing was ideal; Carter used the De Coppet results to great advantage. Toward the end of 1956, working with Peter Wilson, then head of the painting department, Carter convinced Alfred Schwabacher of New York to consign his eleven Impressionist and Post-Impressionist paintings to Sotheby's. Among the treasures were a Matisse still life, a Morisot, and three Renoirs. The amount realized, $83,430, was not as significant as the nature of the sale itself, the first to be held in London featuring the Impressionists. This was followed by the dispersal of the Old Masters belonging to Jacob Goldschmidt of New York, for $379,960. Sotheby's was beginning to show it could get top prices for American clients. With the Goldschmidt figures in front of him, Wilhelm Weinberg, a German banker who had settled in Holland, and then, after the war, moved to Scarsdale, New York, consigned his remarkable collection of Impressionist paintings, drawings, and sculpture to Sotheby's. The quality of these paintings tempted one brave journalist to guess that the total realized from the sale might climb to $800,000. The Queen, the Duke of Edinburgh, and Princess Margaret attended a private showing the day before the sale began. The fifty-six lots, including works by Van Gogh, Seurat, Degas, Renoir, Pissaro, and Daumier brought a total of $914,246. The executors were delighted and of course Carter and Wilson shared that delight. By the end of the 1956/1957 season, American consignments accounted for more than twenty per cent of Sotheby's $8,851,732 turnover.

When it came to evaluating collections of paintings, drawings, jewelry, ceramics, and furniture Carter relied on Peter Wilson, A. J. B. "Jim" Kiddell, Carmen Gronau, and other Sotheby specialists. With books and manuscripts he naturally managed very nicely by himself. Among the American collections steered to London during Carter's early years with Sotheby's were Herbert S. Auerbach's early Mormon newspapers and periodicals, a selection of James Ford Bell's English literature, duplicates from the holdings of the Library Company of Philadelphia, Otis T. Bradley's Bibles and prayer books, and the William A. White/Frances White Emerson's collection of William Blake's illuminated books. The White/Emerson sale held on May 19, 1958 offered seven volumes including first editions of *Thel* (1789), *Songs of Innocence* (1789), and *America: A Prophecy* (1793). The sale brought $114,000, "not much by 1971 standards," as Carter later remarked, "but an eminently satisfactory total at the time."[32]

As collection after collection crossed the Atlantic, from west to east, the officers of Parke-Bernet and members of the New York antiquarian book trade began to take notice. In the spring of 1963, the prominent New York dealer John T. Fleming protested vigorously when the American Academy of Arts and Letters made an arrangement with Sotheby's to sell Archer M. Huntington's collection of autograph letters and historical documents. "What's the point?" Fleming asked. "The valuable part, that's about 60 percent of the collection, is American material and no one in England or Europe collects Americana. The cost of the trip doesn't warrant it for most of us, consequently there won't be competition and the Academy will lose. . . . This is bad business. It's common sense to get a competitive offer."[33] These comments, printed first in the *New York Times* and then in *Antiquarian Bookman*, were, according to Carter, unjustified since the collection was international in scope and called for an international venue. The decision to consign it "to the leading international auctioneer of literary property must surely be considered eminently reasonable." He dismissed the need for a competing offer by reminding his readers that the sale was to be by auction and not arranged by private treaty. The mere suggestion that competition had been stifled was, he thought, "an affront to a distinguished institution, though one which its shoulders are doubtless broad enough to shrug off."[34] The successful results of the sale on November 12, 1963 proved again that Americana letters and documents could attract buyers when offered in London.

In spite of all their prestige and financial resources, Sotheby's occasionally found itself bested by a shrewd and hard-working independent dealer. Such was the case when it came time to settle the Ian Fleming estate. Best known for his adventure novels featuring the dashing counter-espionage agent James Bond, Fleming was also an imaginative book collector. He started buying at Dulau's in Bond Street in the mid-1930s under the guidance of Percy Muir, later settling in as one of Muir's best customers at Elkin Mathews. Fleming avoided the traditional collecting areas of early European printing, English literature, and fine bindings, turning instead to books that influenced change: landmarks in science and medicine, political science, history, religion, and philosophy; seminal works by Einstein, Röntgen, Herbert Spencer, Darwin, Curie, and Marx. When Carter and Randall tried to buy the books for Scribner's in the early fifties, Fleming was not interested. "Fool," Carter chastened him in a one-word wire. As the value of his collection continued to rise, Fleming turned out to be anything but a fool.

Shortly after Fleming's death on August 12, 1964 Carter wrote the executors of the estate introducing himself as an old friend, and offering Sotheby's services in matters pertaining to evaluation and disposal of the books. He tempered his sales pitch by saying that of course the executors would be advised by Muir, who had done so much to build the library in the first place. While Sotheby's would "not think of intruding on any plans you might be making with him, I am confident we should work together in complete harmony if those plans included the possibility of a sale by auction."[35] It was all urbane and friendly, up to the point in 1968, when Carter learned that Muir, along with Mrs. Fleming and the other executors, had signed a contract with Indiana University. For $150,000, Randall, representing the Lilly Library at Indiana University, had purchased Fleming's books along with all the typescripts for the James Bond novels.

Carter's letter to Muir barely disguised his anger. "Sotheby's had, as you know, left this business in your sole charge in the hope, which you and I personally shared, that with your inside track to the widow you would be able to steer it in the direction of New Bond Street on the normal introductory commission terms. It sounded as if the horse had got out of the stable in the direction of the western plains but if it has not I know you will do everything you can to lasso it."[36] Carter registered his unhappiness in even stronger terms in the summer of 1969: "You will recall, or if you don't a glance at *your* file will refresh your memory, that throughout this period (from August 1964 to December 1968) we here had understood ourselves to be working arm in arm with you, and relying on this understanding we made no direct approaches to Mrs. Fleming. Before I put the file away, I think I ought to put on record Sotheby's - what shall I say - disappointment? that so old and trusted a friend should not have thought it right to let us know at some point between September 1965 and December 1968 that he was no longer representing our interest in this business."[37] Muir answered, "Your letter of 26 June was wounding. I imagine that this was its intent. My first duty was to the Fleming estate, not to Sotheby's or any outside party." At the end of the letter, after his signature, Muir wrote a note by hand. "I hope still the old and trusted friend but at the moment a little 'tired.'"[38] Carter had no wish to prolong the fight - if it had been a fight. "My letter was certainly not meant to wound you of all people," he wrote. "It was more of a gentle sigh. Of course your primary duty was to the estate, and if I had been in your shoes I expect my advice to Mrs. F. would have been the same as yours." Even with the apology Carter needed to fire off one more round, "But since we had left our interest, secondary as it might be, squarely in your hands, and since I myself had registered a very active interest long before Ian died, would it have been a dereliction of your duty to the estate to have let me off the hook, if not between autumn 1966 and autumn 1968, at least on receiving my letter of 10th December 1968 instead of leaving me to hear of the fait accompli from Dave? Surely not. So. Having exhaled my sigh of resignation, let us put it out of our minds."[39]

In 1971, Randall invited Carter to attend the opening of a Fleming exhibition at the Lilly Library. Perhaps sensitive to the failed negotiations with Sotheby's, he described the collection in less than flattering terms, "a mish-mash, some swagger things, but neither Ian nor Percy paid any attention to condition, so there are disappointments."[40] If the books had to be sold rather than auctioned, Carter was pleased to see them go to Indiana, "a respectable home; one in which, indeed, I have a cubicle of my own [The John Carter Collection of A. E. Housman] and therefore a personal interest."[41]

CHAPTER EIGHT
Sotheby's Higher and Higher

The 1958 fall season opened at Sotheby's with a sale that topped everything that had gone before. Based on the excellent results of the 1956 sale, Jacob Goldschmidt's executors went directly to Sotheby's with a second collection: seven magnificent Impressionist paintings - two Cezannes, three Manets, a Van Gogh, and a Renoir. On the evening of October 15, at 8:00 p.m., Peter C. Wilson, Sotheby's chairman and chief auctioneer, offered bidders the first of the Cezannes, his *Garçon au Gilet Rouge,* and saw it reach $620,000, a world record for a modern picture. It only took twenty minutes to sell the rest, bringing Sotheby's grand total to $2,202,400. The publicity that followed dwarfed even the exuberant notices given to the Weinberg sale. Clearly, if you wanted to sell paintings, drawings, books, furniture, ceramics, or other works of art, Sotheby's was the place to go. America had proven to be an even richer source than Wilson and Carter imagined. By 1960, the firm needed a full-time presence in New York.

Wilson wanted the New York office to be run with a certain imaginative panache, modeled on his conception of the auction business as an exciting cultural phenomenon. He was a complicated and sometimes imperious man who had started with Sotheby's as an assistant in the furniture department, moved to paintings, and finally in 1957, based on a variety of talents, became chairman. He was a master auctioneer with a bag full of tricks, the raised eyebrow, the deprecatory shrug, the momentary pause, and the come-on smile. With those skills, plus a ready charm and an instant ability to communicate with a hesitant buyer, he was, as Frank Herrmann, the firm's official historian, reported, "Sotheby's ultimate weapon."[1] Wilson liked quick decisions and was intolerant of anyone who was long-winded or equivocal. In meetings he frequently found it impossible to disguise his impatience with Carter's elegant but measured delivery. The New York office, he decided, needed a fresh face.

The man Wilson nominated to run the American branch was a rather surprising choice. Peregrine Pollen, once described in the *Sunday Telegraph* as "urbane and hawk-faced," was a cosmopolitan twenty-nine years old, who had at the time of his appointment worked in the painting department for three years. His credentials for the new post were impeccable - he had grown up on a large family estate in the Cotswolds, gone to Eton and Christ Church, Oxford, served as personal assistant to Sir Evelyn Baring, the Governor of Kenya, and traveled widely in the South Sea Islands, Australia, Canada, and the United States. There was also a family tradition in the arts. Pollen's grandfather, Sir George Holford, owned an outstanding collection of incunabula and fifteenth and sixteenth century Italian paintings. If connections and style meant anything at Sotheby's, and they did, Pollen was well-equipped to assume the New York post. Some insiders wondered how the new appointment would sit with Carter, who had been successful in luring trade eastward across the Atlantic since 1955, and was himself not lacking in connections or style. Would there be dissension in the ranks? Wilson was concerned, and wrote Carter a cautionary note. "Peregrine is going to organize the setting up of the office in New York and to work directly with Sotheby's directors in London. Nothing should be done to weaken his feeling that he has the full confidence of the board and has the right to make decisions on his own."[2] The letter was hurtful. Carter replied,

> I was greatly surprised to receive your "hands off Peregrine" memo. Please reassure any of the partners who share your apprehension that no such warnings were necessary. Peregrine himself, I think you will find, knows that I have no wish to breathe down his neck or jog his elbow. He also knows that I am entirely at his disposal for any help or advice he may feel the need of. Neither will be proffered unasked. So, please let all concerned relax.
>
> As a practical directive from the partners, the memo makes it usefully clear that Peregrine is to be solely responsible, and directly responsible to you, for everything to do with the organization of the new office. This precision in his terms of reference will no doubt be welcome to him as it is to me.[3]

Any underlying rivalries that may have existed between Carter and Pollen were brushed aside as they worked together building Sotheby's image in New York. Carter remembered Pollen as "my friend, always the most loyal and stimulating of colleagues and sharer, during the hectic years between the establishment of Sotheby's of London Ltd. in 1960 and the assimilation of Parke-Bernet in 1964, of so many trials and tribulations as well as many exhilarating adventures."[4] Pollen spoke of Carter in similar terms:

Jake's contribution to Sotheby's was massive and never sufficiently recognized or rewarded by the firm. It was he who introduced Sotheby's to America by taking a space in the office on Lower Broadway of Donald Hyde the collector, and it was from this little base that Sotheby's grew. Jake was never given any credit for starting Sotheby's business in America.[5]

Pollen followed the same plan of action Carter had initiated five years earlier, visiting curators, dealers, bankers, and lawyers. There were catalogs to distribute and business cards to exchange. Now, with a full-time staff and an established address on 57th Street and Fifth Avenue in the Corning Glass Building, things were different. Instead of trying to get in touch with a Sotheby's representative, who only came to the States twice a year, it was now possible to speak with a member of the firm on a daily basis. Part of Pollen's responsibility - shared with Carter - was to keep a close eye on their New York rival, Parke-Bernet. They made it a practice to attend all PB's auctions, with the latest Sotheby's catalogues held ostentatiously under their arms. It was a tease, meant to annoy, and it did. The rivalry had a history going back at least to 1947, when Wilson tried to acquire Parke-Bernet. Major Hiram Parke, the largest shareholder, seemed willing, but after several months of discussion the arrangements fell through. The American firm had just moved into a handsome new building at 980 Madison Avenue, and PB's President, Leslie Hyam, saw no profit in joining the Englishmen. Profits eventually proved to be a serious problem. Although the American firm's gross turnover held up between 1956 and 1963, profits declined. At the same time, staff attrition made it difficult to maintain quality. Arthur Swann, the chief cataloger and head of the book department, died in November 1959, and Hyam, who was the moving force of the business, committed suicide in the fall of 1963.

Swann's shares went to Richard Gimbel, a Philadelphia department store executive, who immediately began to exert his authority by suggesting staff appointments. In an ambitious attempt to replace Swann, he asked Carter to join the firm as head of the book department. From Carter's point of view, the offer bordered on the ludicrous. In his superficially polite letter he listed a number of difficulties:

1. Parke-Bernet's book department is in bad shape. The person would be asked to make bricks out of straw.
2. I think you are right in saying "you are the only person potentially available who has the reputation, the experience and the connections essential to a possible successor." The doubt is whether success is possible.
3. It would be awkward to leave Sotheby's for the opposition. My wife is at the peak of a highly distinguished and successful career (Editor of the Woman's Section of *The Sunday Times*).
4. Both my wife and I dislike New York as a residence.
5. Aside from Hyam, I don't care for the company I should be keeping at PB.
   You will understand you are inviting me (and don't think I underestimate the compliment) to sever all connections here in order to lead a forlorn hope, in uncongenial company, over very difficult terrain, in a direction flatly opposite to the course I have pursued energetically, and not without the blowing of trumpets, for the past five years. Such an invitation can obviously be sincerely considered, in my position and in my time of life, only if it is so heavily weighed with gold as to make it irresistible.[6]

Carter concluded the negotiation two weeks later with an acid note, "I have decided that you and Parke-Bernet will have to get along without me in your campaign to "put Sotheby's in their place." I shall be much interested to see what you can do, both in the matter of personnel and of politics to rehabilitate PB, and although I cannot exactly wish you luck, I hope you have yourself a good time doing it."[7] The rehabilitation never happened. When Sotheby's finally took over in 1964, Gimbel was the most uncompromising of all the shareholders, maintaining to the end a chauvinistic view that only Americans should run an American auction house. He was somewhat appeased later, when Wilson offered him free Sotheby's book catalogs for the rest of his life.

Although in favor of the merger, Carter was not directly involved in the financial negotiations. The principal figures in those months of meetings and administrative maneuver were, on one side, Pollen, Wilson, and their lawyer, Jesse D. Wolff, and on the other, Louis J. Marion, Parke-Bernet's president, Mary Vandegrift, the administrative vice president, and Gimbel, representing the shareholders. There were countless problems and competing bidders, but as Carter remembered, Vandegrift pulled the staff together with the reasonable view that, "if PB was going to be sold anyway it made better sense for the staff that it should be bought by a firm that really understood the auction business and could make it again a prosperous concern, rather than some millionaire who bought it as a speculative flutter."[8] By September 1964, all major differences had been resolved and the Sotheby/Parke-Bernet merger became a reality. In order to maintain a semblance of the past and to avoid any public outcry against the takeover by the British, Sotheby's retained Louis Marion as president. Robert Metzdorf, the head of the book department and an outspoken critic of the merger in general and Carter in particular, resigned immediately rather than serve the English invaders. The editor of *Antiquarian Bookman* reported that one of the first tangible results of the affiliation came with the announcement that Parke-Bernet would reduce their commission charges to12 ½ percent on paintings, drawings, and books sold for more than $5,000 and 15 percent for those sold for $5,000 or less. This change brought New York in line with practices followed on Bond Street.

No sooner had the merger contract been signed, than Carter was on the road promoting its benefits. Speaking to the Baltimore Bibliophiles on September 23, 1964, he praised Parke-Bernet as a first rate fine arts auction house, saying it would survive and prosper under the new management from London. Consignors, he claimed, would now benefit from the opportunity to select either London or New York as an auction site, based on the nature of their collection. One difference between the two houses that called for attention was the manner in which they treated members of the book trade. In London, Sotheby's tried to maintain close ties with dealers, many of whom bought for stock as well as for commission. In New York, on the other hand, the focus had been on individual purchasers. It was Sotheby's intent, Carter said, to "graft on to the new partnership that cordial cooperation which over the years we have established with the trade in both our countries."[9]

Carter's emphasis on good relations with the trade may have been his way of making amends for the unfortunate wording used in a short article he had written three years earlier for *Books: The Journal of the National Book*

League of London. The article began, "In the course of a
century of steady shopping in Europe the Americans have
learned they will usually get a squarer deal in these parts
than they will get elsewhere (including their home pitch).
More important, if possible, they have learned to rely with
confidence on the expertise of English professionals."[10] If
his article had not been reprinted in *Antiquarian Bookman*,
where it came to the attention of American dealers, Carter
might have gotten away with the somewhat condescend-
ing tone. As it was, he found himself in the middle of a
heated exchange. Richard S. Wormser, president of the
International League of Antiquarian Booksellers, resented
what he called Carter's slur on the thirteen hundred members affiliated with the League. "Dealing is not squarer in
one country than in others," he wrote, and furthermore,
"The auctioneer's hammer was designed for use in sig-
nalling the end of bidding, not for tacking up advertising
posters."[11] The venerable Boston dealer George
Goodspeed called the article a gratuitous insult. Carter
apologized in the next issue of *Antiquarian Bookman* -
"What I had *in mind* when I wrote was that a number of
American bookdealers still *think* the British trade superior
to others . . . I am very far from sharing this illusion; and
I much regret the careless phrases which suggested that I
do."[12] In spite of his conciliatory tone, there was a feeling
among some of the dealers in the United States and
England that in joining Sotheby's, Carter had, in fact,
joined the enemy. When he first returned to London in
1955, and aware of possible accusations of conflict of interest, he placed a notice in *The Clique*, the British trade journal of the antiquarian booksellers, declaring he had no
intention of buying or selling, since, as he said, that was
the province of the bookseller. Some members of the trade

were not convinced. In 1958 a rumor circulated, stoutly denied by Sotheby's, that the auction house had gone behind the backs of dealers to solicit bids from private collectors and institutional buyers. The conflict underlined the essential difference between independent book sellers, who offer hard cash and operate on a meager profit margin, and the managers of the powerful auction houses who promise higher prices through public sale. It all came down to profits.

No event brought this competition for profits and power into sharper focus than the struggle that took place in 1964 over the estate of the Chicago collector Louis H. Silver. Among those involved were Sotheby's, represented by Carter, the trustees and administrative staff of the Newberry Library of Chicago, the New York rare book dealer John F. Fleming, and Harry Ransom, Chancellor of the University of Texas. Silver, a wealthy Chicago lawyer and real estate developer, had gathered an impressive rare book collection during the late 1940s and 1950s, working chiefly through A.S.W. Rosenbach and his successor John T. Fleming. Silver's tastes were eclectic, but centered on incunabula, English literature of the Renaissance and Victorian periods, fine bindings, and scientific and technical landmarks. Toward the end of his life, Silver experienced serious financial losses and had to use his library as collateral for loans. After he died in October 1963, the executors of the estate were faced with the difficult question of how to realize the maximum amount of money from the books. For advice, they turned to Fleming, who knew the collection better than anyone else. Just four months before his death, Silver had asked Fleming to dispose of the books. At the trustees' request, Fleming inventoried the library, established its value at $2,687,000, and set about looking for a buyer. Ransom, already famous for his high stakes acquisitions, let it be known that the University of Texas was ready to meet Fleming's price. At the same time, Carter, who had maintained close ties with Silver and his wife over a period of years, began a vigorous campaign in favor of disposal at Sotheby's. The stakes were high since the quality and value of the books in the Silver library made the Poole duplicates, for example, look like so much wastepaper. When Texas appeared to have an edge, Carter wrote imploringly to Silver's widow, Amy, who had been actively involved in the formation of the collection and served as its bibliographer:

> Dear Amy: I won't say, however you know, how deeply disconcerted and distressed and disheartened I am that, after all the weeks of work and thought (and delays after delays at the Chicago end) since the evening you and I and Bob made our agreement for the sale of the library at Sotheby's, we now hear that John Fleming has negotiated its sale to Texas. . . . I will ask you to think hard before the executors require you to sign any contract.
>
> If it was Newberry or the University of Chicago, or Harvard or even Illinois, I would understand. But what did Lou, what do you, care about Texas? It just has a lot of money, some empty shelves, and an overweening appetite.
>
> You yourself admitted, and John Fleming knows perfectly well, that we shall get the estate more money than they are offering. In the process of doing so we shall do three things equally or more important. We shall give (you will give) collectors and scholars and libraries all over the world a chance to buy some splendid books, with the pleasure of keen competition to them (to your profit) which Lou himself so relished when he was collecting; instead of your putting them all behind glass thousands of miles away. We shall give them the kind of sales catalogue you and he would want: the best and truest memorial in

the eyes of future book collectors, the best reference book for future scholars. And, for today and tomorrow, the Silver Library will culminate in a blaze of glory, instead of being carted off as a captive to the most bibliographically unpopular institution in the entire United States.

I know these considerations don't appeal to bankers or lawyers, however intelligent and devoted to your and the family interests. But the 'realists' would call them imponderables, you and I know how much they weigh in Lou's world; the world of humanists and enthusiasts, of scholars and students and book-collectors. So, do, Amy, I beg of you, think of all these things, and think hard, before you are persuaded to sign any contract which they will be presenting to you in lieu of the one on which Mitchell (Edelson) has been working on so patiently for the past six weeks.

Our chairman, Peter Wilson, is, as it happens (and as we have cabled Clarence Beucel and John Stern), due in New York over the weekend. He is as keen as I am that Sotheby's should prove its well-tested mettle with the Silver sale on the lines we agreed, and which you and I and Anthony Hobson discussed so fuly with your advisors in Chicago. Don't let them close the door in our face. Affectionately, John[13]

In retrospect, Carter's all-out attack on Texas seems a poor return for past favors. His long and close relationships with Chancellor Ransom and his ambitious acquisition programs were well known throughout the trade. In 1972, he wrote to Warren Roberts, the director of the Library at the Harry Ransom Humanities Research Center, "I think you know, I have always been a rooter for UT's expansionist policy, in the face of much criticism, not always well informed, from other sources, and I should be very sorry if it were to be curtailed by, of all things, in the state of Texas, lack of funds."[14] In 1959 he

29. *Harry Ransom, Chancellor of the University of Texas, Austin. Determined collection builder, but the loser in the contest to acquire the Louis H. Silver library - c. 1965.*

traveled to Austin, at the invitation of Professor William B. Todd of the English Department, as the featured speaker in a symposium organized to mark the one hundredth anniversary of Thomas J. Wise's birth. Texas was the appropriate place to celebrate that event, since it had the largest collection of the Wise forgeries in the country, having acquired them in 1918 with the purchase of John Henry Wrenn's library. At the conclusion of the symposium, the University of Texas Press published Carter's talk, "Thomas J. Wise in Perspective," along with five other presentations, in a handsome volume entitled

Thomas J. Wise Centenary Studies. As if that were not enough to cement the friendship, in April 1960 Texas purchased Carter's extensive Catullus collection. Now, in a letter that became public as a result of legal proceedings, he labeled the University of Texas library as "the most bibliographically unpopular institution in the entire United States" with nothing to offer except "empty shelves and an overweening appetite." Perhaps the most surprising outcome was that Ransom and Todd continued to correspond with Carter on the most cordial terms.

Carter's letter to Amy Silver may not have changed anyone's thinking, but as an argument for Sotheby's cause, it was a masterpiece. In the midst of these negotiations, Texas was curiously slow to act. They had not sent anyone to examine the books nor paid a deposit nor signed a contract. In the meantime, the books were costing the Silver estate a considerable sum of money in interest, since they were collateral for a large loan. When Lawrence W. Towner, the director of the Newberry Library, found out that the books were still available, he set about immediately to try and raise the required two and a half million dollars. This, obviously, was no small undertaking. His plan included the sale of stock from the endowment to cover the purchase and the sale of any Silver books that turned out to be duplicates or outside the library's fields of interest. Fleming, already unhappy with Sotheby's for removing the Archer Huntington historical documents from the American market a year earlier, was furious at being bypassed. He had appraised the Silver library at no charge to the trustees, expecting a fifteen or twenty percent commission from Texas. Now, there would be no commission from Texas or anyone else. While the loss of the commission rankled, there was also the matter of hurt

237

pride. Everyone in the trade knew of Fleming's involvement with the Silver books. How would all that look now? He sued the estate in the Federal Court in Chicago for $412,500 and obtained a face-saving $92,000 judgment for his work.[15]

The press painted the events surrounding the sale of the Silver books in various shades of gray. John Hayward, who shared Carter's view that disposal by auction was the best solution, wrote a vitriolic editorial for *The Book Collector* condemning both Texas and the Newberry for gluttony. Referring to the Silver library as made up of "800 prestigious show-pieces remote from Newberry's professed interests," he quoted Edmond de Goncourt on the evils of consigning books to the cold tomb of a museum.[16] Carter, although disappointed at not having secured the books for Sotheby's, praised Towner and the Newberry trustees, saying their action was "a legitimate cause for loud huzzas in Chicago and for gnashing of teeth in Texas and other competing locations."[17] He congratulated Towner in a personal note, "Of course all Newberry's friends here are delighted that, if the Silver Library had to be sold en bloc instead of coming back into the market (and as you know we did our best in the latter direction!) it is immensely satisfactory that Lou's library stays in Chicago instead of going off to the wilds and moreover stays in the place to which he was so much attached."[18] Always alert to the possibilities of business, he asked about the duplicates. Where would they be sold? If a decision had not been made, he hoped Towner would consider Sotheby's. The whole situation - a significant number of rarities from an American collector purchased by an institutional library with the chance to auction off the duplicates - certainly must have reminded Carter of the saga of the Poole duplicates, lost to Sotheby's just two years earlier. This time there would be no competing offer from Parke-Bernet, recently absorbed by Sotheby's. The Newberry trustees considered a number of bids. When H. P. Kraus' offer was turned down as too low, he threatened to boycott the sale. In the end, he became one of the major buyers. Christie's book department was considered too inexperienced to handle the complicated cataloging requirements. Finally, perhaps to no one's great surprise, Sotheby's received the authorization to proceed. The books were collated by the Newberry staff, then divided into two groups with the perfectly reasonable idea that English and European titles would draw better prices in London, and that the Americana would do better in New York. In the summer of 1965, the Newberry library sent 386 volumes to London, a shipment made up of Silver duplicates as well as books and manuscripts outside the library's primary collecting areas - among them an *Ars Memorandi* (1470), the Chatsworth copy of the Jenson *Biblia Latina* on vellum (1476), a Coverdale Bible (1535), the Ulm Ptolemy of 1482 in contemporary German pigskin, a Kilmarnock Burns (1786), a Galileo letter, and the manuscript of George Bernard Shaw's *John Bull's Other Island*. Soon after the agreement was signed, Carter forwarded Towner a long memorandum including a timetable for events leading up to the sale along with a list, with price estimates, for the most important items.

Sotheby's catalog for the November sale, dressed in the traditional spinach-green wrappers, promised "Distinguished Printed Books, Autographed Letters and Manuscripts, the Property of the Newberry Library of Chicago." Although unsigned, the preface has the distinctive ring of Carter's prose style. "We venture to think that the international fraternity of book-collectors, rare book librarians and the antiquarian booksellers will join us in saluting the addition of the Newberry Library to the roster of those enlightened institutions who have come to believe, in the words of Dr. Louis B. Wright, Director of the Folger Library, Washington, D. C., that 'if all libraries would take stock of their possessions and sell books that have no predictable use, they would improve their cash position, gain space they need, and serve the public interest.'[19] The decision to sell the English and European books in London turned out to be a good one, as lot after lot brought substantially higher amounts than had been anticipated. Carter was delighted when the *Ars Memorandi*, estimated at $65,000 went to Kraus for $81,000. Lew David Feldman took the Jenson Bible for $64,000 - more than double Carter's estimate - and John Howell traveled from San Francisco to pay $16,800 for the Kilmarnock Burns, and $4,760 for Shelley's *Adonais* (1821). Total sales at the end of the first day were $462,316, the highest amount grossed for printed books in a single auction session up to that time. At the end of the second day, the grand total, $808,914, was more than $300,000 over the pre-sale estimate.

Several years after the sale, Carter sent James Wells, the curator of the Wing Collection at the Newberry, an account of how his original plan to secure the Silver library for Sotheby's had gone awry:

> It was on New Year's day that I heard the news that John Fleming, arm in arm with whom I had been negotiating for three agonizing months with the Silver estate for the consignment of the entire library to Sotheby's, the terms for which had been agreed and the contract awaiting signatures for a month, had ratted on me and organized the

sale to the University of Texas. I remember the date well because I heard the news from Frank Francis to whom, along with practically every other librarian in Europe, John had conveyed this exhilarating news; and my telephone call to him from London that night included an example of that very rare phenomenon, Carter in a practically unprintable rage.

I was, and have always remained delighted, that I had been able to pay John Fleming back in his own coin. He had ditched me and Sotheby's, and, thanks to me, as it turned out, [it was Carter who told Wells that Texas had not yet signed a contract with the Silver trustees] you and Bill [Towner] had ditched him and Texas.[20]

Annual reviews do not usually make for exciting reading, but Sotheby's sales summaries from 1956 to 1964, the first three written by Carter, tell an impressive story of growth. By the end of the 1956-1957 season, sales came to £3,168,476, with twenty- percent of that figure representing art objects and books consigned from the United States. In 1963-1964, Sotheby's realized £4,000,000, from American consignments alone, an amount larger than Parke-Bernet's turnover for *all* sales during the same ten month period. Wilson and the directors had every right to be pleased with their decision to develop the American side of the business.

Shortly after the successful conclusion of the Silver sale, Carter took stock. He had served as Sotheby's American agent for ten years, and helped to bring in dozens of important collections of books and paintings. In January 1966, he sent Peter Wilson a rough draft summary of his accomplishments.

1. Set up the New York agency, beating Christie's to the draw and eventually knocking Parke-Bernet sideways.

2. In October 1964 with the help of PP, [Peregrine Pollen] I reconstituted the PB book department.
3. My contributions to Sotheby's in general in the United States. (Probably my two time a year trips have outlived their use. I would like to discontinue.)
4. I want to continue continuity between New York and London book departments.
5. Book Department here to work with.

For the remaining years of our agreement, I want to serve as above.[21]

The memorandum signaled a turning point. With the New York office now a successful operation under the direction of Pollen, and with Parke-Bernet no longer a competitor, Carter wanted to devote more time to the London office, and to London in general. At the time he wrote the memorandum, Carter's annual salary was £5,000, an amount far below his value to the firm, as he kept reminding Peter Wilson, but enough to assure him "some comfort" as promised in 1955 by his friend Donald Hyde.

One event that focused all of Carter's attention on Sotheby's London book department in the fall and winter of 1967 was the auction of Maurice P. Pariser's collection of Thomas J. Wise books and letters. Pariser, an alderman of the city of Manchester, had spent thirty years collecting Wiseiana. Pre-sale notices of the collection described it as extraordinary, astonishing, and unequaled. In addition to an almost complete run of the forgeries, including the Reading edition of Browning's *Sonnets,* and one of three known copies of Tennyson's *Morte D'Arthur* (1842), the sale offered an impressive gathering of letters to and from Wise, a complete collection of his bibliographies, and privately printed limited editions, including proof copies and a group of publications on the forgery itself. Some of the books were inscribed, and many had letters laid in. The effect was to show Wise in his various guises - book collector, businessman, bibliographer, book dealer, editor, publisher, and forger. Carter and Pollard supplied a few pamphlets from their own shelves to fill gaps.

Writing for *Antiquarian Bookman,* Carter explained his role in the sale. Three years earlier he had helped organize an exhibition of Pariser's collection at the Manchester Central Library. In discussing the eventual disposition of the collection Carter, naturally enough, stressed the advantages of consigning the books and papers to Sotheby's. He promised a sale "with flags flying and guns firing," and with "a bang-up catalogue."[22] The result, an accurate and thoroughly annotated listing of five hundred twenty-two lots, lived up to his promise. Carter wrote the notes, selected facsimile illustrations to highlight important items, and arranged the entries into appropriate groupings. Reading the catalog, codemarked ASHLEY, was like being conducted through a maze by the person who laid out the original plan. For Elizabeth Barrett Browning's *The Runaway Slave at Pilgrim's Point,* Carter supplied four paragraphs of description, history, and comment. Although Robert Louis Stevenson's *Ticonderoga* (1887) had been given a clean bill in *An Enquiry,* Carter's note explained why it should now be considered a forgery. His description of the forty letters exchanged between Wise and Edmund Gosse provided a carefully drawn estimate of both men as bibliographers and book collectors.

Lord John Kerr, the head of the book department, conducted the sale at a brisk pace, moving through one hundred fifty lots an hour. The total received by the end of the second day, $57,376, was not as remarkable as the prices brought by a few star items. Certainly there were ironies. The forgery of the Browning 1847 *Sonnets* (guaranteed as a forgery by Sotheby's) realized $1,680, while a legitimate copy of the first printing of the *Sonnets from the Portuguese*, as they appeared in *Poems* in 1850, sold two weeks earlier for only $115. A genuine copy of *Two Poems* (1854) by Elizabeth and Robert Browning, went for $9.50, while two copies of the forgery of Elizabeth Barrett Browning's *The Runaway Slave at Pilgrim's Point* (1849), reached $100 and $625 respectively. Matthew Arnold's *Alaric at Rome* (1840), a rare book that frequently went for $500 in its authentic printing, brought $1,920 as a forgery, the record high of the sale. When it came time to bid on the Wise correspondence, the New York dealer Lew David Feldman took the entire run of lots 399 through 479, chiefly, it was thought, for the University of Texas. By the end of the second day his successful bids came to approximately $41,000, and represented seventy-five percent of the sales total. It must have reminded old-timers of pre-World War I days, when the irrepressible George D. Smith traveled to London with Henry E. Huntington's bids in his pocket and carried away all the most important books from the country's ancestral collections. Carter admitted that the sale "had been conceived as a sophisticated lark - the kind of off-beat exercise which can justifiably enliven the serious course of a million pound season for hard-worked professionals and other regulars" but, because of Feldman's enthusiasm, "turned out to be also a perfectly satisfactory two days' business."[23]

After 1969 Carter's role at Sotheby's became somewhat diminished. He was still involved in consignments from America, such as the collection of important duplicates acquired from the Pierpont Morgan Library in New York, but the old days of scooping up libraries from Salt Lake City and Minneapolis were over. The firm itself was changing at a rapid pace. A crop of young specialists and managers opened offices in Paris, Johannesburg, Zurich, Munich, Hong Kong, Melbourne, and Florence. While New York still held its primary position in the United States, Boston, Philadelphia, Chicago, Palm Springs, and San Francisco now had Sotheby's offices. Growth lead to complications. If you were in London, it became increasingly difficult to keep track of the international flow of business in Europe, South America, and the Orient. It was unsettling not to be able to remember the name of the new person in charge of the book department in San Francisco or why the early letters of James Joyce were being auctioned in Zurich instead of London. Even the nature of the goods coming up for sale was changing. Where the firm had always dealt in paintings, coins, watches, sculpture, furniture, china, books, and jewelry, it now also offered vintage automobiles, airplanes, country estates, and various kinds of bric-a-brac that would never have crossed its threshold in earlier days. Traditionalists were astonished in 1971 when catalogs from Sotheby's Belgravia featured bright red covers and photographs throughout. The following year, the Board allowed a tobacco company to use the firm's name to promote a new brand of cigarettes. The scheme not only failed to produce any substantial revenue, but gave Christie's, Sotheby's cross-town rival, a chance to come up with a catchy jibe - - "Buying Sotheby's can ruin your health." The cigarettes vanished as quickly as they had appeared. In 1965 a change occurred that affected Carter directly. Anthony Hobson, who had been in charge of the book department for fifteen years, decided to turn that responsibility over to a younger man. The directors chose Lord John Kerr, who at one time had worked as a cataloger for E. P. Goldschmidt, and later had an antiquarian book shop on High Street in Oxford. Kerr understood the fine points of bibliography, and was adept at the rostrum. Carter might have wanted to move up but under Sotheby's hierarchical system one needed to be a director to head a department. Instead, he kept his small office and his part-time assignment - serving more and more as a consultant, rather than as an active participant in the daily flow of business.

Even after sixteen years, some of Sotheby's directors, including Wilson, still found Carter an enigma. He was respected, of course, for his work in establishing the firm's strong base in the United States and for his bibliographical accomplishments, but it was a little like the old joke about the Senator and his constituents - sure, you got us seventy million dollars to build a dam last year, but what have you done for us lately? In 1968 he was asked to serve as a board member on a new subsidiary, Sotheby Publications Ltd. The chief function of the board seemed to be to try to keep Philip Wilson, the chairman's son, from overspending his modest publication budget - an unexciting assignment at best. A larger project came Carter's way in 1972. Based on his years of service and his proven ability to turn out lucid prose, the directors asked him to write a history of the firm.[24] He was an excellent choice, but the assignment was not without problems. The author would be required to sort through of a vast array of documents, fill in spaces where documents didn't exist, and cajole recollections from a large number of people, some of whom might not be willing to cooperate. Carter agreed, but with reservations, as he explained to Randall: "I have rashly undertaken to consider writing a history of the firm, which unfortunately has virtually no archives whatsoever."[25] The more he thought about the task, the less he liked it. Again writing to Randall he complained, "The Sotheby history will be a nightmare of a job, there being virtually no records and I shall probably regret the idea of undertaking it."[26] By the end of the summer, citing health reasons, Carter told the directors he would not be able to do the history, but offered to look for a suitable replacement. He had been impressed with Frank Herrmann, who had just completed a carefully organized exhibition, *The English as Collectors,* for the National Book League and was under contract with Chatto & Windus to do a book based on the exhibition. In January 1973 Herrmann signed a contract to do the history with help from Carter and Munby as paid consultants.[27] That help was sadly cut short when Munby died in December 1974, and Carter the following March. Herrmann's book, *Sotheby's: Portrait of an Auction House* (1980), included a tribute to Carter "who asked me to write the book and forged my early links to Sotheby's."

Carter's decision to retire, relayed to the directors in 1971, came as no great surprise. The press release issued from the New York office summarized his career in three bland paragraphs, and concluded with the information that he would continue as a board member for Sotheby Publications and serve as a consultant for Lord John Kerr in the book department. The release mentioned pioneering work in America, but shifted quickly to identify Peregrine Pollen as the current president of the New York office.

Carter was proud to have worked for the leading auction house in the world and satisfied with his role in establishing the firm's presence in the United States. His name never appeared on the letterhead, as he might have wished, under the heading "Directors." As an Associate, however, he had often been able to choose the jobs that suited him - a rare kind of benefit.

Shortly after Carter gave his notice, Ernestine announced her retirement from *The Sunday Times*. She had worked on the paper first as Woman's Editor from 1955 to 1968 and then as Associate Editor from 1968-1972. Everything seemed to be changing at once, and not necessarily for the better. In 1957, they had moved from a small house at 16 Bedford Gardens to 26 Carlyle Square - a desirable Chelsea location on the North side of King's

30. Ernestine Carter - c. 1950.

Road. With a splendid drawing room and large dining
area the house was designed
for entertaining. The Carters had a wide circle of
friends, and enjoyed having
them over in the late afternoon for drinks, followed
by dinner, and an evening at
the theater or ballet. On
these occasions, hired cars
would transport guests to
the event and back to
Carlyle Square for a late-
night buffet. Bedrooms on

31. The Carter's residence at 26 Carlyle Square in Chelsea. They lived here from May 1957 to December 1970.

the second floor provided ample space for visiting friends
from America. A live-in couple attended to the daily
chores and upkeep. The property was difficult to support
on full salaries and impossible on retirement incomes. In
late 1970, the Carters moved to what one friend described
as "a small, dark house" at 113 Dovehouse Street. They
were still in Chelsea, but far removed from the pleasures
of Carlyle Square. Unaccustomed to economize, the
Carters tolerated their new situation with a mixture of
resignation and disappointment.[28]

CHAPTER NINE

Organization Man

One of the advantages of Carter's half-time appointment with Sotheby's was the freedom it gave him to work on independent projects. The heading on his stationery now read, "John Carter 26 Carlyle Square, London SW3 - Bibliographic Consultant" and in one particular case, "On behalf of the Pierpont Morgan Library." He explained his circumstances to Randall in a letter of June 6, 1957, "As you know, I am retained by the Pierpont Morgan Library as their London Consultant, and of course if I hear of anything up their street, which cannot be got for Sotheby's (e.g. in trade hands) I should give Fred [Frederick B. Adams] the tip. But apart from this, I am available."[1] Between 1955 and 1969, Carter sent Adams hundreds of notes on books, manuscripts, drawings, and painting he felt might fit the library's needs - among other things, the etchings of Bernard Bellotto, the calligraphy of Edward Johnston, Stanley Morison, and Wilfrid Blunt, a collection of Scottish bindings, and the manuscripts of the novels of Mrs. Humphry Ward. The two men were close friends, shared many professional interests, and saw each other socially as well as at meetings of various bibliographic societies. In addition to his work for the Morgan Library, Carter took on consulting assignments for Cooper Union University in New York, the University of Buffalo,

University Microfilms in Ann Arbor, Michigan, and the Metropolitan Museum of Art. He also acted as London agent on a retainer basis for a few private collectors.

Carter's work arrangement at Sotheby's also gave him more time to devote to professional and social organizations. He had been a member of the Bibliographical Society since 1934, served on numerous committees, and in 1969 was elected president. In that position, he chaired the monthly council meetings, set agendas, appointed committee members, and generally acted as a spokesman for the organization. He was fortunate to have old friends like A.N.L. Munby, John Sparrow, Simon Nowell-Smith, and Howard M. Nixon serving as members of his executive council. When it came time for him to deliver his presidential address in November 1969, he chose to discuss recent trends in book collecting - continuing remarks he had made on the same topic as the Sandars Reader in Bibliography twenty-two years earlier. He began by paying tribute to two of his early mentors, Michael Sadleir and Stanley Morison: Why, he asked, had the Society never seen fit to award Sadleir its gold medal?

With that grievance out of the way, he proceeded to the main part of his address - an outline of changes that had taken place in the rare book market and in collecting since 1947. The most profound difference, he said, had occurred soon after the end of the war with the rapid increase in library book budgets, particularly in American libraries, enabling them to dominate the rare book market. As a result, when a fine book came into the hands of say, Quaritch, or Maggs, the short list of names of potential buyers would now include significantly more institutions than private collectors. Bookdealers, well aware of the trend, had become much more sophisticated in pursuing the institutional dollar. When it came to evaluating changes in bibliography, Carter pointed to the availability of more sophisticated tools, including the Hinman machine-collator, and beta-radiography, a process that allowed researchers to examine watermarks in more depth than was previously possible. There had been marked improvements in catalogs during the last twenty years, and of course, prices had risen, sometimes in breathtaking leaps. Some things had not changed. Americans collectors still maintained an edge on the English in clubbability, and American librarians continued to outclass their English colleagues with attractive exhibitions and well designed publicity brochures. It was heartening, Carter said, that the British Museum had "discovered sherry," but there was much more to be done to insure a healthy flow of information between booksellers and collectors. Another area where the Americans had pulled ahead was in the acquisition of modern authors' original manuscripts - with the University of Texas being the prime example of determination and apparently unlimited funds. Perhaps thinking his audience had heard enough about American achievements, Carter launched into an entertaining description of the London book trade between the wars. His walking tour began on Museum Street with Paul B. Victorius' shop, and wound up on Marylebone High Street with the Francis Edwards establishment. These were men, Carter implied, too often neglected in the Society's lofty concerns with bibliographic theory. Then, he mentioned the Geoffrey Keynes - Fredson Bowers debate - was bibliography a powerful research procedure as defined by Bowers, or simply a useful handmaiden to research, as argued by Keynes? Carter left the decision to the audience but implied his own preference for Keynes' point of view. The address was delivered with elegance and wit, but, according to one listener, startled the audience - "since it seemed altogether too close to home for comfort. But the elegance and wit of its style, masked by an almost throw-away delivery, were so breathtaking, that few could detach themselves enough to realize that they were listening to an *apologia pro vita sue.* If this was the world in which his work had been done, as he seemed to say, it was also (which he did not even suggest) a world he had done much to make."[2]

Beginning in 1929, the Society began to award medals to those who had made an outstanding contribution to bibliography. Between 1929 and 1990, twenty-nine scholars had been so honored - among them Montague Rhodes James, George Watson Cole, Wilberforce Eames, Alfred W. Pollard, Arundell Esdaile, Victor Scholderer, Geoffrey Keynes, and Robert B. McKerrow. The presentation of the medal was an occasion of great ceremony. In 1969, after a hiatus of several years, the Society awarded the medal to Graham Pollard and Fredson Bowers. Carter, then serving as president, wrote to his friend, "Nothing could have given me greater pleasure than to preside over the Council's decision to give you the gold medal, and I hope the mint will construct it in time for me to pin it on you before my term in office runs out."[3] What of Carter himself? Why had he been neglected? Finally, in the fall of 1974, the Council added him to the list, but by that time he was too ill to participate in the ceremony. The announcement came with an ironic footnote. With the price of precious metals at an all-time high, his medal would be cast in silver-gilt instead of gold. Carter handled the explanation with characteristic self effacing charm, "It matters not the metal," he said, "so the heart be sound."[4]

After 1955, Carter devoted a considerable amount of time to the editorial boards of *The Book Collector* and the Soho Bibliographies. In both cases, he began his work with high enthusiasm but soon found himself bogged down in management and financial problems. The first issue of *The Book Collector* appeared in the spring of 1952, with Ian Fleming, John Hayward, and Percy Muir on the editorial board. The second number, Summer 1952, announced the appointment of the bibliographer Philip Gaskell as editor. The quarterly had a history that could be traced back to 1935, when Muir, with help from Carter, Randall, Sadleir, and others, edited *Bibliographical Notes and Queries*. The immediate forerunner of *The Book Collector* was *Book Handbook, An Illustrated Guide to Old and Rare Books*, issued serially in nine parts, from February 1947 to March 1952 and edited by Reginald Horrox, a bookseller from Bracknell, Berkshire. According to introductory matter, *Book Handbook* would "give information on interesting points about books, about their authors, printers, or publishers, and about their previous possessors. This will lead us to include within our purview bookplates and handwriting, autograph letters, historical documents, armorial and other bindings, illustrations and so forth."[5] Early issues featured articles on Richard De Bury and the *Philobiblon,* the use of wood engravings in book illustration, the Shakespeare Folios, the ghost stories of Montague Rhodes James, and the life and achievements of Robert Bage, an eighteenth century novelist and paper maker from Derby. In a handsomely illustrated article, L. J. Lloyd described the library of the seventeenth century French collector Jacques Auguste de Thou. This was followed by a short article by George Bernard Shaw on reading Marx and Engels. The journal also included a section called "Notes and Notices," made up of reviews and comments about people and activities in book production, bibliography, and collecting. In 1952, the editors of *The Book Collector* adopted the "Notes and Notices" format in a feature first called "Commentary," then, "News and Comments."

The Book Collector

INCORPORATING BOOK HANDBOOK

EDITORIAL BOARD

IAN FLEMING   JOHN HAYWARD
P. H. MUIR

★

VOLUME I   NUMBER I   SPRING 1952

CONTENTS

ENGLISH BOOKBINDINGS I by Howard M. Nixon	2
ENGLISH LITERARY AUTOGRAPHS I by T. J. Brown	5
THE HISTORY OF A MANUSCRIPT by B. J. Timmer	6
ISAAC TAYLOR THE ELDER by H. A. Hammelmann	14
ELKIN MATHEWS IN THE 'NINETIES by P. H. Muir	28
THEATRICAL COLLECTING by Ifan Kyrle Fletcher	41
BIBLIOGRAPHICAL NOTES AND QUERIES	53
BOOK REVIEWS	61

★

32. Contents page from 'The Book Collector'
volume 1, number 1, Spring 1952.

Among the articles included in the first number of *The Book Collector* were Part One of Howard M. Nixon's long running series on English bookbinding, Muir's recollection of the early days of the Elkin Mathews book shop, and Ifan Kyrle Fletcher's essay on collecting theatrical memorabilia. The editors clarified their debt to Horrox with a three-word note at the head of the contents page - "Incorporating Book Handbook." In 1939 Muir had promised that *Bibliographical Notes and Queries* would rise again, and true to his word it appeared in the first issue of *The Book Collector*. That feature continued until 2002, when it was made redundant by web newsletters. In the midst of closing Scribner's London office and moving to Washington D.C., Carter had little time to become actively involved in the new journal. He did however, contribute regularly to "Bibliographical Notes and Queries," sometimes under his own name and sometimes, for the sake of variety, or just for fun, under one of his favorite pseudonyms, "Harriet Marlow," or "George Waynflete." One of Carter's questions in the Spring 1952 issue, unanswered from the time he first submitted it to *Bibliographical Notes and Queries* in 1939, concerned Thackeray's *Pendennis*. Did the second volume, he asked again, always contain the preface?

As soon as he returned from Washington in the summer of 1955, Carter joined the Editorial Board. A paragraph in the Winter 1955 issue carried his credentials - "Mr. John Carter has been appointed as member of the Editorial Board. In this capacity, he will bring to the service of THE BOOK COLLECTOR both his bibliographical knowledge and the great experience of antiquarian book collecting on both sides of the Atlantic which are reflected in his two best-known books: *Taste & Technique in Book Collecting* and *ABC for Book Collectors.*"[6]

It only took three years for the cost of producing *The Book Collector*, approximately £1000 an issue, to overrun the balance built by subscriptions and advertisements. In the spring of 1955, just before Carter joined the board, Lord Kemsley, the principal share-holder, decided to withdraw his support from the journal, and from the Queen Anne Press, the journal's publishing house. The decision came as a complete surprise. Fleming took care of the immediate money problem by purchasing a large number of shares. Muir and Hayward appealed to collectors for support, and Carter sent a three-page letter to a number of friends in America. The Editorial Board, he said, wanted to maintain the standard of excellence that had characterized the early issues - "We now have a new and excellent publisher and although the annual subscription has had to be raised from $3 to $5, it is still, in my view, an absurdly good value for money. What is needed to keep it firmly on its feet is a minimum of an extra 500 subscribers."[7] While the goal of adding five hundred names to the subscription list was unrealistic, the letter and other efforts did generate enough support to keep the journal going. The addition of a "new and excellent publisher" was indeed an important step. The board moved quickly and wrote a contract with the Shenval Press of London, a house known for excellent design and careful typographic work.

For the first few years the affairs of *The Book Collector* were guided, on paper at least, by an editor and an Editorial Board. As issue followed issue, however, a pattern emerged that for all practical purposes made the board redundant. According to Muir, "With the second number . . . John Hayward began to assume the control which eventually made the Editorial Board superfluous. . . . The board ceased to meet and the journal became avowedly, what it had long been in fact, the exclusive product of John Hayward's fertile brain."[8] Fleming supported the journal in its time of need, but seldom took any serious interest in the day-to-day problems associated with its management. By 1955, with the popular success of the James Bond novels, his time was taken up more and more with the pleasant duties associated with being an author people wanted to meet. According to one of his biographers, owning *The Book Collector* meant little to Fleming beyond soliciting advertising from wealthy friends, a useful activity to be sure, and holding monthly editorial lunches at Victoria Square, where he served unpalatable Chianti.[9] Fleming and Hayward disagreed on almost everything to do with the journal from page make-up to editorial policy. All this came to a head in September 1957. Fleming claimed the journal's poor financial condition was due to Hayward's inept editorial leadership. Why, he asked, would anyone want to subscribe when the articles were uniformly leaden, stuffy, and unreadable? In a memorandum to the members of the board Carter rose to Hayward's defense:

> Though neither ILF [Ian Fleming] nor PHM [Percy Muir] has of late had as much to do with the week-to-week conduct of The Book Collector as I have, they know just as well as I do (and so do RH [Robert Harling of the Shenval Press] and our faithful publisher) that without JH (and let me be clear, that would mean without me also) The Book Collector would not last two issues. If that is what, privately, the Collector Ltd. wants, its course of action is simple. I imagine a couple more letters like that of September 13 would do the trick. As I do not believe that this is in fact what ILF at least does want, I submit that there are only two ways out of the present impasse, which are as follows:

A. The Collector Ltd., should recognize that <u>The Book Collector</u> in anything like its present form (and a <u>Sunday Dispatch</u> version of it, though it would undoubtedly lose more money while it lasted, is a pipe-dream), depends for its success on one man: the present editorial director. It should then resign itself to letting him run the magazine with as many contributions of ideas as the editorial board can muster, but without interference, on the lines which have made it the best thing of its kind in the history of book collecting.

B. The Collector Ltd., having reaped any available tax advantage from the past losses made by *The Book Collector* and performed a most valuable service to the world of bibliophily, should take evasive action ahead of the incidence of any future profit, and at the same time rid itself of a strong-minded editor, by selling the magazine to someone who likes it the way it is.[10]

The memorandum implied that Fleming had used the past losses to gain valuable tax advantages for himself - an accusation Fleming denied. " The Company was formed at my personal expense," he reminded Carter, "to keep the Book Collector under the editorship of John alive and for no other purpose whatsoever."[11] When it came down to a matter of supporting Hayward or letting the journal die, Fleming finally voted for survival.

Later, in describing *The Book Collector's* early years, Carter avoided any mention of the controversy, and ended his summary on a high note:

> Doubtless there have been shortcomings, misjudgments, disappointments in the forty Numbers which THE BOOK COLLECTOR has provided in return for a very modest subscription during the first ten years of its life. Yet, whatever its faults, it seems to me that it had done something more than provide a comprehensive chronicle,

a shrewd commentary, a lively picture, an informative guide, a bibliographical stimulus, for the bibliophiles of the 1950s throughout the English speaking world. It has contrived, as few English language specialist publications do, to avoid being parochial. It has never forgotten, or allowed its readers to forget, that their addition is world-wide: penetrating iron curtains; making nothing of the merely geographical distance between say, Geneva, Switzerland and Bloomington, Indiana; assuming (and thereby surely promoting) an international sodality of book collectors capable of overlooking ideological barricades and of maintaining some degree of equanimity among the drums and tramplings of nuclear argument."[12]

You can almost hear the crash of cymbals.

As Muir pointed out, Hayward was the person chiefly responsible for *The Book Collector's* success. But he was, at the same time, responsible for some of its problems. With an autocratic, sometimes intransigent, manner, he set extremely high standards for himself and his colleagues. He was seldom inclined to compromise, and his waspish remarks fell on friend and foe alike. Even Carter felt the sting. In the winter of 1962, Hayward complained to Carter about postage bills incurred in corresponding with authors, collectors, and librarians in England and the United States. He chided Carter for presenting a postage bill for £64, based on some two hundred fifty letters sent over a two- year period. Hayward sent a check on his personal account along with a cheeky note saying of course Carter would do the right thing and tear the check up.[13] A more serious breach occurred in July 1964, when Carter supported the Newberry Library's expenditure of over two million dollars for the Louis Silver collection. Hayward claimed the acquisition was a "display of gulosity" and a "prodigious gormandizing feat." Further, the books were "merely show-pieces, of no use to scholars and remote from the Newberry's interests."[14] As a result of this and other differences, Carter resigned from the Editorial Board, and Muir followed suit. Carter's resignation brought a curt reply, "This will bring an end to affairs that have been causing mutual embarrassment, even more so now that you are to be associated with Parke-Bernet."[15] Fleming, the last of the original board members, died in August 1964, and for the next four issues, Hayward's name stood alone on the masthead. As his health worsened, the business of editing the journal became more and more difficult. He had been confined to a wheelchair for many years, but now he was unable to leave his flat in Cheyne Walk. At work on the Winter 1965 issue, he died peacefully on the morning of September 17, 1965.

At once, Carter, Muir, and Munby faced the question of the journal's future. Certainly it would survive if the right editor could be found. Outside St. Luke's Church in Chelsea, following Hayward's memorial service, they surrounded the man they hoped would take the job. The events that followed are best told by Nicolas Barker, then an editor with Macmillan's:

> It was a cold grey day outside, and three or four men (I recall Percy Muir, John Carter and Tim Munby), their hands in raincoat pockets and, in John Carter's case, hat pulled down over eyes, cornered me against the north aisle. I was, they said had to be, the next editor of THE BOOK COLLECTOR. I protested my incapacity; I didn't have a tithe of John's bibliographic, let alone editorial skill, still less his wide circle of acquaintance; besides editing THE BOOK COLLECTOR had been a full-time job for John and I had one already. The gang of three or four

were reassuring: all I had to do was edit; others would help with the writing of editorial matter, rounding up articles and reviews; James Shand (I think he was the fourth rain-coat and second hat), publisher as well as printer, would look after all the business side. All right, I said, I would see the next number through the press."[16]

The Summer 1966 issue, the first to carry Barker's name as editor, also identified the editorial board: Carter and Muir - familiar names, of course, to regular readers.

There had been a break in Carter and Hayward's forty-year friendship, but all that seemed trivial now. Carter wrote a memorial for *The Times* in which he described Hayward as a man with "unquenchable determination" and a "gallantry of spirit . . . whose incidental intransi-gence, whose occasional waspishness were forgiven by his friends out of admiration for the indomitable resolution of which they were the necessary safety-valves."[17] Carter enthusiastically took up the task of making the Winter 1965 issue a tribute to Hayward's career. He solicited com-ments from a range of collectors, editors, librarians, and bibliographers who had known and worked with Hayward - everyone from the American collector Mary Hyde, to the English novelist Graham Greene. The forty pages of tributes filled nearly half the Winter number, making it one of the largest ever issued up to that time. Carter's introduction included a memorable turn of phrase. The contributors, he wrote, reflected "the overlap-ping bands of the Hayward spectrum."[18]

Carter continued to be an active member of the Editorial Board almost up to the time of his death. He read proofs, suggested authors, wrote reviews, and submitted daunting inquiries to "Bibliographic Notes and Queries." *The Book Collector* was one of the chief anchors of his professional life.

It may have been Carter's unhappy experience with Lord Kemsley that made him cautious when it came to dealing with Lord Bernstein, the president of Granada, a London media conglomerate. In 1963, Granada took over Rupert Hart-Davis's publishing lines, including what must have seemed a highly suspect commodity, the Soho Bibliographies. Carter was still working for Scribner's in 1951, when Hart-Davis asked him to join the Soho Advisory Board. He accepted as a favor to his old friend and fellow Biblio member and because he believed in supporting bibliographic endeavors. The Hart-Davis firm, founded in 1946, had gotten off to a good start with *Fourteen Stories* by Henry James, and *Democracy and the Arts* by Rupert Brooke. Over the next few years, it produced a number of best sellers, including *Sealskin Trousers* by Eric Linklater, *The Theory & Practice of Gamesmanship* by Stephen Potter, and *Elephant Bill* by J. H. Williams. In 1950, Allan Wade asked his old friend Hart-Davis if the firm would be interested in publishing a bibliography of William Butler Yeats. There was no question about Wade's credentials, as he had devoted himself to the project for over forty years. At almost the same time, Geoffrey Keynes joined the firm as a non-executive director. He brought both bibliographic expertise and financial resources. Thus, the Soho series was born. Carter, Hayward, Munby, and William A. Jackson, director of the Houghton Library at Harvard University, made up the Advisory Board. The undertaking was unique. University presses sometimes issued scholarly bibliographies, but for a commercial publisher to do so was highly unusual. According to a prospectus, the bibliographies would provide a complete record of an author's published work, including not only books, but periodical contributions, and translations. Individual works by an author would receive full bibliographical descriptions,

A BIBLIOGRAPHY
OF THE WRITINGS OF
W. B. YEATS

ALLAN WADE

RUPERT HART-DAVIS
SOHO SQUARE LONDON
1951

*33. Wade's work on Yeats was the first volume to be issued
in the distinguished Soho Bibliography series. Carter was a
member of the Advisory Board from 1951-1970.*

although not as full as the American bibliographer Fredson
Bowers recommended in his major work *Principles of
Bibliographic Description.* In discussing the question of bibliographic style Carter once confided to Jackson that it took
him four stiff drinks of bourbon whiskey to make his way
through the Bowers formulas.[19]

Carter threw himself into organizing the series. He wrote James Babb and Donald Gallup at Yale, and Herbert Cahoon at the Pierpont Morgan Library, to get their suggestions for a compiler to do a bibliography of James Joyce. In the meantime, Hart-Davis brought out the first three Soho volumes - Wade's *W. B. Yeats* (1951), Carter and Sparrow's *A. E. Housman* (1952), and Gallatin and Oliver's *Max Beerbohm* (1952). All had been subjected to Hayward's meticulous editorial checking. In spite of positive reviews, sales were disappointing. The board reduced the production from 750 to 350 copies for the next five volumes. With compilers at work on both sides of the Atlantic, it took an agile mind to keep track of the various works in progress. Carter created four categories - published, in press, on ice, and headed for the refrigerator. Sadly, promised volumes on Churchill and George Moore never made it past the refrigerator door. The Joyce bibliography came out in 1953, followed by Woolf's *Norman Douglas* in 1954 and, after a three-years gap, Keynes' *Rupert Brooke*, Woolf's *Baron Corvo*, Leon Edel and Dan Lawrence's *Henry James*, and B. J. Kirkpatrick's *Virginia Woolf*. As the reputation of the series grew, institutional libraries placed standing orders, guaranteeing a sale of from 500-600 copies. It was a measure of success when, by 1962, Wade's *Yeats*, Keynes's *Brooke*, and the Edel/ Lawrence *James* went into second editions. Reviewers praised the individual volumes, although Simon Nowell-Smith criticized the series for what he claimed was a lack of uniformity in style and content. Some of the volumes included critical publications on the authors, most did not. Only a few included reference to letters and manu-scripts. And what was the novice to make of the wide dif-ference in bibliographic style between Wade's *Yeats*, with its title page transcriptions and detailed collation notes, as against Carter and Sparrow's bare bones approach to Housman? It was difficult to argue with Nowell-Smith's point: "tactful guidance by a general editor would be welcome."[20] Selling slowly but steadily, the Soho Bibliographies nevertheless came to be recognized as a useful contribution to literary scholarship.

After Jackson died in 1965, Carter recruited Gordon N. Ray, the director of the J. S. Guggenheim Memorial Foundation in New York, to take his place. "All the Sohovians," he wrote, "are much pleased that you are willing to join the advisory board of the Bibliography series. We don't plan to impose on your much occupied time by asking you to vet manuscripts or the like. . . .What we need . . . is an ear to the bibliographic ground in the United States."[21] During the five-year period before Ray joined the Advisory Board, the Hart-Davis firm had gone through several reorganizations, ending up in September 1963 as a subsidiary of Granada Publishing. The Granada managers had no interest in bibliography, and the series languished. They issued two titles in 1964, and one more in 1965, but none for the next several years. In a letter to Ray, Carter claimed the series had no future under the present management and told him the London members of the board planned to resign unless Granada agreed to transfer the bibliographies to another publishing house. When nothing happened, Carter appealed directly to Lord Bernstein. It was obvious, he wrote, that the firm had no interest in the bibliographies aside from collecting revenue from the sales of the older volumes. His tone grew harsher as the letter progressed, "Neither I nor any of my advisory colleagues have felt justified in encouraging bibliographies for a series whose future seemed so uncertain. . . .You cannot expect labours of love from a (let's face it) fairly distinguished board of advisers when the publisher does so little to deserve them."[22] The only solution, Carter maintained, was to transfer the series to another publisher, preferably Macmillan, where it would be under the care of the astute bibliophile Nicolas Barker. Since Carter was so unhappy with the present management, J. C. Reynolds, the director of the Hart-Davis unit of Granada, suggested he resign from the Advisory Board. Carter did so, with one last shaft: "You prefer to hold onto the Soho bibliographies and dogs have a legal right to their mangers. Remove my name from the Advisory Board, book jackets and catalogues."[23] Carter's letter did the trick. In less than a month, the Granada officers asked Barker to take over the series. Carter was pleased. In a letter to William Cagle, an American librarian at work on a bibliography of Conrad, he summed up the situation as an "amicable solution to a long standing problem."[24] Barker accepted the appointment on the condition that new bibliographies be added, and older titles revised. In order to improve sales in the United States, he suggested a cooperative arrangement with an American publisher. When Barker moved from Macmillan to Oxford University Press he took the Soho series with him. The members of the new advisory board were Rupert Hart-Davis, Gordon Ray, and Simon Nowell-Smith. Carter was too ill to participate, but it must have pleased him to know that Keynes' *A Bibliography of George Berkeley, Bishop of Cloyne*, the nineteenth title in the series, would be guided by Barker's careful editorial supervision and graced by the colophon of the Oxford University Press.

In addition to his editorial responsibilities with *The Book Collector* and the Soho Bibliographies, his work for the *Times Literary Supplement*, occasional consulting, and the job at Sotheby's, Carter devoted a considerable amount of time and effort to the 1963 "Printing and the Mind of Man" exhibition and the publications that grew out of it. When Stanley Morison learned that the eleventh International Printing Machinery and Allied Trades Exhibition, IPEX, would be held in London in the summer of 1963, he asked the organizers to consider sponsoring an exhibition of machinery and books to illustrate the history of printing, and, by implication, the debt civilization owed to that invention. It was a large idea, but Morison, who had written a score of well-received monographs on printing history, and had served as typographic adviser to Cambridge University Press, the Monotype Corporation, and *The Times*, specialized in large ideas. There was even a precedent. In the spring of 1940, the Fitzwilliam Museum at Cambridge University opened an exhibition to celebrate the quincentenary of the invention of printing. As the emphasis was on content rather than fine printing, there were classic works on travel, cooking, politics, sport, philosophy, and religion, as well as ground-breaking books in the history of science and technology, many loaned from the collections of John Maynard Keynes and Ian Fleming. The arrangements for the exhibition were carried out by a highly talented group of printers and bibliophiles under the direction of one of Carter's best friends, Brooke Crutchley, the assistant university printer. The members of Crutchley's advisory committee were John Dreyfus, then a trainee at the Press, Morison, Muir, Carter, Beatrice Warde, Paul Hirsch, and Graham Pollard. Carter suggested setting aside a portion of the exhibition to highlight books issued in 1859 - among them Darwin's *On the Origin of the Species,* Dickens' *Tale of Two Cities,* Mill's *On Liberty,* George Eliot's *Adam Bede,* and Fitzgerald's *Rubaiyat of Omar*

Khayyam. The exhibition opened on May 6, 1940, and closed ten days later as German forces invaded the Low Countries. It was simply too dangerous to display precious books in so public a place when the Luftwaffe was expected to strike England at any moment. The exhibition catalog, which incidentally served as a model for those working on the 1963 exhibition, came out the day the books were returned to their owners.

Carter, who coined the sonorous phrase "Printing and the Mind of Man," identified Morison as the originator, the supercharger, the conscience, and mentor of the 1963 exhibition. That may have been true, but Morison himself would have been the first to acknowledge the importance of the elaborate committee structure that furnished the backbone for the undertaking. Leading the way was the Honour Committee, under the patronage of the Queen, and including the Prime Minister, the Duke of Wellington, the President of the Roxburghe Club, the Head Master of Eton, the President of the Bibliographical Society, and many other worthies. The working groups included the Supervisory Committee, the British Museum Committee, the Historical Sub-Committee, and the Technical Sub-Committee. These groups did the planning, made the decisions, and carried direct responsibility for the exhibition's success. Carter was a member of the Supervisory Committee, serving along with Robert W. Boardman, representing IPEX, Sir Frank Francis, Director and Librarian of the British Museum, Jack Matson, President of the Association of British Manufacturers of Printing Machinery and Managing Director of the Monotype Corporation, and Stanley Morison. The difficult task of choosing specific books to be exhibited was placed in the able hands of the Historical Sub-committee chaired by Percy Muir.

The Preface to the 1963 catalog explained the premise and the purpose of the exhibition:

> The invention of printing with movable type was crucial to the whole of Western civilization. The purpose of the historical exhibition annexed to IPEX 1963 is to illustrate the internal development of that invention, in the technical progress of printing as a craft; the external development, in the finest achievements of printing as an art; and, beyond the limits of the art and craft of printing, to demonstrate the impact of printing on the mind of man and the effect it has had on the history of the last five hundred years.[25]

It was the responsibility of the Supervisory Committee to see that the exhibition carried out those aims.

The largest exhibition halls in London, Earls Court and Olympia, were given over to a display of the mechanical tools of printing - a variety of presses, typecasting machines, and punch cutters, along with early models of the Linotype and Monotype machines. To illustrate the impact of printing on the human mind, the committee selected and displayed 420 influential books and documents beginning with the Gutenberg Bible, and concluding with a copy of Winston Churchill's speech to the House of Commons on August 20, 1940 (in which he declared, "Never in the field of human conflict was so much owed by so many to so few."). The preface to the exhibition catalog characterized the books as "decisive battles against ignorance and darkness in the history of man." Morison was determined that no literature or music be included in the final display, but the members of the Historical Sub-Committee were just as determined that Homer and Shakespeare, for example, be included. The impasse was broken after Muir and his entire committee threatened to resign if Homer was left out. With that classic victory in hand, the committee pressed forward and gained acceptance not only for Shakespeare, Dante, and Goethe, but Lewis Carroll and Walt Whitman - not to mention Lord Baden-Powell's *Scouting for Boys.* Although most reviewers praised the exhibition, a few claimed the selection of books was narrowly anglo-centric - a difficult argument to refute.

The exhibition at Earls Court illustrated both the evolution of printing technology and the impact of printing on learning. A separate exhibition at the King's Library of the British Museum featured the physical appearance of the book. The display began with the Gutenberg Bible, ' and progressed through the work of Nicolas Jenson, William Caxton, Robert Estienne, Christopher Plantin, John Baskerville, William Bulmer, William Morris, T. J. Cobden-Sanderson, Bruce Rogers, and Hermann Zapf. The books were chosen to represented the best typography of their day.

The catalog for the exhibition, designed by John Dreyfus, and with wood- engravings by Reynolds Stone, won universal praise. The annotations were accurate and well written. The catalog's description of Samuel Johnson's *Dictionary of the English Language*, for example, reveals both the charm and importance of the book:

> This is the most amazing, enduring, and endearing one-man performance in the field of lexicography. Johnson's lucid and often idiosyncratic definitions have kept their freshness, and the *Dictionary* may still be consulted for instruction or pleasure. Johnson's endeavours to 'fix' the English language once and for all, however, were nullified by Webster and shown to be delusive by the *Oxford English Dictionary*.[26]

PRINTING
AND THE
MIND OF MAN

CATALOGUE OF THE
EXHIBITIONS AT
THE BRITISH MUSEUM
AND AT
EARLS COURT, LONDON
16–27 JULY 1963

ORGANIZED IN CONNEXION WITH THE
ELEVENTH INTERNATIONAL PRINTING MACHINERY
AND ALLIED TRADES EXHIBITION

34. Cover design, by Reynolds Stone, for the 1963 catalog, Printing and the Mind of Man exhibition. Carter served on the Supervisory Committee.

While many regarded the catalog as a useful reference guide to some of the world's most notable books, Morison saw it as a preliminary exercise, a creditable effort to be sure, but only a beginning. He was determined to produce a more comprehensive work. When Morison pushed, few people were willing to stand in his way. So it was that on August 28, 1963, without any clear idea of the financial burden involved, the Supervisory Committee approved Morison's plan to produce a new and expanded volume. The committee gave the task of coordinating all phases of the production to Carter and Muir as joint editors. With unwavering belief in the importance of the project, and complete faith in Morison, the members of the Historical Sub-Committee, H. A. Feisenberger, S. H. Steinberg, Nicolas Barker, and Howard Nixon, agreed to continue. Over the next year and a half the editors and the committee worked on a variety of fronts at the same time. The duty of the committee "was to supply, in as full measure as seemed appropriate to each case, background and perspective as well as analysis and exposition: that is to say, to expand a carefully considered list of landmarks, furnished with annotation sufficient to explain why we had chosen them, into a book which could be not merely consulted but read."[27] The annotation for Johnson's *Dictionary* was expanded from a succinct sixty word summary in the 1963 catalog to a four paragraph essay, including contemporary reviews of the book, an outline of its four major parts, and a summary of its importance in the field of English lexicography. One of Carter's tasks was to balance the committee's laudable desire for a high quality book with the reality of a severely restricted printing budget. Jack Matson originally promised financial support from the Association of British Manufacturers of Printers' Machinery, but in September 1964 withdrew the offer. When it appeared the project might collapse, Morison gave the committee £3,000 from his personal account. Carter lined up a distinguished group of artists and scholars to work on various aspects of the book's production.

Denys Hay, an Edinburgh historian, wrote a ten thousand word essay, "Fiat Lux," on the spread of printing and its influence on learning. Once more John Dreyfus supervised the book's design and guided it through production at Cambridge University Press. Carter's friend Desmond Flower, now chairman of Cassells, took on the responsibility for sales and distribution. Early reviews in *The Times* and *The Daily Telegraph* were cordial, but George Steiner, writing anony-

> # PRINTING
> # AND
> # THE MIND
> # OF MAN
>
> EDITED BY JOHN CARTER & PERCY H. MUIR
>
> Second edition
> revised & enlarged
>
> KARL PRESSLER · MÜNCHEN

35. Jacket design for the 1983 second revised edition of Printing and the Mind of Man edited by Carter and Muir.

mously in the *Times Literary Supplement*, renewed charges of Anglo-Saxon bias that had been directed at the earlier edition. After dismissing the editors' claim of a representative European balance, he wrote, "The preponderance of English books among the 466 titles chosen is not merely an engaging oddity; it suggests a number of cases of essential myopia. *The Anatomy of Melancholy* is included but Rabelais's immensely more influential *Gargantua and Pantagruel* is not." In a curious phrase, Steiner claimed the annotations were delivered in "a certain Catholic voice and Hibernian inflection."[28] Denis Brogan's review supported Steiner on the matter of bias, but gave the compilers credit for the quality of the annotations.[29]

After Cassells allowed *Printing and the Mind of Man* to go out of print for more than ten years, Muir began to campaign for a revised second edition. His friend Karl Pressler, the Munich publisher, agreed to bring the work back in print. With a new introduction by Muir and an added bibliographical section by Peter Amelung, the revision came out in 1983. Reviewers praised *Printing and the Mind of Man* as a scholarly guide to the impact of printing on the mind of Western man.

If Carter's work on *Printing and the Mind of Man* was his most professionally rewarding activity during the decade of the sixties, his appointment as a Fellow at Eton College was the most personally satisfying. Carter had maintained close ties with Eton over the years. He frequently gave advice on costly purchases. "When you can, buy books from Anthony Rota," he advised the Eton librarian, Michael C. Meredith, "but don't ask for a discount, as his books are correctly priced unlike many other bookshops in London."[30] On another occasion when Meredith asked about what appeared to be a desirable edition of Thomas Hardy's novel *The Trumpet Major*, Carter advised against the purchase with a crisp negative evaluation: "It's spine had been glued."[31] From years of experience in the trade Carter knew the difference between a fair price and one that had been inflated. When a book of Eton interest appeared in a catalog or came up at auction in London or New York, he was able to provide expert analysis. It is difficult to imagine a consultant with better credentials.

In 1967 Eton's governing board elected Carter a Fellow of the College. He immediately set about to improve the College Library's physical facilities as well as its holdings. The collection contained many distinguished volumes, including a Gutenberg Bible in a signed contemporary binding, but the library rooms were dark, uninviting, and underused. Few improvements had been made since 1728, when the building was opened. Soot from the coke-burning stove covered the woodwork and the books with an overlay of grime. Carter asked for funds to strip and refinish the woodwork, add shelving, and replace the ancient heating and lighting facilities. In the fall of 1969, after a year and a half of upheaval from construction work, the Prime Minister, Harold Macmillan, opened the newly-restored rooms. To mark the occasion, Carter commissioned Cambridge University Press to print a history of the library and a checklist of notable books in the collection. Robert Birley's *The History of the Eton College Library* had been published earlier in *The Library,* but was updated and enlarged under Carter's supervision. *One Hundred Books*, also by Birley, was a personal selection made to demonstrate the range of the Library's holdings. Both pamphlets were decorated with a bookplate designed by Reynolds Stone, and wrapped in Eton blue. Even before the restoration started, Carter urged the trustees to appoint a librarian-archivist to supervise the collections. In the past, library management had been given over to retired masters, untrained in bibliography or library procedures. On Carter's advice, the trustees appointed Patrick Strong, a trained archivist, who, with Noel Blakiston and Neil Ker, brought Eton's collections into workable order.

Following his efforts to improve the College Library, Carter supported the campaign to build a collection of twentieth-century authors begun by Michael Meredith in the School Library. Carter obtained first editions and autographed manuscripts from a number of Eton authors - Cyril Connolly, Anthony Powell, Peter Fleming, and

Harold Acton. These were displayed at the dedication of the School Library's refurbished quarters, on March 7, 1971, an occasion marked by a visit from Queen Elizabeth, the Queen Mother.[32] During the last ten years of his life, Carter made regular Saturday trips to Eton. It was satisfying to see the dark old rooms now brightened with new furnishings, to handle a perfectly restored binding on a sixteenth-century prayer book, and to discuss future plans with the librarians. Carter was proud of his contributions to the Eton libraries and even more so his Eton heritage.

Carter marked his allegiance to both Eton and King's College, Cambridge, by serving for over twenty-five years as the official rose-bearer at the Ceremony of the Lilies and the Roses. The celebration took place on May 21, marking the date on which King Henry VI, founder of both Eton and King's, was murdered in 1471 in the Tower of London. In the early 1920s, Carter's father commissioned a marble tablet to be set in the Wakefield Tower to mark the spot where the King had died. Each year on the anniversary of the event, he arranged for a bouquet of Eton lilies to be placed on the stone. Beginning in 1947, Carter took part in the ceremony, placing the white roses of King's beside the lilies of Eton. It was an occasion to honor his father, Eton, and King's.[33]

Although Carter probably would have been offended to be called an organization man, there was some justification for the label. He was the unofficial secretary for the Biblios for over forty years, Secretary, then President, of the Double Crown Club, Chairman of the Library Committee of the Garrick Club, councilor, vice-president, then President of the Bibliographical Society, coordinator for bibliographical articles in the *Times Literary Supplement,* and member of the editorial boards of *The*

Book Collector, and the Soho Bibliographies.[34] His work on the Supervisory Committee for *Printing and the Mind of Man* was crucial to the success of that project. He reorganized Scribner's rare book department in New York, and did the same at Parke-Bernet in 1965, when Sotheby's took over. He liked to see things done properly. Members needed to know the date and location for the next meeting of the Biblios. A replacement was needed on the Advisory Board of the Soho Bibliographies. Someone had to edit the revised version of *Printing and the Mind of Man.* He took on these tasks willingly and completed them successfully.

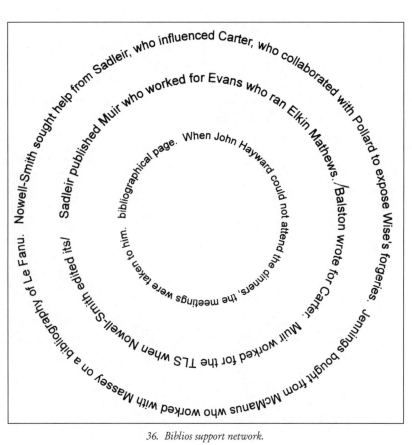

Nowell-Smith sought help from Sadleir, who influenced Carter, who collaborated with Pollard to expose Wise's forgeries. Jennings bought from McManus who worked with Massey on a bibliography of Le Fanu. Sadleir published Muir who worked for Evans who ran Elkin Mathews./Balston wrote for Carter. Muir worked for the TLS when Nowell-Smith edited its/ bibliographical page. When John Hayward could not attend the dinners, the meetings were taken to him.

36. Biblios support network.

CHAPTER TEN

Circles and Inner Circles

Lewis and Lilly (The Collectors) – Morison (The Typographer) –
Munby (The Librarian) – Hayward (The Editor) – Randall and Muir
(The Bookdealers) and Pollard (The Bibliographer)

A mong Carter's circle of friends were bookdealers, collectors, librarians, bibliographers, academic administrators and faculty members, curators, editors, printers, publishers, writers, and graphic artists. Old and young, American and English, professionally trained and self-taught, many of them urbanites, some, like Desmond Flower and Tim Munby, connected by the old-school tie, and some, like Graham Pollard, who seldom bothered with a tie at all. They possessed a rich variety of tastes and talents. Carter's friendship with Hayward, Pollard, Sadleir, Morison, Muir, Simon Nowell-Smith, Dudley Massey, and Richard Jennings went back to the late 1920s. The word *circle* is appropriate for this group of friends who supported each other on many levels (see figure 36). A publisher was often willing to take a chance on a new book if the manuscript came from someone within the circle. A journal editor sometimes looked across the table at a dinner party and saw a potential contributor. Librarians and curators turned to friends when they needed someone to write a preface, or prepare annotations for an exhibition catalog. Carter profited as much as anyone from these fraternal exchanges. Sadleir, the founder of the Biblios, published Carter's first four books at Constable & Company, while Rupert Hart-Davis, another Biblio, issued his next four. In 1934, under Carter's editorial guidance, Muir, Pollard, Sadleir, and Randall each contributed essays to *New Paths in Book-Collecting*. Muir could not have kept *Bibliographical Notes and Queries* alive without substantial contributions from Carter, Sadleir, Sparrow, Nowell-Smith, and Randall. Carter reviewed books by Muir, Sadleir, and Morison for *Publishers' Weekly* and the *Times Literary Supplement*, and they returned the favor. His comments and letters to the editor appeared regularly on the back-page of the *Times Literary Supplement*, a publication controlled by a series of friends; Morison from 1945 to 1947, Alan Pryce-Jones from 1948 to 1958, and Arthur Crook from 1959 to 1974. Members of the circle even rewarded each other socially - Sparrow and Sadleir nominated Carter for membership to the Garrick Club, Frederick B. Adams and Wilmarth S. Lewis endorsed him for the Grolier Club, and Morison supported his application to the Double Crown Club. The adage one hand washes the other comes to mind.

With a distance of time and place it is risky to try to be precise about personal relationships. Friends change, and archival and published records can be misleading. Carter counted many collectors as friends but only a few, such as Wilmarth S. Lewis and Josiah K. Lilly, became members of his inner circle.

Both Lilly and Lewis were intelligent, determined collectors with abundant means to satisfy their enthusiasms. Beyond that, the similarities end. "Lefty" Lewis, a Yale-educated Californian, started buying Horace Walpole books, letters, and manuscripts from A. W.

37. Wilmarth S. Lewis, indefatigable Horace Walpole collector and honorary American corresponding member of the Biblios.

Evans at the Elkin Mathews shop around 1925, two years before Carter came down from Cambridge. Muir knew Lewis as a regular customer but didn't become well acquainted with him until after Evans retired. Carter probably met the American at one of the late afternoon gatherings that drew collectors, dealers, and their friends to the Conduit Street shop. Since Lewis bought his first rare books - a copy of Gray's *Odes* and a Garrick leaflet - products of Horace Walpole's Strawberry Hill Press - at the Scribner's Bookstore in New York, it was only natural that he would find Carter, Scribner's rare book specialist in London, a congenial companion. Between 1935 and 1973 the two men kept in touch on a regular basis. Letters, post-cards - one of Carter's favorite means of communication - and cables flew back and forth across the Atlantic as Carter offered Lewis tantalizing eighteenth century books and pamphlets as potential additions to his growing Walpole library.

In December 1951 Carter called Lewis' attention to what he identified as Walpole's own set of the *Detached Papers*. These were sample title pages, labels, cards, and various loose pieces printed at Walpole's Strawberry Hill Press. The collection was at the moment on display at the Bibliotheque Nationale, but Carter promised it would be available in a matter of a few months after the exhibition closed. He wrote Lewis on December 27, 1951:

> I hope to procure an exact list of the contents, and I will send you a copy of this when I can. I have not yet got to any discussion about the price which the owner would take, but there is no disposition to part with it except for a sizable hunk of currency. I shall, of course, do the best I can in your interest, but the owner needs some money for a particular purpose, and we shall not get a bargain.

However, it is, I imagine, something which you ought most certainly to have, and I shall be much disappointed if I don't manage to land such a handsome piece of the True Cross for you in 1952.[1]

Lewis was indeed interested and replied immediately, "Of course I would like to have this, and I am perfectly willing to pay more for it than anyone else would pay - but not a great deal more! That is, I hope Lady Cynthia Colville (who Owen Morshead has told me is the present owner) will not get delusions of grandeur."[2] Later in the month, Carter discovered there had been a mix up in the matter of ownership. He cleared up the confusion in a letter of January 9:

> Despite the information supplied by Sir Owen Morshead, the book is not the property of Lady Cynthia Colville but belongs to the Marchioness herself. . . . I need not, I am sure, explain that Lady Crewe is not, in general terms, in need of money. But, for your private ear, she wanted to lay hands on a certain sum for a particular project, and was receptive to the suggestion that this could be raised by disposing of a few pieces from the library, of which this Strawberry Hill volume was suggested as one. It was owing to the good offices of our friend John Hayward, whose advice she took, that I was given the opportunity of looking over the suggested items, and he and I naturally thought immediately of you for this particular book. . . . If Lady Crewe cannot get a pretty good price for the book she will not sell it at all; and it has therefore been a question of arriving at a price which I, acting on your behalf, thought not unreasonable, and which the Marchioness' advisers in this matter consider to be satisfactory (I should explain that I offered to conduct the negotiations on this particular book on the basis of a modest commission payable by the seller).

The figure, then, which I am authorised to transmit to you for the purchase of this book is $1,500. I realize that this is no bargain price, and I realize too that, in the course of your indefatigable quest, you have procured many things either at nominal prices or as gifts. This however, is, for the reasons which I have already explained, a straight business transaction, and although only you can say whether the book is worth this price to you, it seems to me a fair one."[3]

Lewis was satisfied and replied, "I am very grateful to you for all the trouble you have taken about HW's set of Detached Pieces and accept the price of $1,500 with pleasure. As you suggest, it is on the stiffish side, but what can one expect under the circumstances? In any event, I am delighted to have the lot and am writing John Hayward to thank him for his part in the transaction."[4]

Shortly before Lewis made the final arrangements to buy the *Detached Pieces*, Carter wrote him about another Walpole-related volume owned by Lady Crewe. This time is was a holograph manuscript of John Hall Stevenson's verses entitled "The Muses Upon Ye Banks of the Forth - A Tribute from Ye North Upon his Majesty's Accession to ye Throne - To which is Added a Collection of Monkish Epitaphs from an Ancient Manuscript at Strawberry Hill." Carter found it difficult to place a value on the manuscript. In a letter of January 5, he wrote, "John Hayward and I have had much debate about the proper price which is not, as you will recognise, easily determined with a piece of this kind. The Marchioness, however, is in no give-away mood, and we have to get $350 for it, which I hope you will find not unreasonable."[5] Lewis was happy to pay the amount asked. After thanking Carter for his help in another matter he wrote, "And please send the <u>Monkish Rhymes</u>. I shall be delighted to have them, and I feel that, as usual, you have found just the right price. I shall write the sage of Chelsea [John Hayward] to thank him, once more, for his help in delicate negotiations."[6] Carter and Lewis liked to refer to these Walpole finds as "Bits of the True Cross" or simply BTC's.

The Lewis-Carter friendship was a mixture of business and pleasure. Whenever Lewis visited England he tried to coordinate his schedule with the meetings of the Biblios. As an occasional visitor to that informal group, he was awarded a formal title, "Honorary Foreign Corresponding Member." In May 1957, the Biblios abandoned their usual London venue, and gathered in Cambridge to honor Lewis on the occasion of his appointment as Sandars Reader in Bibliography. Whenever Carter visited the States, he always tried to spend a night or two with Lewis in Farmington, Connecticut. It was a pleasant interlude between appointments in New York and Boston, and offered easy access to the Yale campus in New Haven, where he could do business with the university librarian, James Babb, and perhaps have lunch with the determined bibliophile Professor Chauncey Brewster Tinker.

Carter and Lewis understood each other very well. Each man got what he wanted from the social and business exchange. In 1952, Carter wrote an enthusiastic review of Lewis's *Collector's Progress.* He praised it as "a story which will entertain and instruct many others besides collectors and eighteenth century specialists: not only by its wealth of anecdote and its easy, often racy style, but by the singularly agreeable impression which it consistently conveys both of its author's dedicated humanism and of the pleasing warmth generated in all sorts and kinds of people by exposure to Mr. Lewis's enthusiastic ingenuity and persistence as a collector."[7]

In turn, Lewis rolled out his warmest praise for *ABC for Book Collectors*. It was, he said, "a delight - clear, accurate and witty. ABC books are not meant to be read straight through but I have gone from ABBREVIATION to YELLOW-BACK without skipping and been instructed and entertained on every page. . . . It is perhaps unwise to pronounce a book 'a classic' on its publication, but if ever that inflated word is to be so risked it may be of the book under review."[8]

Once Carter joined Sotheby's the tone of the correspondence changed slightly. No longer selling books directly, Carter provided what might be called bibliographic tips to his friend in Connecticut. He recommended the well-printed Folio Society books as a good investment. Had Lewis heard about two BTC items coming up in the Hutchinson sale in March? Did he know about the lady in Northumberland who claimed to have two hundred letters from Edward Walpole to his family? Would Lewis like Carter to look into the situation? In return, Lewis provided hospitality at Farmington and introductions to wealthy friends who, from time to time, might be talked into parting with valuable books and paintings.

After Carter died in 1975, the officers of Eton College set up a Memorial Library Fund in his honor. The Yale Edition of Horace Walpole's *Correspondence*, edited by Lewis, was the first purchase made from the fund. When he heard the news, Lewis wrote Ernestine a warm letter of appreciation, "How very dear of you to subscribe to this edition with the first use of John's Memorial Fund! I can't tell you how touched I am by your doing so, and I think John would be pleased, too. This takes me back to my first meeting in March 1926 with Graham in Birrell and Garnett. I see John coming in with the latest Wise excitement as clearly as if it were yesterday."[9]

While Lewis enjoyed being "one of the boys," Lilly, the president of a large family-owned pharmaceutical company in Indiana, insisted on a certain distance. There was no lack of friendliness on his part, neither was there any wish to be chummy. After exchanging scores of letters over a twenty-five year period, Carter and Lilly continued to address each other as "Dear Mr. Lilly," and in return, "Dear Mr. Carter." The two men met through Randall, who had done business with Lilly as an independent dealer and as a representative of Max Harzof for a number of years in the early 1930s before joining Scribner's. In December 1936, Randall wrote Lilly that he planned to bring Carter, "my London agent," along on his next trip to Indianapolis.[10] When Carter and Lilly got together there was an immediate rapport. The previous month Carter had delivered a talk before the Bibliographical Society on the history of the 1786 Lausanne edition of William Beckford's *Vathek*, coincidentally, a book Lilly had recently purchased from Scribner's. Carter praised Lilly's judgment for buying what he called "a nice book and a rare book, and also a highly interesting one."[11] Applying a touch of salesman's flattery, Carter told Lilly he was sorry not to have left behind a mint copy of *Pauline*, 1833, Robert Browning's earliest publication, since, "I would rather you had it than anyone else."[12] Lilly liked to work from lists, and over the next several years Carter supplied titles from the Grolier Club's *One Hundred Books Famous in English Literature* and Asa Don Dickinson's *One Thousand Best Books.* In answer to Lilly's inquiries, he also recommended reference titles. In a long letter of September 28, 1938, he suggested Carteret's *Trésór du bibliophile,* as well as Tchemerzine's *Bibliographie d'editions originales ou rares d'auteurs français des Xve, XVIe, XVIIe et*

XVIIIe siècles for continental editions, and Hain's *Repertorium Bibliographicum,* and, the British Museum's *Catalogue of Books Printed in the 15th Century* for incunabula. It happened that Scribner's had copies of all these in stock, at what Carter called reasonable prices.

In the spring of 1938, Lilly decided to narrow his collecting fields and dispose of his British and Continental literature. After all, he reasoned, one person can only do so much. Carter argued that such a procedure would be a grave mistake:

> It does seem to me that it would be a thousand pities to disperse the nucleus of a collection already distinguished and capable of expansion into something really significant. There are very few collectors in your country to-day who are paying proper attention to first editions of the masterpieces of Continental literature, and in that fact, as well as their intrinsic interest, lies the importance and value of this department of your library.[13]

Lilly accepted this reasoned argument and kept his literature holdings intact.

In the fall of 1938, Randall wrote to ask if he and Carter could again pay a visit to Eagle Crest, the Lilly estate outside Indianapolis. Lilly replied, "I give you fair warning that if you and your friend from dear old London call upon me you will find me in great financial distress and in no position to entertain anything stronger than a first edition of GENTLEMEN PREFER BLONDES."[14] Lilly must have felt better about his bank balance the next year, when he cheerfully spent $15,000 for the Audubon Elephant Folio. At the same time he urged Carter to speed up the supply of wanted titles from the Dickinson list. Carter said of course he could supply the titles faster if

Lilly was willing to relax his standards of condition. It was, however, an approach Carter could not recommend. "I confess" he wrote, "that I don't want to do this, because I don't think you would ultimately be happy with 'moderate' or even 'good' copies. For instance, of the titles you were interested in from Maggs' catalogue, only 'The Little Minister' was really fine. 'Diana of the Crossways' was fair (and fair is not enough for this book). . . . I am constantly faced with the same situation with other books on the list, but I feel sure that we shall get the books in the right condition in time."[15] Two days later Carter was back again promoting the "right kind of books," in this case, books in the language in which they were first written. He explained at some length why some of the Greek classics appeared in Latin before Aldus, the noted Venetian printer, brought them out in Greek. The Latin editions, he wrote "are also in many cases handsome and desirable books for their own sake; but they are none the less translations and nothing more. Needless to say, the decision in this matter rests entirely with you. I think myself it would be a pity not to have the great Greek authors in their proper language."[16] It is difficult to say whether Lilly followed Carter's advice, as he essentially suspended buying during the war years.

As soon as the war was over, Randall picked up negotiations with Lilly where he and Carter had left them five years earlier. He planned a trip to Indianapolis late in 1945 and wanted to bring Carter along. Lilly was conditionally agreeable: " I should be very happy to have a visit from you and John Carter. If you arrive here with six suitcases full of letterpress I am off you for life."[17] Since Lilly expected to visit London in the spring, Carter and Randall decided to wait it out. In the meantime he had developed two new collecting interests - science and medicine. With Carter's help, he began to add first editions by Copernicus, Kepler, Bacon, Jenner, Darwin, Freud, Osler, Harvey, and Vesalius. It was a difficult collecting field, as Carter reminded him.

> It has to be recognized that most of the really swagger books are desperately rare, and that some of the corner-stones of the collection you envisage will have to be fit-ted in as and when they can be found but also many books, recognized as really significant in the various departments of science, even though they be by compar-ison modest in price, and may therefore seem at first sight not worth your attention. For the fact is that there are still a great many scientific books of which the full sig-nificance is only recognized by the experts, and which have therefore not yet reached the higher price brackets, as the more obvious things have done. . . . Many books not yet fully recognized will undoubtedly quadruple in price within the next decade or so, and I shall not want to pass up on your account things which we might after-wards regret missing."[18]

Lilly added books along the lines Carter suggested, although his active collecting days were coming to a close. In 1954, he decided to transfer his library to Indiana University. Carter heard about the plan through Randall and wrote at once. "I was naturally much interested, since more good books that have passed through my hands have ended up on your shelves than on those of any other col-lector in America. . . . I hope you won't think my contin-ued interest in your library intrusive; but I should certain-ly appreciate (and wd' of course keep in confidence) any news of your plans as they develop."[19] Lilly was somewhat taken aback by the letter since he thought his plans were known only to an inner circle. "I am a little embarrassed," he wrote, "that our mutual friend Randall mentioned the possible gift to Bloomington prior to my having taken the matter up with the authorities there but I guess no harm will come of it. Frankly, I think I will get a great deal of pleasure in giving my books away over a period of years to university libraries where they may serve a useful purpose."[20] Carter's long relationship with Lilly was one of the most satisfying of his bookselling career.

Anyone assembling a list of the members of Carter's inner circle would undoubtedly place Stanley Morison's name near the top. On more than one occasion Carter identified Morison as the conscience of the group. During a BBC round-table radio discussion Carter said, "I think most of his friends would agree that there were certain things which one avoided doing, or decided not to do - certainly it was true of me - because I didn't think that Morison would approve of it; and to that extent I think of him sometimes as a sort of conscience of my own. And many other people, I think, would remember the influence, sometimes by precept, sometimes by example, that Morison had on the course of their careers, their work, what they should do next."[21]

Carter got to know Morison in the late 1920s through Graham Pollard. According to legend, Morison was making his way around London's bookshops in 1926 showing Frederick Warde's facsimile edition of the Arrighi writing books when he stopped by Birrell & Garnett's shop late one night, and found Pollard still at work in a back room. Out of that meeting a friendship developed based on common interests in Marxist politics, trains, good food and drink, and the history and development of letter forms. Pollard brought Morison around to the dinner meetings of the Biblios, where he was no doubt already known, at least by reputation. By 1927, the year Carter started working for Scribner's, Morison had already published a number of short general texts including *The Craft of Printing* (1921), *A Brief Survey of Printing* (1923), *Type Designs of the Past and Present* (1926), and *A Review of Recent Typography in England, the United States, France & Germany* (1927). He had also written dozens of articles on topics ranging from calligraphy to the proper use of Baskerville type. Morison was not a regular member of the Biblios, but attended the dinners whenever he could, attracted by the group's brash informality. He was particularly drawn to Carter and Pollard's investigation of a suspicious group of nineteenth century pamphlets, partly because the analysis centered on the dating of letter forms and partly because it challenged the reputation of T.J. Wise, one of England's established bibliographical pundits. Wise turned out to be a perfect target for Morison's dislike of the overblown. It was Morison's careful analysis of the type faces used in the Reading 1847 printing of Browning's *Sonnets* that gave Carter and Pollard the technical ammunition they needed to continue and expand their investigation.

The Carter-Morison friendship was based on a respect for each other's intelligence and a mutual no-nonsense view of people and events. There was no room for pretense or compromise. In addition, both men enjoyed the high life. The wine list at the Garrick Club was particularly attractive.

Morison had a habit of chastising his friends, including Carter, when he thought they were wasting their time. A person should settle in a job and see it through. What was to be made of a career that bounced from London to New York, back to London, then to Washington, D. C., and back again to London - from bookselling to government service to the auction room? Morison also worried about Carter's publication record. It had gotten off to a splendid start in the 1930s with the *Enquiry* and the books on Victorian binding styles but, as time went by, there seemed to be a decline in substance. Morison thought Carter should make an effort to produce something substantial, perhaps a bibliography drawn from his Catullus collection, or a scholarly history. Even on small matters Morison could be uncompromising. He dressed entirely in black, the same sensible style year after year. Why would Carter waste time and money assembling a fashionable bespoke wardrobe? When a book or article didn't please him, he made his disappointment known. He had no patience with what he considered mediocre. As noted earlier, Carter's *ABC for Book Collectors*, he guessed, might be useful after it reached a fifth edition. It was the kind of criticism that friends received, if not with pleasure, at least with the understanding that the critic wished them no harm, in fact wished them great success. That success, he warned them, would only come as a result of rigorous application. It was the A. E. Housman message all over again. In spite of his reputation as a merciless critic, Morison was also ready to deliver praise and support. In the summer of 1953, when Carter was taking up his duties in Washington, D. C., Morison wrote, "I imagine you climbing peaks of diplomacy, Everestian in daunt and dimension. You are much missed in this valley."[22] Even with such direct expressions of friendship it was always "Dear Carter," "Dear JWC," or, sometimes in a playful mood, "Dear Waynflete." In July 1942, Morison thanked Carter for sending a set of *The Fleuron* to replace a copy destroyed, along with his other books and papers, the previous spring in a massive air raid.

The loss had been particularly devastating, since Morison along with Oliver Simon had founded the journal in 1923, and carried it forward for the next seven years. Carter, Oliver Simon, Brooke Crutchley, Francis Meynell, the founder of the Nonesuch Press, and Graham Pollard financed the gift. Morison was touched. "Dear Carter," he wrote, "I was greatly cheered on my return from Liverpool to have your generous letter and the parcel of the Fleuron v. I-VII complete with the original jackets and I shall guard it as I only hope more carefully than the set effectively done in by the old Hun."[23]

In order to celebrate Morison's sixtieth birthday in 1949, Carter drew together a listing of his published works. The objective, Carter remarked in his preface, was utilitarian. This was to be "nothing more than a handlist, intended to serve as a series of signposts now and as a basis for amplification, correction and addition in the future."[24] The description of individual titles was appropriately straightforward, with no attempt to supply detailed collations or title-page transcriptions. The annotations, often written by Morison himself, provided one of the handlist's most attractive features. Commenting on his article "Toward an Ideal Italic," published in *The Fleuron* in 1926, Morison wrote, "The historical portion, still worth reading, leads to an argument favouring the reduction of the cursive, and the increase of the inscriptional element in the design of italic."[25] He was not pleased with a contribution made to the 1925 *Gutenberg Festschrift* concerning the type used in the Aldus masterpiece, *Hypnerotomachia Poliphili* (1499). "Valueless" he commented, "except for a small point, not well made, about cl and st."[26] Crutchley supervised the printing of the handsome volume at the Cambridge University Press. Carter correctly anticipated amplifications and corrections. P.M. Handover published "A Second Handlist 1950-1959" in *Motif 3* in 1960, again with Morison's annotations. The final version, *The Writings of Stanley Morison,* compiled by Tony Appleton, came out in 1976 with brief biographical essays by Crutchley and Dreyfus. As a supplement to the main body of the text, Appleton added an extended list of books and articles about Morison and his work. Carter, who died the year before the book came out, would have been pleased with the simple dedication in his name.

Also in honor of Morison's sixtieth birthday, the BBC asked Carter to prepare what they called an appreciation. Carter's talk explored the range of Morison's varied contributions, and focused on his interest in the development of letter forms. In the process of explaining how that interest affected all of the typographer's work, Carter produced one of his delightfully sinuous sentences: "It is Morison's broad view of the relation between different kinds of letter-forms, and their arrangement- whether incised on stone or metal or wood; written with the quill or reed or pen on vellum or paper; multiplied by types cast from matrices struck by engraved punches; or reproduced by one of the numerous photographic processes - it is this horizontal as well as vertical approach which gives his interpretation of typographic developments its commanding force, and makes so persuasive his exposition of the principles and practice appropriate to typography's various mediums and purposes."[27] It was not only a lucid explanation of Morison's approach to his work, but a breathtaking demonstration of Carter's all-flags-flying prose style.

Printing and the Mind of Man, and the various publications that resulted from the 1963 exhibition brought Carter and Morison together for the last time. Carter was part of Morison's grand plan from the beginning and remained one of its chief supporters through the publication of the expanded Catalogue in 1967. Carter and Muir were able to get a completed copy of the final text to Morison shortly before he died on October 11, 1967. The obituary in *The Book Collector*, written by Nicolas Barker, closed with the words, "It is not given to most people to alter any part of their environment so completely as Morison did by changing the letters we all read to the forms in which we now see them. He was a great man, and will be greatly missed."[28]

Carter got to know Tim Munby just before the outbreak of World War II. Munby came down to London from Cambridge to work first for Quaritchs' then for Sotheby's. With a mutual interest in book collecting, and a shared background at King's, they developed an easy friendship. After the war, with Carter back at Scribner's, and Munby returned to Sotheby's, the friendship continued. In 1947, Munby became Librarian of King's College. From that post he quickly established himself as a bibliographic scholar, with a series of studies on the life and collecting habits of the omnivorous nineteenth century bibliophile Sir Thomas Phillipps. Carter and Munby worked together on the professional level with shared interests in collecting and the book trade. On the personal level, they simply enjoyed each other's company. Munby's duties at Cambridge made it difficult for him to take part in the London social scene, but he enjoyed his status as a "country" member of the Biblios. During the last years of his life, health problems made it difficult for him to travel

By nature reluctant to discuss his joys or frustrations, Carter was unusually open with Munby. He didn't want to be considered for the post of Cambridge Librarian, he

*38. Carter with A.N.L. "Tim" Munby, genial scholar and librarian of
King's College, Cambridge - c. 1965.*

told his friend, because the appointment would limit his
freedom of movement. In 1953 he asked Munby's advice
about a career change. When Munby suggested a King's
College fellowship Carter dismissed the possibility saying
he couldn't think of a subject he would be qualified to
examine. He simply wanted to return to the book trade
and work with American collectors.

Nicolas Barker described Munby as "the most
humane, as well as one of the most learned bibliographical scholars of this century."[29] It was the humane side of
Munby's character that appealed to Carter. This was a
man who collected writing instruments, enjoyed boating,

hunting, and carpentry, a good laugh, a good meal, and seaside vacations with his family. He provided a refreshing contrast to some of Carter's city friends for whom gossip and character assassination often seemed the chief ingredients of conversation. Carter was pleased when Munby asked him to act as godfather to his son Giles, an honor he acknowledged on the dedication page of *Books and Book Collectors*. As Carter's health declined he asked Munby to prepare an obituary to be forwarded to *The Times* on his death. The tribute emphasized Carter's affection for Eton, King's College, and the Garrick Club, his sartorial splendor, and his personal charm. It was a testimony of admiration. The obituary appeared in March 1975, three months after Munby's sudden death on December 26, 1974.

Munby, the amiable librarian, and Hayward, the flamboyant editor, exhibited radically contrasting personalities. Carter first met John Hayward in 1924 at Cambridge. The two men had a common interest in collecting, and often spent Saturday mornings scanning the books displayed in Gustave David's bins in the Cambridge Market Place. Collecting was a King's tradition going back at least to the early decades of the century when John Maynard Keynes, Stephen Gaselee, and Arthur Cole scoured David's shelves for bargains. In spite of a progressively disabling disease of the nervous system, Hayward was able to take part in these hunts with the same vigor he applied to his participation in various University musical and theatrical productions. His chief academic interest was in Restoration literature. The Nonesuch Press published his *Collected Works of the Earl of Rochester* in 1926 while he was still an undergraduate and *The Complete Poetry and Selected Prose of John Donne* two years later.

During the late 1920s Carter and Pollard and their fellow Biblios were deeply involved in uncovering the origin of the mysterious nineteenth century pamphlets. According to Muir, "After dinner, whenever there was anything especially striking to impart we developed the occasional habit of going on to see John Hayward, then living in Bina Gardens, who with his keen mind was usually able to add something to the purpose."[30] Collector, editor, anthologist, critic, textual expert, and bibliographer, Hayward was a man of many interests and accomplishments. For several years Hayward shared his flat with T. S. Eliot and was credited for providing the poet with welcome editorial assistance.

In an 1950 BBC presentation in honor of Morison, Hayward analyzed the purposes and pleasures of book collecting in a talk entitled "Why First Editions?" As the basis of literary research, Hayward explained, first editions are held to be essential. But shouldn't the sheer satisfaction of owning first editions be recognized as equally important? "Pleasure," he claimed, "may be as good a justification for collecting as any other. The pleasure of pursuit, the pleasure of discovery, the pleasure of possession - they all combine to gratify the mind and the senses."[31] While part of Hayward's reputation came from his writing, an equal part rested on his sharp wit - often on display for an elite group of poets, publishers, collectors, librarians, and artists who gathered at his flat at 19 Carlisle Mansions. According to his obituary in *The Times*, he was a man both feared and admired. Friendship with Hayward was never easy but those who knew him best excused his irritating performances with an appreciation for his indisputable talents - talents that he demonstrated in forty-eight issues of *The Book Collector*.

Carter's closest friend among American booksellers was David Randall. They began their careers in the book business at about the same time; Carter with Scribner's in London, and Randall working for E. Byrne Hackett at the Brick Row Bookshop and then for Max Harzof at the G. A. Baker firm in New York. Carter met Randall in 1929 on his first trip to New York. The two young dealers found they shared many of the same beliefs. It was time, they agreed, to wean collectors away from their blinkered concentration on standard sets of English literature, fine bindings, color plate books, and early European printing. In his contribution to *New Paths in Book Collecting*, "American First Editions, 1900-1933," Randall asked why collectors didn't pay as much attention to Ernest Hemingway, William Faulkner, Robert Frost, and Robinson Jeffers as they did to Emily Dickinson and Walt Whitman. When the head of Scribner's rare book department resigned in 1935, Carter knew the right person for the job. Working with energy and imagination, Carter and Randall became known as Young Turks of the rare book world. Beyond the basics, they knew how to scramble. They cut prices when necessary, raised prices when they thought they could get away with it, dumped stock that had been gathering dust in the vaults, and kept a vast assortment of dates and sale prices in their heads. They remembered that Galsworthy's earliest works were issued under his pseudonym, John Sinjohn, and that *Spicilegium Poeticum*, a volume of poems by Manley Hopkins, printed for private circulation, was not by the noted nineteenth century poet and Jesuit priest, Gerard Manley Hopkins, but by his father. If they wanted to make a two-week buying trip in the Midwest, start handling classic medical texts, set up a new bookkeeping system, move the rare books in the New York store from the balcony to the main floor, or buy a Gutenberg Bible, they usually got their way.

Letters exchanged over a period of thirty years reveal a shrewd, hard-working team. The Carter-Randall axis, as they called it when they worked for Scribner's, operated effectively from 1935 to 1953, with a gap of four years for Carter's wartime service. In 1956 Randall was appointed director of the Lilly Library in Bloomington, Indiana, and a year earlier Carter joined Sotheby's. Although they now reported to different employers, their interests remained constant and interwoven. In the fall of 1960 Carter traveled to Bloomington to attend the dedication of the Lilly Library.[32] The following spring he addressed the Friends of the Library at a dinner honoring H. Bacon Collamore, who had presented his A. E. Housman collection to the University. Five years later, Carter sold his own substantial Housman collection to the Lilly. To underline the importance of the acquisition, Randall asked Carter to prepare a brief article for publicity purposes. Once started, Carter found it impossible to be brief. It was, after all, a collection he had built over a period of nearly forty years. He had specific ideas about how his text should be handled. "I have taken a good deal of trouble with it" he wrote Randall; "it is, as it were, my farewell to Housman. It won't, you'll agree, lend itself to cutting; in short I want it (like my "Farewell Catullus" which Texas published in their Quarterly) printed as is. Would it be possible to have it as a separate leaflet, uniform with and to go with your Report? It would make, I should guess, 6 pages in the larger of your normal type sizes and probably 4 in the smaller. Think about this, my dear Dave; and oblige me if you can.[33] The leaflet was issued as Carter requested.

One of the last Carter-Randall transactions involved arrangements for the "Printing and the Mind of Man" exhibition to be mounted at the Lilly Library in the fall of 1973. The date would mark the tenth anniversary of its impressive London debut sponsored by the International Printing Machinery and Allied Trades Association. The Lilly was an appropriate location since it owned seventy-five percent of the books shown in the original 1963 exhibition and Carter was, for obvious reasons, the appropriate person to deliver the featured address. Sadly, he had to cancel. He explained the situation to Randall. "I have been under the weather the past few months and was sent yesterday to a specialist who, among other things, set a firm veto to my planned trip. With much regret and apologies I must cry off. I'm terribly disappointed (being in low spirits anyway) but there it is."[34]

Over the years there had been many occasions to celebrate - the success of the Scribner's catalogs, especially those featuring the first editions of works by Bach, Handel, Mozart, and Wagner, the discovery and sale of the Gutenberg Bible, and the sale of Blake's *Jerusalem*. Not all of Carter's promotions ended in success. Did Randall have any interest in either the Graham Greene or Ronald Firbank archives, or in Carter's own extensive archive of books and letters on the T. J. Wise forgeries? He did not. There were also questions of a more personal nature. Who was Carter considering as a replacement for Robert Metzdorf at Parke-Bernet? This question led Carter to inquire, "How long does your stint at Lilly continue? And what are your plans thereafter? I am still having trouble with the book department at PB and I hear myself saying (as I did when we took over and Metzdorf resigned in a huff) if only I had Dave on the other end we could make this into something. I don't expect to stay on at the grind-stone for ever though having no money and no pension I may have to."[35] Occasionally, Randall's freewheeling approach annoyed Carter. When *The New York Times* reported Randall as saying he discovered the Gutenberg Bible in England and brought it to the United States, Carter objected. "Wouldn't it be better," he asked, "to indulge in a little historical accuracy?"[36] Late in 1961, Carter told Randall about an inscribed copy of the first edition of Housman's *Shropshire Lad* about to come up at auction in London. The copy happened to be inscribed to a Mrs. Wise, and Carter hoped no one would notice it was *the* Mrs. Wise. He implored Randall, a notorious gossip, to "keep your old lip buttoned in talking about this copy."[37] It was the kind of request that could only come out of a twenty-five year close working relationship.

A superficial examination of the Carter-Randall friend-ship might conclude it was based on an attraction of oppo-sites - Randall the brash, off-the-cuff opportunist - Carter the elegant perfectionist. Beyond those externals, Carter and Randall agreed on the basics - hard work and creative salesmanship. Carter liked to quote Michael Sadleir: "In nature the bird who gets up earliest catches the most worms, but in book-collecting the prizes fall to birds who know worms when they see them."[38] In recognizing the important worms, Carter and Randall had few equals. They confided in each other, sipped each other's bourbon, supported each other's successes, and covered each other's mistakes. Their long partnership was one of the most suc-cessful in the history of the Anglo-American book trade.

Percy Muir dedicated his memoir, *Minding My Own Business*, "To J.W.C. affectionately." In a note written to celebrate Muir's eightieth birthday Carter acknowledged

the tribute. "In nearly half a century in the rare book business, few things, I think, have given me greater pleasure
than Percy Muir's dedication to me of that lively chronicle of an old friend and colleague's career, *Minding My
Own Business.*"[39] Carter and Muir's friendship was based
on a mutual enthusiasm for collecting, bibliography, and
the daily give-and-take of the rare book trade. The two
men got acquainted shortly after Carter came down from
Cambridge in the fall of 1927. Muir, ten years Carter's senior, was working at Dulau's in Bond Street at the time, but
shortly made the transition to Elkin Mathews Ltd., an
environment he described in lively detail in a series of articles published first in *The Book Collector,* and then brought
together much altered and shortened in *Minding My Own
Business.* Carter and Muir both had an amateur interest in
music, and with that as a base, started to acquire and catalog examples from the work of European masters.
Encouraging returns from Elkin Mathews and Scribner's
sales catalogs in the early 1930s showed there was a market
waiting to be exploited. In the process of buying musical
first editions, along with standard works in religion, philosophy, science, and technology, Scribner's became Elkin
Mathews' best customer. Muir never forgot the debt he
owed Carter for providing a flow of orders during the difficult Depression years of the late 1930s and on into the
early war years.

Carter and Muir worked together on a wide variety of
projects, starting in 1935 with *Bibliographical Notes and
Queries,* and extending to 1967 with the publication of
Printing and the Mind of Man. In between there were the
years they served on the Editorial Board of *The Book
Collector.* Through it all, their friendship not only endured
but ripened. Carter's last contribution to *The Book*

Collector paid tribute to Muir on his eightieth birthday. "I have every confidence," he wrote, "that, despite the pressing claims of his garden and his increasing reluctance to set eyes on London, Percy Muir will continue to maintain during his new decade those contributions to the enjoyment, instruction and entertainment of the bibliophile world which has owed so much to its predecessors."[40]

One of the first people Carter met after he started work at Scribner's was Graham Pollard, a graduate of Jesus College, Oxford, and already established at Birrell & Garnett's bookshop on Gerrard Street. Pollard was a rebel, casual in appearance, in corduroy pants and broad brimmed hats, and sporting party card No. 1 in the Young Communist League of Great Britain. His interests - book production and distribution, newspaper and periodical publication, writing books, bookbinding, and type design - caught Carter's attention. The two men became a working team around 1929 based on their investigation of the dating and distribution of a number of nineteenth century pamphlets. The product of their research, *An Enquiry Into the Nature of Certain Nineteenth Century Pamphlets*, is a classic study in bibliographic detective work and a tribute to their creative determination. In 1942 Pollard took a post at the Board of Trade, but never lost interest in the history and development of book production. He was the kind of meticulous researcher who liked to trace the origin of obscure facts, no matter how long it might take. It was a work pattern that drove Carter to distraction. In 1948 Rupert Hart-Davis agreed to publish *The Firm of Charles Ottley, Landon & Co.*, a pamphlet the partners were working on as a supplement to the *Enquiry*. After numerous attempts to get Pollard to supply a corrected final draft, Carter wrote, "Are you not

39. Graham Pollard · c. 1973

pushing your insouciance a little far? I can get no answer
to my letters, you remain incommunicado by telephone
without even the civility of a message from your secretary
to say why you are unable to ring me back."[41] Two years
later Carter found himself in the same situation, waiting
for Pollard to complete the index for the *Handlist of the
Writings of Stanley Morison*. "I shall be greatly disappointed," he wrote, "if the Morison handlist is to be put to
press without your index and I hope you will be able to
get at this immediately."[42] Work on the revision of the
Enquiry, which stretched over almost three decades, was
another case in point. In the early stages of the revision,

Carter wrote Pollard saying "Cape [the publisher] is getting apprehensive about the standing type of "the Enquiry," and is anxious to know what prospects there are of the second volume being completed. This, as you know, depends on you."[43] In 1969, as noted earlier, Carter had the pleasure of pinning the Bibliographical Society's Gold Medal on Pollard in honor of his bibliographical achievements. The citation, read by Carter, summarized their long working relationship:

> In presenting to you Mr. Graham Pollard, I take a more than special satisfaction; it is indeed a sensation so intimate as to be almost incestuous. For in half a dozen of his minor published works my own name is joined with his on the title-page. Of these, one is directly pertinent to this evening's exercise, for it was a joint tribute, on his sixtieth birthday, to an earlier Gold Medalist, Stanley Morison, to whom both of us were for many years deeply indebted and affectionately attached. Of the others (most of them concerned with the doings of an earlier President of this Society) I shall say no more than that, despite a certain tendency to procrastination in recent years (known to our publisher as "Pollard's pace"), no collaboration in a series of technical memoranda can ever have been more harmonious; nor, I think, has any co-author been more comfortably conscious of his debts than I am.[44]

It was a handsome tribute based on over forty years of close collaboration.

CHAPTER ELEVEN

Causes and Opinions

S hortly after the end of the war in Europe, Carter
began to speak out against the government's export
and import controls, particularly as they applied to
works of art, books, and manuscripts. The restrictions, put
in place in 1939 under the Import, Export and Power Act,
were intended to safeguard the flow of sterling to and from
Great Britain - a necessary wartime regulation. As time
went by, however, the Board of Trade, whose duty it was
to oversee the enforcement of the act, regularly refused to
issue export licenses for works determined to be national
treasures. This raised an outcry from dealers, consignors,
and buyers. To meet these objections, the Board set up a
review committee made up of government officers, and
the directors of several leading libraries and museums. The
committee, naturally enough, was unsympathetic to the
complaints of those who favored a more liberal export policy, and the restrictions continued.

In what he later characterized as a tremendously
pontifical article, entitled "The Heritage of Culture,"
Carter, writing anonymously, urged the government to
develop a more reasoned approach to the export of pictures, sculpture, books, and manuscripts.[1] What happens, he asked, when institutions such as the British
Museum lack the funds to buy articles declared too
important to export? The owner is left without a buyer

and the auction house without a sale. In Carter's view three things needed to be considered in order to make the system work more efficiently:

> First, whether it is right, as a matter of public policy, to take official measures to safeguard against export of things of historical or nationally sentimental value; if so, on what principles they are to be scheduled in advance, or adjudged when they come into the market: and, thirdly, whether they should be simply prohibited from export . . . or whether the desired result would not be more satisfactorily achieved by providing the national libraries with a purchasing fund which bore some real relation to their importance and their responsibilities to international scholarship - and encouraging their administrators to an energetic and enlightened use of it.[2]

Those in the Office of the Treasury who were working on the question of export control, took Carter's arguments seriously.

In 1950, the Chancellor of the Exchequer appointed a committee under the chairmanship of Viscount Waverly to study the problem. During a period of several months in 1951, the Waverly Committee heard testimony from over 150 concerned museum directors, rare book and fine arts dealers, librarians, government officers, private collectors, and auctioneers - both English and American. The committee concluded that the state had a right to ban the export of objects of national importance only if one of three conditions were met: the object must be closely allied with the country's history or its national life, it must possess outstanding aesthetic importance, or it must have significance for the study of a particular branch of learning. Objects less than one hundred years old, or valued at less than £1,000, a figure later raised to £2,000, could not be banned. In a supplementary regulation, the committee declared the originals of manuscripts, documents, and archives could not be exported unless the buyer arranged for a copy to be made for deposit in an appropriate British library or museum. Responding to one of Carter's recommendations, the committee declared that in certain cases, when objects of great value were beyond the means of British museums and libraries, the government was urged to provide the money through an act of Parliament. Finally, the committee established a permanent Reviewing Board and an Advisory Committee to set policy. The report was approved by the Chancellor of the Exchequer, passed by Pariament, and became operational early in 1953.

Before the final approval of the Waverly report, and while he was still employed at Scribner's, Carter became involved in an important case testing the government's right to control exports. In early 1952, working through Scribner's, William Stirling of Keir sold his hand-colored copy of William Blake's *Jerusalem* and five Blake paintings to the American collector Paul Mellon. The British Museum objected to the sale, and in June the reviewers of the Board of Trade turned down the request for an export license. Carter, representing Scribner's, raised the question again in December in what was historically the first appeal to be heard by the Reviewing Committee now operating under the Waverly report guidelines. He argued that the content would not be lost by the transfer to America since an excellent facsimile had just been published by the Trianon Press for the William Blake Memorial Trust. His second argument raised the question of access. National treasure or not, how could anyone, he asked, defend the present situation? Located in a private library in northern Scotland, the book could hardly be said to be available, either to scholars or those with a mild curiosity about Blake.

In exchange for the *Jerusalem,* and in order to settle some of the concerns voiced by the British Museum, Mellon agreed to give one of the Blake paintings, a Madona and Child, to a public gallery in England, and sell the others for £5,000, a price considerably below their value on the international market. After six months of lively debate, the Reviewing Committee approved the export license. The victory for free trade was duly noted in *The Book Collector.* Those who regretted the loss of the *Jerusalem* could find some consolation "in knowing the nation has acquired as a direct result of the sale five Blake paintings of the first quality (formerly of Kier) the finest of them, a Madonna and Child, as a generous gift from the anonymous purchaser."[3] The editor went on to celebrate Carter's role in securing the necessary approval:

> The long and difficult negotiations were conducted by Mr. John Carter, London director of Charles Scribner's Sons of New York, who is to be congratulated on a transaction even more remarkable perhaps than his purchase of the Shuckburgh copy of the 42-line *Bible* in 1951. Like the *Bible,* the *Jerusalem* was flown to New York in his personal charge.[4]

Carter said delivering the *Jerusalem* to Mellon was one of the most satisfying moments of his professional career.

Even with the Waverly resolutions in place, controversy over the export of books and paintings never entirely disappeared. Early in 1964 the Director of the Metropolitan Museum in New York objected when a

Raphael drawing was denied an export license. He attacked the system as unduly oppressive - "This is apt to happen when we try to acquire new works at auction. In European houses, such as Sotheby's where the Raphael was up for auction, It's not really a free-market, for the country can forbid a work's sale or export as it did in this case."[5] Carter rose to the defense:

> We at Sotheby's warmly sympathized with Dr. Rorimer's . . . disappointment and frustration in this particular case (we have another fine Raphael drawing coming up on March 11th, in case the Metropolitan likes to have another try). But surely it is going a little far to say that London is not really a free market just because once in a while the perfectly well-known regulations for protecting national treasures in Great Britain are enforced.[6]

He went on to point out that during the 1962-63 season some forty thousand works of art were exported from England to the value of fifty million dollars. In only two cases were export licenses denied. "Sotheby's have fought scores of cases on behalf of clients," he concluded, "and along with the fine art trade in London as a whole, has helped over the years to secure numerous simplifications and alleviations in the regulatory procedure. As firm believers in free trade we shall continue to do so."[7]

Carter was only marginally involved in the negotiations that followed the discovery of several sections of the manuscript of Caxton's translation of Ovid's *Metamorphoses*, but he followed the proceedings with great interest. This was based on his friendship with the participants, his position at Sotheby's, and his concern for the continued efficient operation of the Waverly Committee regulations. On June 27, 1966, Sotheby's auctioned Books one through nine of the *Metamorphoses*. The aggressive American dealer Lew David Feldman won the manuscript, presumably for his favorite customer, the University of Texas, with a record breaking bid of £90,000. This was a serious loss to the nation, as the Pepys Library at Magdalene College, Cambridge, owned the rest of the Ovid manuscript, Books ten through fifteen. Although neither Magdalene not the British Museum could match Feldman's bid, transfer of the precious document to America seemed unacceptable. Representatives of the British Museum lodged an objection, and under the terms of the Waverly report, the matter was duly transferred to the Reviewing Committee. After several months of delay, the Committee declared, "if within three months an offer of £90,000 were made to purchase the manuscript by, or on behalf of, the British Museum, the Pepysian Library, the Cambridge University Library, or any public institution in the United Kingdom, then an export license would not be granted."[8] When the government declared itself unable to provide financial support to any of those institutions, a number of Magdalene faculty members started an ambitious fund drive on their own. Supported by appeals in *The Times* and the *Times Literary Supplement*, they raised nearly £20,000 in two weeks. This was encouraging, but the end of the ninety days grace period was drawing near. The events that followed had all the suspense of an old-fashioned melodrama.

On a trip to England, the American publisher George Braziller read about the case of the Caxton Ovid and thought he knew how it might be resolved for all parties concerned. By coincidence, a facsimile edition of *The Hours of Catherine of Cleves*, recently published by his firm, had been made possible by joining two manuscript segments. The reproduction sold well and produced a solid profit for the company. Shortly after he arrived in England, he met with the members of the Cambridge Appeal Committee and convinced them that the purchase price could be raised by issuing a carefully printed, attractively bound facsimile. All that was needed was a patron to support the project with a £70,000 loan. Braziller, to everyone's surprise, found such a person in Eugene B. Power, President of University Microfilms of Ann Arbor, Michigan. Power had long been interested in books and manuscripts, but the idea of putting $200,000 into this slightly bizarre scheme must have tested his imagination. Carter, always able to provide an apt summary, described Power's dilemma: "There was a distinct element of the quixotic in the idea of one American asking another American (a total stranger) to put up a large sum of money, at a few days' notice and wholly unprepared, in order to save something for a small college in England from a third American."[9]

After weighing the possibilities and still uncertain about his role, Power made two telephone calls to England, one to Sir Frank Francis, Director of the British Museum, the other to Carter, who had worked for him as a consultant in the late 1950s. Assured of the importance of the project, Power authorized a £70,000 two-year interest-free loan to insure the manuscript's future as part of the Magdalene College collection. With the money in hand, Sotheby's informed Feldman that the Board of Trade ruling, denying export, would stand. One year later, Braziller published the facsimile in a handsome limited edition. For Magdalene College in particular, and for scholarship in general, the Ovid affair had a happy ending, but as Carter pointed out, with the emergency negotiations and a last minute rescue, it was one more example of "our preference for wringing hands rather than putting them deep into the pocket."[10] Beyond this criticism there was one final negative outcome. Originally, Carter suggested a printing of five hundred copies. Encouraged by the rapid sale of his *Catherine of Cleves*, a modestly priced volume, Braziller doubled that number. By the summer of 1969, several hundred copies remained unsold. In reply to an appeal from Power, Carter promised to make every effort to publicize the book in the *Times Literary Supplement* and *The Bookman*, but, as he reminded Power, somewhat testily, his own position in favor of a limited printing had been overruled. In answer to Power's inquiry on cost saving, Carter was adamant about maintaining the original price: "To reduce the price in hopes of attracting orders would, as I think everybody would agree, be out of the question, it would be a breach of faith with the original subscribers, many of whom (e.g. Eton College Library) subscribed not because they needed the book but to support a good cause."[11]

Carter's earliest articles in *Publishers' Weekly*, the collection of essays he gathered and edited in 1934 under the title *New Paths in Book Collecting*, and the Scribner's catalogs he and Randall produced in the 1930s and 1940s, were all part of a cause. His goal was to broaden collecting habits. It took time, but eventually many collectors were won over. One who refused to follow Carter's suggestions was Lord Rothschild. For over a dozen years, beginning in 1936, and with unlimited funds, he mounted an all-out attack on the eighteenth century. The record of his accomplishments, *The Rothschild Library, A Catalogue of the Collection of Eighteenth Century Printed Books and Manuscripts*, was a sumptuous two-volume, privately-printed showpiece. The catalog exhibited all the tendencies Carter deplored - over emphasis on original condition, a preponderance of high spots and association copies, and a complete disregard for the popular writers of the day, Maria Edgeworth and Regina Maria Roche, for example, in favor of established names such as Defoe, Fielding, Goldsmith, Gray, Pope, and Prior. Carter's review of the catalog was a masterpiece of thinly-veiled derision:

> To assemble a splendid collection, rich in rarities and masterpieces and remarkable for its very high average of condition, is an enviable thing.
>
> To publish a scholarly and ample catalogue of it is an admirable thing.
>
> Many bibliophiles have done the former, a few the latter; and Lord Rothschild has an honoured place among the best of them. The very quality of his achievement, however, and still more its deliberate restriction of period and scope, inevitably (and perhaps to him unwillingly) provoke the question whether the Rothschild library has exerted, or will exert, any significant influence on the taste, as distinct from the technique of other book collectors. His design called for concentration rather than initiative, for devotion rather than imagination.
>
> He has ridden - and won - an extremely stylish race over a well-known course, rather than explored open country. It is doubtful whether, even in twice the dozen years of his activity, anyone could do what he set out to do, either in assembly or exposition, better than he has done it. And if he has no ambition to open anyone else's eyes to unexplored avenues of bibliophily, who shall say that *incipit* is necessarily a more deserving word than *explicit.*[12]

The review emphasized Carter's fundamental belief that collectors should use their imaginations and explore new paths.

It would be an oversight to pass on without a mention of Carter's cause célèbre, the investigation of the Wise forgeries. Perhaps it is enough to say that as the co-author of the *Enquiry* he had two objectives: the explicit, to test the authenticity of a group of suspect pamphlets, and the implied, to warn collectors about the danger of accepting established wisdom. The *Enquiry* succeeded on both levels.

Carter, never timid in expressing his views, was particularly adamant in defending the integrity of the auction business. In a letter to the editor of *Antiquarian Bookman* he wrote:

> From p. B 16 of *Yearbook* section II I learn (in my 38th year in the rare book business) that auctioneers and property owners are "hoods," engaged in felonious conspiracy to manipulate or kite prices of books and manuscripts: thus defrauding the public and confusing the professional appraisers of the United States whose "civic duty" it is to protect not only the public but also, it seems, the government.
>
> I am appalled, as I am sure all your readers must be, by the notion of such skullduggery. Dr. Robert F. Metzdorf, that practised dispenser of alarm and despondency, cannot of course conceivably be attributing these goings-on to Parke-Bernet, of whose book department he was until quite recently in charge. He must therefore presumably be referring to the London auction houses - Sotheby's, Christies, Hodgsons and the rest - who were so often the target of his calumnies and complaints when he was in the auction business himself.
>
> As a professional appraiser it is Dr. Metzdorf's duty to know, and no doubt he does know, that it is illegal in England to bid against your own reserve; and that he is thus accusing the allegedly conniving London auctioneers of deliberate fraud. Will he now please come out from the undergrowth of innuendo; naming names and quoting chapter and verse for this apparently habitual malfeasance; so that appropriate action may be taken.[13]

Metzdorf never replied.

Regular readers of the Letters to the Editor columns of *The Times*, *Antiquarian Bokman*, the *Times Literary Supplement*, and half a dozen other journals and newspapers came to know Carter as a man of strong opinions. He objected when the government released an exchange of letters leading to a ministerial resignation. He chided the Post Office for issuing what he considered poorly designed stamps. He complained when newspaper editors allowed the use of what he called double-barrelled, simile-adjectives - April-fresh and thermometer-slim and complained once more when they removed quotation marks from expressions like "mods" and "rockers." Why, he asked, were so few women placed on the Honours List? He protested vehemently when Christie's advertised itself as "London's Leading Auction House." In a letter to the editor of *Antiquarian Bookman*, Carter reduced that claim to ashes. It was simply a matter of record, he wrote, that Sotheby's was founded twenty-two years earlier that Christie's and had for a decade produced an annual turnover exceeding its rival by over one hundred percent. Christie's might be most stately and most lovable and nearest to Buckingham Palace, Berry Brothers, and White's Club, but was by no means the leading auction house in London. Besides, as Carter reminded his readers in a delicate change of emphasis, "Our chairman is the taller by about half a foot."[14]

CHAPTER TWELVE

Summing Up

C hanges don't happen overnight, but in Carter's case they came rather quickly. After his work on the folio edition of *Printing and the Mind of Man*, completed in 1967, his publication record slowed. He contributed a handful of short articles to *The Book Collector*, reviews to the *Times Literary Supplement*, a scattering of letters to the editors of *The Antiquarian Bookman* and *The Times*, and a survey of private libraries in America to *American Libraries*, but that was the extent of it. His situation at Sotheby's also changed. When Parke-Bernet became an official branch of Sotheby's in 1965, and was able to offer consignors terms in New York equal to those in London, there was no further need for an agent to travel around the United States promoting the advantages of sales on Bond Street. With that job done, Carter became less active in the day-to-day flow of business in the book department and became more of a consultant - something of an outsider. From the time he joined the firm in 1955, without funds to secure a directorship, his status had always been marginal. The Sotheby's officers, although never completely sure about the appointment, accepted Carter as a man who obviously knew how to cultivate the American market. As an associate, he was not eligible to be a candidate when it came time to replace Hobson as head the book department, and for the same reason was never asked to call an auction, although his knowledge of books and his personal style would undoubtedly have made him an effective auctioneer. When Peter C. Wilson, Sotheby's chairman asked Carter to write the firm's history, it must have seemed, however graciously advanced, a make-do kind of assignment, and, uncomfortably, the phrase "putting the horse out to pasture" comes to mind.

It wasn't merely a diminished role at Sotheby's that troubled Carter in 1970 as he reached his sixty-fifth birthday. Other things were closing in. His health had never been robust, and now the years of high-pressure living began to take a toll. A knee injury suffered on the playing fields of Eton troubled him throughout his life. In the fall of 1970, he was admitted to a hospital in London for undisclosed reasons. Ernestine wrote to friends that he was very ill. He returned to the hospital in 1973 with a broken collarbone, and before that healed he suffered a mild stroke. "I'm still shaky all up my right side," he reported to Randall, "doctors seem helpless."[1] As a result, he was forced to cancel a trip to Bloomington where he had been asked to read a paper at the opening of the Lilly library's "Printing and the Mind of Man" exhibition. Three months later he wrote to Randall and his wife, "I had a small stroke, my second early in December, and though out of hospital I am still immobile and rather groggy. Happy (we all need it) New Year to you both and let's stay away from doctors."[2] Unfortunately, the New Year brought little good news. Again, he unburdened himself to Randall, " The first Horblit sale is scheduled for June 10. I devoutly hope I shall be better before then. At present I am still much below par, as you can see by my script, with all, very dispiriting."[3] A friend visiting in December noticed a hesitancy in speech and some loss of memory. Carter died on March 18, 1975.

Although health problems controlled his later years, there was much for Carter to look back on with satisfaction. As a professional dealer, and that was all he ever claimed to be, he had, with Randall's help, transformed Scribner's moribund book department into a thriving outlet, respected by those in the trade and by collectors both in the United States and overseas. His influence with American collectors and librarians, an area of expertise he could justifiably claim as his own, brought Sotheby's a series of important sales that helped establish the firm as the leading auction house in the world. His nomination as Sandars Reader in Bibliography at Cambridge, his election to the Presidency of the Bibliographical Society and his appointment as a Fellow at Eton College were all distinct honors. But again, his major accomplishments were in his writing. For over four decades he turned out a series of books, articles, reviews, and notes that were unrivaled in their elegant turn of phrase, concise analysis, and sound critical judgment. No one who has ever looked at a Carter draft, covered with his carefully inserted corrections and emendations, can miss his concern for both style and content. Even his post cards, and he sent hundreds, often written in a fine italic script, carry a distinctive flavor. In his writing, arguments are made, evidence produced, and conclusions reached all with a light touch. There is a winning charm in his style that few writers on the book arts, or any other arts, have been able to match. "If he ever wrote a bad sentence," the novelist and book dealer Larry McMurtry mused, "I haven't found it."[4]

Behind Carter's sophisticated professional manner there were several contradictions. The *Dictionary of National Biography* and most other reference sources identify him as a bibliographer, a title he never claimed for himself. He was, as he often said, a professional book dealer. His manner could be haughty, and although some called him a snob, others, including such rough and tumble characters as the book dealer I.R. Brussel and the editor of *Antiquarian Bookman*, Sol Malkin, admired him and considered him a friend. It seemed strange to some that he achieved more success as a rare book expert in the United States than in England. On the personal side, he maintained close friendships with rebels like Stanley Morison and Graham Pollard without subscribing to their political or religious beliefs. He was a politician without being interested in politics. His publications varied from scholarly essays in *The Transactions of the Bibliographical Society* to frivolities written for *The Bookseller*. After maintaining a close friendship with a colleague like Percy Muir for over thirty years, he could write a vitriolic letter in response to a perceived professional slight. He consistently turned down offers from libraries that would have given him a secure future. Neither friends or family were exempt from what might be called a penchant for social intimidation. On one occasion, in the stately Garrick Club dining room, he ordered partridge for his young nephew, Sebastian, and watched him struggle with it, while he ate scrambled eggs. He was conscious of his own heritage as the son of a country parson but was comfortable with the wealthy and powerful. His dress was elegant, if somewhat on the raffish side, perhaps, as a friend suggested, modeled on the image of his favorite screen actor Humphrey Bogart playing Philip Marlow in *The Big Sleep*. In England he was considered more American than British, but in the United States, with his pipe, monocle, elegant suits, and languid cultivated manner, he was taken as the personification of the

English gentleman. He was a traditionalist who criticized those who hid behind tradition. Carter balanced all these contradictions with consummate ease.

One contradiction deserves further comment. His dismissal of the title bibliographer seems excessively modest. He had, after all, been the co-author of one of the best known bibliographical studies of the century, served as President of the Bibliographical Society; won that organization's Gold Medal, and worked on the Advisory Board of the Soho Bibliographies. While it is true he never produced a "bibliography," so-named, preferring instead the less pretentious "Checklist" (Housman 1940) or "Handlist" (Cory 1949, Housman 1952, Morison 1950), he understood the purposes of bibliography and was able to transmit bibliographic information in concise and readable prose. He had no wish to pose as a bibliographical authority, having had the opportunity to observe that kind of pretension at first hand in the person of T. J. Wise. Carter believed in a common sense approach to bibliography. For him it meant an accurate, well-organized, annotated list, with an emphasis on satisfaction for the user. The Morison Handlist was a "utilitarian project" aimed at "scholars and amateurs in those typographic and calligraphic studies which owe him so much."[5] The Housman Handlist was for "the convenience of collectors and amateurs rather than for the instruction of literary critics,"[6] and the Cory Handlist was a "signpost for potential readers."[7] Carter placed more emphasis on provenance and publishing history than on detailed collations and title page transcription. In this he simply followed his own definitions of "Bibliography" and "Hand-List," from *ABC for Book Collectors*:

BIBLIOGRAPHY. The systematic description of books according to subject, class, period, author, country or district; or of the products of a particular press or publishing house. Bibliography may be enumerative, analytical or descriptive; ranging in method from a HAND LIST to a heavily annotated catalogue.[8]

HAND-LIST. Defined by SOED as 'a list of books, etc., in a form handy for reference', this term is commonly applied today to something considerably fuller than a SHORT TITLE list or a librarian's 'finding list', but considerably less full than a descriptive bibliography.[9]

Carter's common sense approach didn't come from any lack of interest in establishing accurate bibliographic detail. To the contrary, his contributions to the literature in behalf of accuracy are on display in myriad forms. From 1935 to 1939 in *Bibliographic Notes and Queries,* and continuing from 1952 in *The Book Collector*, Carter laid down a barrage of exacting questions and enlightening answers. As the author of thousands of catalog notes written first for Scribner's and then for Sotheby's, he observed the strictest kind of bibliographic control. His letters and cards to Josiah K. Lilly and Wilmarth S. Lewis, for example, are packed with informed comments on editions, printings, issues, binding states, and other details dear to the heart of the bibliographer and the discriminating collector. Carter's books and articles on nineteenth century binding variants are decidedly bibliographic in content. In his talk "Nineteenth Century English Books: Some Bibliographical Agenda," given at the University of Illinois Library School in 1951, Carter praised such notable figures as Henry Bradshaw, Robert Proctor, R B. McKerrow, A.W. Pollard, and W.W. Greg. They deserve applause, he insisted, for their attention to an uncharted and confusing period in the early history of printing. Regrettably, he commented, no one, aside from Sadleir, had taken much interest in the nineteenth century. Carter's remarks included a few barbs directed toward Fredson Bowers, a bibliographical theorist at the University of Virginia. It was encouraging, Carter said, that Bowers had at least considered nineteenth century problems in his scholarly monograph, *Principles of Bibliographical Description* (1949), but unfortunately his approach had been both dogmatic and inappropriate to the time period under consideration. Carter referred to Bowers as "a bibliographical pundit," a left-handed compliment at best, and identified him as possessing "a powerful, indeed an autocratic intelligence, addicted to formula and impatient of imprecision, at large in an area whose bibliography is still in a highly fluid, and therefore vulnerable, state." Finally, Carter found Bowers's intricate formula "unnecessarily elaborate for many of the books for which it is designed." It was unfortunate, Carter claimed, that Bowers's "attack on the nineteenth century has been conducted from a seventeenth-century base, and the tactics occasionally show signs of the rigidity natural to a cautious man operating in comparatively unfamiliar territory." Carter closed his remarks saying, "Professor Bowers's magisterial treatise is at once a landmark and a challenge."[10]

When it came to choosing the appropriate words, Carter had few rivals. When he applied "pundit," "autocratic," "addicted," "impatient," "rigidity," and "magisterial," to one man, his opinion was abundantly clear. It is quite possible that in arranging his remarks about Bowers's style Carter looked over his shoulder and saw the shadow of T. J. Wise, another bibliographical pundit who was autocratic, addicted, and magisterial. The argument was not over the importance of detail, but rather over the use of a bibliographic style appropriate to the material examined. It was a matter of applying what Falconer Madan identified in 1908 as the "Digressive Principle," a certain judicious elasticity in the bibliographic treatment of modern (anything printed after 1800) books.[11] While Carter was one of the first to question Bowers's approach, he would not be the last. Donald C. Gallup, the distinguished bibliographer of T. S. Eliot and Ezra Pound, wrote that signature collation was unnecessary for books published in the twentieth century.[12] In his 1953 presidential address before the members of the Bibliographical Society, Geoffrey Keynes, the compiler of bibliographies of Jane Austin, William Blake, Sir Thomas Browne, John Evelyn, and John Donne, among others, described bibliography as, "a fundamentally humane pursuit, shedding light not only on an author's printed texts, but also on his literary history, his life in general, his personality, and should often have as its main objective the establishment of the basic and final text of all his writings."[13] Responding to Bowers's claim that the old tabby cat of bibliography had grown into a tiger, Keynes countered, "The old tabby cat, innocent of streamlined brilliance, can still be well worth stroking by our firesides. It all depends on the kind of material that happens to be our object at the moment."[14] It was the same point Carter made two years earlier in his talk at the University of Illinois.

One major disappointment clouded Carter's bibliographic accomplishments. He and Pollard both considered the *Enquiry*, as it appeared in July 1934, to be a work in progress. The nature of the *Enquiry* was such that new information kept coming in. In 1945, Carter and Pollard had to cope with the important disclosure that a document in the Pforzheimer library proved Wise's guilt and H. Buxton Forman's complicity. Arrangements for publication of a supplement proceeded, fell backwards, and proceeded again, finally coming to rest in 1964 at the University of Chicago Press. The officers of the press agreed to republish the original 1934 volume along with a supplementary volume to bring the story up to date. It was not to be. Carter found it difficult to get revisions from Pollard and the press grew tired of waiting. The agreement collapsed. In 1983, John Collins and Nicolas Barker, edited a second edition the original volume and a supplement - *A Sequel to an Enquiry into the Nature of Certain Nineteenth Century Pamphlets.*

In Carter's view social success was nearly as important as professional success. The trick, and he managed it with a deft hand, was to blend the two. In this he had the complete support of Ernestine, who had her own circle of influential friends and who thoroughly enjoyed the whirl of London and Washington society. Hard working, determined, and articulate, the Carters were a formidable and sometimes intimidating couple. Carter was particularly adept at personal relations, especially when they suited his purpose. Give him a lunch date with an American collector, and chances were that the gentleman's, or preferably the lady's, paintings or books would shortly wind up in one of Sotheby's sales rooms. If he often got what he wanted out of these negotiations, it was equally true that the person sitting across from him at the luncheon table, pleased that the family treasures could elicit enthusiasm from such a charming Englishman, got what he or she wanted as well. Carter's frame of reference was large - prominent dealers, curators, bibliographers, editors, museum officers, librarians, and collectors all had their place in his address book. He was on a first-name basis with celebrities such as the radio broadcaster Edward R. Murrow, novelist Graham Greene, and, with ties formed in Washington, Secretary of State Dean Acheson, and Supreme Court Judge Felix Frankfurter. As a devoted balletomane, he enjoyed a long friendship with the British ballerina Margot Fonteyn. There was no need to drop names since it was clear from his conversation and demeanor that he knew and was known by the people worth knowing. If this was snobbery, so be it. Within Ernestine's circle it was the same. Trendsetters like Elizabeth Arden, Mary Quant, Jean Muir, and Gina Fratini all recognized her as an influential fashion journalist. It was said that when she recommended a certain style of dress on Sunday, the London stores would be out of stock by noon on Monday.

Both Carters earned good salaries during their lifetimes, but it was never quite enough. The upkeep on a large house and the cost of maintaining fashionable wardrobes along with a constant round of travel and entertaining meant expenses almost always exceeded income. Giving up the Carlyle Square house was a painful necessity. Old friends remained, although they were scattered - Tim Munby and Brooke Crutchley were in Cambridge, John Sparrow in Oxford, Rupert Hart-Davis in Yorkshire, and Percy Muir in Norfolk. This made it difficult to get a good turn-out for the monthly Biblios dinner meetings, but the Biblios carried on. Simon Nowell-Smith, one of the founding members, continued to attend, as did Dudley Massey, Howard M. Nixon, and Roger Senhouse. American friends David Randall, Michael Papantonio, William A. Jackson, and Wilmarth S. Lewis kept in touch on a regular basis and came by whenever they were in London. And there were new friends like Nicolas Barker, editor of *The Book Collector,* and Michael Meredith, the Eton School librarian. As for immediate family, Carter saw his brother Will whenever he came down from Cambridge on business. The Rampant Lions Press, under Will's direction, had become highly regarded on both sides of the Atlantic for its hand-somely designed and carefully executed printing. Carter and his brother worked together on several publications, beginning in 1938 with *Clerihews,* a pamphlet of light-hearted verse. In later life, however, even with the loyalty of old and new friends, the Carters felt discouraged. Health problems weighted them down as did the facts of reduced incomes and reduced status. It was time to be fru-gal but neither of them wanted to face that fact.

Money had always been a problem for Carter, since other people seemed to have more than he did. Certainly it was true at Eton, where some of the boys took summer vacations in Africa or the Far East and had parents with shooting lodges in Scotland. As a scholarship boy Carter spent his summers in school, or at home with the family. The atmosphere at Cambridge, another structured society, was somewhat the same. There were those who could trav-el down to London on a regular basis to enjoy the latest West End reviews, and others who had to be satisfied with the local cinema. There is no evidence that Carter felt abused by these circumstances, and in fact he looked back on the Eton and Cambridge years with deep appreciation. Still, it is impossible to believe that the differences in sta-tus and privilege made no impact. From the time Carter started working at Scribner's in 1927 until the close of the London office in 1953, money was a constant concern. In dozens of letters to Scribner's home office in New York,

Carter argued his case. He needed an increased salary because (a) housing costs had risen in London, (b) he had recently married, (c) he deserved the same salary as his New York counterpart whom, by the way, he had recruited, (d) he was asked to take on extra responsibilities, (e) he wanted to maintain Scribner's high standards but was unable to do so on his present wage. It was much the same after he joined Sotheby's. Over the years an archive of Carter's appeals grew in Peter Wilson's files.

By nature, Carter was a careful person. As his health deteriorated, he wanted to be sure the events surrounding his funeral would be carried out according to his wishes. In early 1970, he gave Ernestine an outline for the memorial service. He wanted it to take place in the Eton College Chapel, and burial to be alongside his father and grandfather in the cemetery on the Eton Wick road.[15] The service would follow the King James Bible and Edward VI's Prayer Book, with readings from John Donne's "Death, Be not Proud." "If a contralto could be found to sing "Swing Low Sweet Chariot," he wrote, "it makes a good anthem but probably, not practical."[16] He wanted the choir to sing Housman's "O thou that from thy mansion" as harmonized to J. S. Bach. The Rampant Lions Press would print the order of service. On Monday, May 5, 1975, all was done as he wished - Lord Redcliffe-Maud, a friend from Eton days, delivered the address honoring Carter's life and unique accomplishments.

It is impossible to look closely at Carter's career and not notice the stamp of his mentors: A.E. Housman for his challenging ideas on the application of intelligence to all serious endeavors, Michael Sadleir for his originality and bibliographic perception, Stanley Morison for his wide-ranging curiosity and William Johnson Cory for his lucid views on the goals of education. All left their marks, but Cory's precepts - pay attention to minute points of accuracy and strive for self-knowledge - were perhaps the most influential.

In his address at the memorial service Redcliffe-Maud emphasized Carter's independent personality.[17] From his early days at Sunningdale and Eton, where he excelled both as a student and as an athlete, he seemed to know who he was. By the time he entered Cambridge, he had established a controlled way of dealing with people and situations. One bent, if necessary, but never sacrificed the freedom to maneuver. Carter's study of textual criticism with Housman, that austere intellectual with a passion for truth, reinforced his belief in the importance of disciplined independence. He turned down library positions because he knew he wouldn't enjoy a regimented life. He avoided the detailed kinds of research that lacked personal appeal. A bibliography of Catullus would certainly have been an important contribution, but it was a task for a scholar and he knew he wasn't one. He wrote about things that interested him - happily, they also interested a wide range of bibliophiles.

Carter's fame rests on his eloquently crafted books and articles, many unique for their time. Who else could have written the concise, sometimes saucy definitions that make up *ABC for Book Collectors* - a book that continues to sell at the rate of several thousand copies a year? Who else could have so convincingly pilloried T. J. Wise? Could anyone else have pulled together the various strands that made *Printing and the Mind of Man* the classic reference source it turned out to be? As for his career as a bookdealer, who else could have charmed American collectors into buying hundreds of thousands of dollars worth of rare books during one decade, and then selling them back to a London auction house in the next? Could anyone else have managed to locate Blake's *Jerusalem* and a Gutenberg Bible in England and sell them to collectors in the United States in the course of a year? As for his diplomatic career, could the British ambassador to the United States have chosen a more urbane and knowledgeable personal assistant? Carter carried off these accomplishments, as one admirer observed, with a "felicity in style and analytical tenacity."[18]

Beginning collectors often ask experienced librarians, bibliographers, bookdealers, and curators to recommend good background reading on books and book collecting. Over the last seventy years the advice has never changed - "Read John Carter; he's the best!"

NOTES ON ABBREVIATIONS

Citations to books are given in shortened form. Richard Ollard's *An English Education, a Perspective of Eton*, for example, is given as Ollard. Full citations can be found in the Selected Bibliography. Frequently cited journals and newspapers, books, people, and the location of library archives are also given in abbreviated form.

People –
NB: Nicolas Barker
JWC: John Carter
RHD: Rupert Hart-Davis
HG: Herbert Gorfin
JH: John Hayward
CK: Charles Kingsley
AAK: Alfred A. Knopf
WSL: Wilmarth S. Lewis
JEL: Josiah E. Lilly
SM: Stanley Morison
PM: Percy Muir

ANLM: A.N.L."Tim" Munby
GP: Graham Pollard
DR: David Randall
MS: Michael Sadleir
CS I: Charles Scribner
CS II: Charles Scribner
CS III: Charles Scribner
CS Jr: Charles Scribner Jr.
PCW: Peter C. Wilson
TJW: Thomas J. Wise

Newspapers, Journals and Reference Sources –
AB: *Antiquarian Bookman*
ABC: *American Book Collector*
BC: *Book Collector*
BN&Q: *Bibliographical Notes & Queries*
DNB: *Dictionary of National Biography*
NSN: *New Statesman and Nation*
NYT: *New York Times*
PW: *Publishers' Weekly*
PBSA: *Papers of the Bibliographical Society of America*
TLS: *Times Literary Supplement*

Archives –
BOD: Bodleian Library, Oxford University
CA: Cambridge University Library

ECL: Eton College Library
IND: Indiana University, Lilly Library
KCL: King's College Library, Cambridge University
PML: Pierpont Morgan Library
NL: Newberry Library
PR: Princeton University Library
SC: Sebastian Carter. Family papers
TX: University of Texas, Humanities Research Center
UCLA: University of California at Los Angeles
YLW: Yale University, Lewis/Walpole Library

Books –
ABC: *ABC for Book Collectors*, 1952
BBC: *Books and Book Collectors*, 1956
ENQ: *An Enquiry Into the Nature of Certain Nineteenth Century Pamphlets.* 1934
NP: *New Paths in Book Collecting*, 1934
PMM 1: *Printing and the Mind of Man*, 1963
PMM 2: *Printing and the Mind of Man*, 1967
PMM 3: *Printing and the Mind of Man*, 1983
TNT 1: *Taste & Technique in Book Collecting*, 1948
TNT 2: *Taste & Technique in Book Collecting*, 1970

CHAPTER ONE NOTES

1. JWC to ANLM, 12 Feb. 1949. KCL
2. Frank Herrmann, "John Carter," *DNB* 1971-1980, p. 125.
3. Birth and death dates for Carter's immediate family: Rev. Thomas B. Carter 1871-1934; Margaret Theresa Carter 1875-1942; Mary Carter 1907-1940; Elizabeth Carter Hale 1908-1988; William Carter 1912-2001. SC
4. *Eton Chronicle,* 18 Dec.1901.
5. A detailed history of the Stone family is given in Faith Compton Mackenzie's *As Much As I Dare,* 1938.
6. Mackenzie, p.162.
7. JWC quoted in *Current Biography*, 1959, p. 57.
8. Orwell, p.19.
9. Information provided by Nicolas Dawson, Sunningdale Headmaster, in a letter to the author, 3 Nov. 2000.
10. Ollard, p. 19.
11. Brownrigg, p. 40.
12. W.E. Gladstone, quoted in Ollard, p. 197.

13. Penelope Fitzgerald, *The Knox Brothers*, Washington D.C.: Counterpoint, 2000. p. 44.
14. Ollard, p. 95.
15. Ibid.
16. JWC to Margaret Stone Carter, 23 July 1921. ECL
17. The Wall Game, played against a 120 yard wall bordering the college playing field, is described in detail in Brownrigg, pp. 65-70.
18. "John Carter." *Eton College Chronicle*, 30 Nov. 1923.
19. Connolly, p.233.
20. A sample of Eton recollections includes, Cyril Connolly, *Enemies of Promise* - Henry Green, *Pack My Bag* – Anthony Powell, *To Keep the Ball Rolling* - Edward Lyttelton, *Memories and Hopes* - H. S. Salt, *Memories of Bygone Eton* and Bernard Fergusson, *Eton Portrait*.
21. JWC, "Farewell, Catullus," *Texas Quarterly*, Autumn 1960, p. 275.
22. Ibid., p. 276.
23. William Johnson Cory, quoted in Ollard, pp.64-65.
24. JWC, "A Hand-List of the Printed Works of William Johnson, Afterwards Cory," *Transactions of the Cambridge Bibliographical Society*, 1949, pp. 69-87.
25. Ollard, p.18.
26. Williamson, *A Century*, p. 76.
27. Arthur Watkins, "John Carter," typescript, n.d. SC
28. JWC, "Farewell Catullus," p. 276.
29. Leslie, p. 87.
30. Carter dedicated his first book, *Binding Variants in English Publishing 1820-1900*, to Professor Turner.
31. JWC, "Farewell Catullus," p. 277.
32. A. E. Housman, "The Application of Thought to Textual Criticism," in *A. E. Housman Selected Prose*, pp. 131-132.
33. Ibid., p. 150.
34. Arthur E. Cowley, quoted by JWC in his presidential address to the Bibliographical Society, 1969, *TNT* 2, p. 218.

CHAPTER TWO NOTES

1. Scribner's was the only American publishing firm in the early decades of the century to have a fully staffed London office.
2. The history of Elkin Mathews and the expansion of the business under the direction of A. W. Evans and his partners is described in Percy Muir's *Minding My Own Business*, 1956.
3. PM to JWC, 19 Jan. 1940. IND
4. JWC to PM, 24 Jan. 1940. IND

5. Meynell, p. 157.

6. GP to JWC, 1931. BOD

7. Of the dinner meeting of 31 January 1934, Carter wrote, "An animated, even acrimonious, discussion succeeded the paper which was 'The Rise of Process Engraving' presented by F. J. Newbery. Mr. Fairleigh and Mr. Rooke stated their abhorrence of reproductions in general and the half-tone process in particular. Messrs Hewitt, Foss, Lewis and Cleverdon took them up on various points, demolishing some of Mr. Fairleigh's more irrelevant tirades to the satisfaction (it seemed) of the majority present, and Mr. Balston made a speech which was remarkable as being the only one pertinent to Mr. Newbery's paper." Moran, p. 30.

8. CK to CS II, 30 Sept. 1927. PR

9. CK to CS II, 28 Dec. 1927. PR

10. CK to CS II, 20 March 1928. PR

11. CK to CS II, 14 April 1928. PR

12. CK to CS II, 14 Jan. 1930. PR

13. CS II to CK, 18 Jan. 1929. PR

14. JWC to GP, 10 Feb. 1929. BOD

15. John Champion to Mrs. Insley Blair, 5 Jan. 1929. In possession of the author.

16. Ibid.

17. JWC, *TNT* 1, p.57.

18 Randall p.18.

19. Dauber & Pine *Catalog One Hundred*, 1931.

20. Ibid.

21. JWC, "I.R.Brussel LOGS," *AB*, 25 Dec.1972, p. 2096.

22. JWC, *TNT* 1, p. 216.

23. Ibid.

24. Charles Heartman, "Collecting," *American Book Collector*, Jan. 1932, p. 4.

25. The 1970 edition of Carter's *Taste & Technique in Book Collecting* was dedicated to "Two good friends of the bibliophile fraternity, S.C. Roberts of Cambridge (who got me appointed Sandars Reader) and Frederick G. Melcher of New York (who commissioned my first article on book-collecting) p. xiv.

26. JWC, "Original Condition," *PW*, 15 Nov. 1930, p. 2279.

27. JWC, "Looking Forward," *PW*, 20 June 1931, p. 2891.

28. JWC, "Looking Backward," *PW*, 17 Jan. 1931, p. 331.

29. CS III to CK, 23 May 1929. PR

30. CK to CS III, 4 June 1929. PR

31. Arthur Scribner to CK, 10 Jan. 1930. PR

32. CK to CS III, 9 Sept. 1929 PR

33 CK to CS III, 28 Dec. 1929. PR

34. CS III to JWC, 10 June 1931. PR

35. JWC to CS III, 30 Aug 1929. PR Carter's aunt Faith was married to Montague Compton Mackenzie.

36. CS III to JWC, 1 Sept. 1929. PR

37. CK to CS III, 4 July 1930. PR

38. CS III to CK, 16 July 1930. PR

39. JWC, "Hawkshaw Rides Again," *BC*, Summer 1963, p. 178.

40. JWC, "Introduction," Scribner's Catalog 98, 1934.

41. JWC, "Hawkshaw Rides Again," p. 180. According to Randall, the day the catalog was put in the mail a lady walked into Scribner's and bought the entire collection, she claimed, for leisure reading. Years later the books came back on the market and Randall bought them for the Lilly Library at Indiana University. Randall, p. 211.

42. CK to CS III, 8 Dec.1932. PR

43. JWC, "Introduction" Scribner's Catalog 102, 1935.

44. Ibid.

45. Muir, p. 157. Muir described his successful buying trip in detail in Chapter 16, "Adventures in Search of Music."

46. For a complete account of the transaction see Muir, pp. 193-197 and Randall pp. 59-60.

47. JWC, "Introduction" Scribner's Catalog 113, 1938.

48. JWC, "Introduction" Scribner's Catalog 117, 1938.

49. Ibid.

50. JWC to JH, Handwritten note in Scribner's Catalog 137, 1952 ECL

51. JWC, "Bibliography and the Book Trade," *PBSA*, third quarter 1954, p. 221.

52. CK to SCII, 22 July 1932. PR

53. CS III to JWC, 3 Aug. 1932. PR

54. CS III to JWC, 8 Aug. 1934. PR

55. *The Colophon*, Summer 1935, p. 158.

56. JWC and DR, typescript, 14 May 1935. PR

57. CS III to CK, 7 May 1935. PR

58. In the margin of a typed letter of 10 August 1935, JWC wrote to CSIII that his marriage plans had "come unstitched."

CHAPTER THREE NOTES

1. JWC, "Looking Backward," *PW*, 17 Jan. 1931, p. 330.

2. JWC, "Looking Forward," *PW*, 20 June 1931, p. 2890.

3. JWC, "Sadleir Rides Again," *TLS*, 30 Oct. 1970, p. 1280.

4. MS, "Decentralization or Deadlock," *The Colophon*, Winter 1930.

5. JWC, "Looking Backward," *PW*, 17 Jan. 1931, p. 330.
6. JWC, "An Unsolicited Review," *BC*, Spring 1969, p. 57.
7. JWC, "Memorandum for Contributors" typescript, n.d. BOD
8. JWC, *NP*, p.10.
9. JWC, Foreword in *Catalogue of an Exhibition Arranged to Illustrate New Paths in Book Collecting.* London: J. and E. Bumpus, 1934.
10. JWC, "An Unsolicited Review," *BC*, Spring 1969, p. 60.
11. Charles Heartman," *ABC*, Dec. 1935, p. 57.
12. Ibid.
13. [Simon Nowell-Smith], *TLS*, 27 Dec.1934, p. 918.
14. MS, Letter to the Editor, *TLS*, 10 Jan. 1935. p 21.
15. Ralph Wright, *NSN*, 13 April 1935, p. 534.
16. *Life and Letters*, Nov. 1934, p. 242.
17. JWC, "An Unsolicited Review," *BC*, Spring 1969, p. 59.
18. Sadleir chose *Evolution of Publishers' Binding Styles 1770-1900* to launch his acclaimed Bibliographia Series. Between 1930 and 1938 he issued eight handsomely designed volumes in the series.
19. JWC, "Notes on the Early Years of Cloth Binding," *Book Collector's Quarterly*, April 1932, pp. 46-56.
20. JWC, Preface, *Binding Variants in English Publishing 1820-1900*, London: Constable, 1932.
21. Ibid., p. 89.
22. Ibid., p. 84.
23. E.A.Osborne, *PW*, 16 July 1932, p. 209.
24. *TLS*, 7 July 1932, p. 525.
25. JWC, Preface, *Publisher's Cloth* London: Constable, 1935. pp. 5-6.
26. *TLS*, 11 March 1939, p. 156.
27. Patricia Herrmann to the author, 4 Dec. 2002.
28. JWC and MS, "The Nomenclature of Nineteenth Century Cloth Grains," *BC*, Summer 1953, pp. 54-58.
29. JWC to Philip Gaskell, 9 Oct. 1972. CA
30. PM, *PW*, 21 Jan. 1939, p. 230.
31. JWC, 2 Sept. 1943. BOD
32. JWC, *TNT2*, p. 211.
33. JWC, "The Edition or Impression Controversy." *PW*, 16 April 1932, p. 1733.
34. Ibid.
35. JWC, *TLS*, 29 Sept. 1932, p. 411.
36. JWC, *TLS*, 27 April 1933, p. 300; 4 May 1933, p. 316.
37. A. E. Newton, *BN&Q*, Jan. 1935, p. 12.
38. "Appeal to Subscribers," *BN&Q*, April 1936, p. 1.
39. Ibid.

40. JWC, "London Rare Book Notes," *PW,* 15 June 1940, p. 2297.

41. JWC, "Michael Sadleir, a Valediction," *BC,* Spring 1958, p. 58.

42. JWC, "The Iniquity of Oblivion Foil'd," *BC,* Autumn 1966. pp. 279-282.

43. Cassell printed one copy bound with a portfolio of Nash's original drawings for sale for 350 guineas.

44. *TLS,* 19 Jan. 1933, p. 36.

45. Herbert Read, *Philosophy of Modern Art* London: Faber & Faber, 1952, p. 180.

46. In 1946 the Rampant Lions Press published a limited edition of *The Last Chapter of Urne Buriall.*

47. *PW,* 19 Nov. 1932, p. 1926.

48. JWC, *PW,* 20 Aug. 1932, p. 585.

49. JWC, "A Notable Bibliography," *PW,* 21 May 1932, p. 217.

50. JWC, *PW,* 20 Aug. 1932, p. 585.

51. JWC, *PW,* 16 Jan. 1932, p. 287.

CHAPTER FOUR NOTES

1. JWC, "Thomas J. Wise and His Forgeries," *Atlantic Monthly,* March 1945, p. 100.

2. Sidney Cockerell and F. S. Ellis, "A Warning to Collectors," *Athenaeum,* 20 Nov.1897.

3. George D. Smith, *Price Current of Books,* 8th number, 1898.

4. George D. Smith, "To All Young Collectors and Some Old Ones," *The Library Collector,* March 1901.

5. JWC to TJW, 19 Dec. 1932. TX

6. TJW to JWC, 20 Dec. 1932. TX

7. JWC, letter to *TLS,* 29 Sept. 1932.

8. TJW to JWC, 27 April 1933. CA

9. JWC, letter to *TLS,* 4 May 1933.

10. TJW to JWC, 5 June 1933. CA

11. JWC to TJW, 15 June 1933. CA

12. TJW to JWC, 9 Sept. 1933. CA

13. JWC to TJW, 23 Sept. 1933. CA

14. Mr. Mudie, quoted by JWC in "How We Got Wise," *Sunday Times Magazine* 8 March 1940. p 41.

15. JWC, "Graham Pollard," in *Studies in the Book Trade in Honour of Graham Pollard.* Oxford: Oxford Bibliographical Society, 1975. p. 5.

16. SM to GP, 9 Jan. 1933. TX

17. Flora Livingston to JWC, 6 April 1933. TX

18. JWC and GP, *ENQ,* p. 167.

19. Flora Livingston to JWC, 18 Jan. 1933. TX
20. JWC to Herbert Gorfin, 20 Aug. 1933. TX
21. TJW quoted by JWC in *Gorfin's Stock,* Working paper no. 4. Oxford: B.H. Blackwell, 1970, p. 10.
22. Herbert Gorfin quoted in *Gorfin's Stock,* pp.10-11.
23. JWC to Miss L.M. Gorfin, 11 Aug. 1950. TX
24. JWC to Miss L.M. Gorfin, 15 Aug. 1950. TX
25. J.P.R. Lyell, "Report," 12 Dec. 1933. TX
26. JWC to MS, 28 Dec. 1933. TX
27. Both affidavits are printed in full in *Gorfin's Stock,* pp. 3-11.
28. Wells, pp. 4-5.
29. TJW, letter to *TLS,* 24 May 1934.
30. *The Sunday Times,* 24 June 1934.
31. "First Edition Forgeries," *The Times,* 29 June 1934.
32. *Daily Herald,* 30 June 1934. p. 1.
33. Ibid.
34. JWC to MS, 9 June 1934. TX
35. John Sparrow, "A True Detective Story," *Spectator,* 6 July 1934.
36. Dorothy Sayers, "Authenticity of Famous First Editions," *The Sunday Times,* 1 July 1934.
37. John Hayward, "Fraud Detected," *NSN,* 7 July 1934, p. 17.
38. DR, "A Bibliographical Sensation," *PW,* 7 July 1934, p. 54.
39. Philip Brooks, *NYT,* 15 July 1934, p. 2.
40. R.B.McKerrow, *The Library,* 4th series, number 3, 1934, p. 383.
41. Ibid.
42. JWC and GP, *ENQ,* p. 3.
43. Ibid. pp.152-153.
44. Ibid. p.[v.].
45 Geoffrey Keynes, to JWC, 6 July 1934. TX
46. Max Harzof to JWC, 29 June 1934. TX
47. Holbrook Jackson to JWC, 17 July 1934.... TX
48. W.T..Howe to JWC, 30 June 1934. TX
49. TJW, letter to *TLS,* 12 July 1934, p. 492.
50. Herbert Gorfin, letter to *TLS,* 19 July 1934, p. 511.
51. JWC to Viscount Esher, 8 Aug. 1934. TX
52. Viscount Esher, letter to *TLS,* 22 Aug. 1934, p. 577.
53. Philip Brooks, *NYT,* 3 July 1949.
54. JWC and GP, Introductory statement printed in all four Working papers.
55. JWC to William Todd, 10 Aug. 1971. TX
56. Among the radio and television productions were, "The Clandestine Activities of Thomas J. Wise," written and produced by Stephen Potter from material supplied by John Carter, for which he received a fee of

thirty guineas - "The Case of the Kernless f," BBC Home Services Broadcast 13 April 1961, and "The Wise Forgeries," BBC television production, 12 November 1966. Carter received £250 for making his home available for two days of shooting for the 1966 program.

57. TJW letter reproduced in Fannie Rathchford's, *Between the Lines,* Austin: University of Texas Press, 1945, pp. 10-11.

58. JWC to Carl Pforzheimer, 14 Feb. 1936. TX

59. William Jackson to JWC, 26 June 1935. TX

60. JWC to GP, 13 Oct. 1938. BOD

61 GP to JWC, 20 Oct. 1938. BOD

62. JWC, "The Thomas J. Wise Forgeries," *Atlantic Monthly,* Feb. 1945, pp. 93-100.

63. Edmund Blunden, letter to *TLS,* 28 Sept. 1946, p. 472.

64. JWC, letter to *PW,* 26 Oct. 1946.

65. JWC and GP, "T.J. Wise and Buxton Forman: Further Light on the 19th Century Pamphlets," *TLS,* 1 June 1946, p. 264.

66. DR, *PW,* 8 June 1946, p. 3056.

67. Fannie Ratchford, letter to *PW,* 17 Aug. 1946, p. 717.

68. JWC, "Thomas J. Wise in Perspective," in *Thomas J. Wise Centenary Studies,* Austin: University of Texas Press, 1959, p. 19.

69. D. F. Foxon, "Another Skeleton in Thomas J. Wises' Cupboard," *TLS,* 19 Oct. 1956.

70. John Collins and Nicolas Barker, *A Sequel to An Enquiry,* London: Scolar Press, 1983, p. 124.

71. JWC to GP, Sept. 1969. BOD

CHAPTER FIVE NOTES

1. A photograph reproduced in *PW,* 27 Sept. 1941, p. 2291, shows Carter, Dust and Hale standing outside the front door of Scribner's 23 Bedford Square office. The caption says "Carter is wearing, in deference to wives' prior claim to their husbands' clothes ration cards, an overcoat made in 1925."

2. JWC to Helen Clapitt, 4 Nov. 1939 IND

3. JWC to CS III, 13 Sept. 1939. PR

4. JWC to CK, 13 Sept. 1939. PR

5. JWC to CS III, 1 Nov. 1939. PR

6 CS III to JWC, 9 Nov. 1939. PR

7. CK to CS III, 3 Feb. 1936. PR

8. JWC to CS III, 22 July 1936. PR

9. Ernestine described the wedding in her autobiography, *With Tongue in Chic.* p. 51. The wedding party traveled to Harrison, New York in an ancient Rolls Royce there to be married by an inebriated Justice of the Peace. A photograph used as a wedding announcement shows the couple bundled into heavy coats standing outside the town clerk's office looking very happy.

10. Philip Hofer to PM, 24 Jan. 1937. IND

11. This copy came to Scribner's with a distinguished provenance - from W. A. White, through A.S.W. Rosenbach, to W. A. Clark to Harrison Post to Tone Price, and finally to Scribner's. At the auction of John Carter's personal library on 24 March 1976, the rare book dealer Martin Breslauer bought the copy for $1,800, the highest price given for any item at the sale.

12. CK to CS III, 15 July 1937. PR

13 CS III to CK, 23 July 1937. PR

14. JWC to CK, 3 April 1938. PR

15. JWC, "To Our Friends the Antiquarian Booksellers." 20 Sept. 1939.

16. JWC to PM, 26 Oct. 1939. IND

17. PM to JWC, 28 April 1940. IND

18. JWC to PM, 29 April 1940. IND

19. JWC to PM, 30 Sept. 1941. IND

20. PM to JWC, 12 Mach 1943. IND

21 JWC to PM, 21 April 1941. IND

22. JWC, "The Rare Book Trade In London," *PW,* 13 Jan. 1940, p. 132.

23. JWC, "A Bookseller's Day in London," *PW,* 2 Nov. 1940, p. 1764.

24. JWC to Helen Clampitt, 4 Nov. 1938. IND

25. JWC to CK, 15 Jan. 1949. PR

26. CK to CS III, 15 Jan. 1940. PR

27. JWC to CS III, 12 July 1940. PR

28. JWC to CS III, 20 July 1940. PR

29. JWC to CS III, 13 May 1945. PR

30. CS III to JWC, 13 Dec. 1945. PR

31. JWC to CS III, 7 Oct. 1949. PR

32. For a detailed account of the Blake transaction, see Chapter 11.

33. JWC to DR, 15 Jan. 1950, IND

34. DR to Estelle Doheny, 21 Jan. 1950. IND

35. DR to JWC, 22 Jan. 1950. PR

36. JWC to John Howard, 30 Jan. 1950. PR

37. JWC, "Operation Shuckburgh," *Bookseller,* 17 Feb. 1951.

38. DR to Lawrence Clark Powell, 13 Dec. 1951. UCLA

39. Gordon Ray to Lawrence Clark Powell, 20 Dec. 1951. UCLA

40. The purchase of the Sadleir books is described in some detail in "In Search of Sadleir," by Bradford A. Booth in *Bradford Booth & the Sadleir Collection: Three Dedicatory Essays.* (Los Angeles: The Friends of the UCLA Library, 1973) pp. 385-390, and in *The Sadleir Collection,* Address Delivered by Frederick B. Adams, Jr., and David Randall at the Dedication Ceremonies, University of California at Los Angeles Library November 13, 1952. Los Angeles: Friends of the UCLA Library, 1953.
41. JWC to George Schieffelin, 14 July 1952.
42. Ernestine Carter to CS Jr., 16 Sept. 1953. PR
43. Ernestine Carter to CS Jr., 23 Sept. 1953. PR
44. JWC to ANLM, 18 Oct. 1953. KCL
45. JWC to ANLM, Nov. 1953. KCL
46. JWC, "The Dry Martini," in Ernestine Carter *Flash in the Pan.* London: Hamish Hamilton, 1953, p. 129.
47. JWC, "Sotheby's of London, New York: the Early Days." *Art at Auction 1970-197,* pp. 34-47.

CHAPTER SIX NOTES

1. JWC, "Fashions in Book-Collecting," *Virginia Quarterly Review,* Spring 1950, p. 385.
2. JWC, "Off Subject Books," *The Colophon,* Autumn 1935, p. 201.
3. JWC, "The Library of Frank Hogan," *The Colophon,* Winter 1939, p.55.
4. JWC, "Rarity," *ABC,* p. 152.
5. Frank Herrmann, "John Carter," *DAB,* 1971-1980, p. 124.
6. JWC, "Stock Taking," *PW,* 20 Dec. 1941. p. 2241.
7. John T. Winterich, "Through Fire and Flood with the Colophon," *PW,* 22 Nov. 1947, p. 2398.
8. JWC, "Bibliography and the Rare Book Trade," *PBSA,* 3rd quarter 1954, p. 219.
9. JWC, "On Collecting A.E.Housman," *The Colophon,* Winter 1938, pp. 54-62.
10. JWC, "A Footnote," in *A.E.Housman, A Collection of Manuscripts, Letters, Proofs, First Editions, Etc.* Formed by H.B. Collamore of West Hartford, Connecticut. Presented to the Lilly Library, Indiana University. Bloomington: The Lilly Library, 1961, pp. 35-36.
11. JWC to DR, 2 March 1961. IND
12. DR, "The John Carter Collection of A. E. Housman," Bloomington: The Lilly Library, 8pp., [1965] Limited to 600 copies.
13. A.E.Housman quoted in *A.E. Housman Selected Prose,* edited by John Carter. Cambridge: Cambridge University Press, 1961, p.1.

14. JWC and JS, "A.E.Housman an Annotated Check-List," *The Library*, Sept. 1940, p. 160.

15. A.E. Housman quoted in *A.E.Housman an Annotated Hand-List*, edited by John Carter and John Sparrow. London: Rupert Hart-Davis, 1952. p. 35.

16. William White letters in *TLS*, 26 Sept. 1952, p. 693; 12 Feb.1954, p. 432; Tom Burns Haber letter in *TLS*, 2 Oct. 1953, p. 756.

17. JWC letter to *TLS*, 24 Oct. 1952, p. 445.

18. Tom Burns Haber, *A.E.Housman*, Boston: Twayne, 1967, p. 105.

19. JWC, "The A.E. Housman Manuscripts in the Library of Congress," *BC*, Summer 1955, pp. 110-114.

20. DR, p.163.

21. JWC to DR, 2 March 1961. IND

22. M.I. Finley, *NSN*, 15 Dec. 1961, p. 926.

23. A.E.Housman, "The Application of Thought to Textual Criticism," in *Selected Prose*, p. 150.

24. A.E. Housman to S.C. Roberts, 3 July 1928. CA

25. JWC, "Farewell Catullus," *Texas Quarterly*, Autumn 1960, p. 282

26. William B. Todd to Harry Ransom, 19 April 1960. TX

27. Lord Beaverbrook quoted by JWC in *PW*, 2 Nov. 1940, p. 1764.

28. JWC, "London Rare Book Notes," *PW*, 19 April 1941, p. 1678.

29. JWC, "A Bookseller's Day in London," *PW*, 2 Nov. 1940, p. 1765.

30. JWC, "Clough to Churchill," *PW*, 2 Aug. 1941, p. 311.

31. JWC, ed., *Clerihews*, Cambridge: Rampant Lions Press, 1938.

32. [JWC], ed., *Clerihews*, Cambridge: Rampant Lions Press, 1946.

33. JWC to Brooke Crutchley, 22 April 1952. CA

34. Cover photograph *AB*, 31 July 1948.

35. JWC, *TNT* 1, p. x.

36. Among the many titles on the topic are Thomas F. Dibdin, *The Bibliomania*, 1809; Holbrook Jackson, *The Anatomy of Bibliomania*, 1931; A.E.Newton, *The Amenities of Book Collecting, 1918* and *This Book Collecting Game*, 1928; A.S.W. Rosenbach, *Books and Bidders*, 1927; Iola Williams, *The Elements of Book-Collecting*, 1927 and John T. Winterich, *A Primer of Book Collecting*, 1927.

37. JWC, *TNT* 1, pp. 9-10.

38. Ibid., p. 186.

39. John T. Winterich, *PW*, 31 July 1948, p. 162.

40. Frank C. Francis, *Library*, June 1950, p. 72.

41. Donald Wing, *Yale Review*, Winter 1949, p. 378.

42. [John Hayward], *TLS*, 1949, p. 660.

43. Geoffrey Keynes, to JWC, Nov. 1948. TX

44. Larry McMurtry, "Mad About the Book," *New York Review of Books,* 20 Dec. 2001, p. 58.
45. Scribner's was not interested in publishing the book. After an aborted discussion with Little Brown, Carter sold the American rights to R.R. Bowker.
46. JWC, Memorandum to Percy Muir, John Hayward, John Sparrow, Tim Munby, Dudley Massey and Simon Nowell-Smith, 20 Sept. 1950. KCL
47. AAK to JWC, 7 May 1951.
48. JWC to AAK, 14 June 1951. CA
49. JWC to RHD, 9 May 1951. CA
50. JWC, "Preface," *ABC,* 1952, p.9.
51. Ibid., p. 8.
52. MS, *Spectator,* 19 Sept. 1952.
53. WSL, *BC,* Winter 1952, p. 271.
54. SM, quoted by JWC in "Preface," *ABC* 1960. p. 11.
55. JWC, *Bookseller,* 29 Sept. 1952, p. 74..
56. JWC, "Preface," *ABC* 1953, p. 10.
57. JWC to AAK, 30 Aug. 1956 CA

CHAPTER SEVEN NOTES

1. JWC to Frederick B. Adams, 25 April 1954. PML
2. Frederick B. Adams to JWC, 4 May 1954. PML
3. JWC to C. Vere Pilkington, 16 Dec. 1953. CA
4. C. Vere Pilkington to JWC, 17 Feb. 1955. CA
5. JWC to Frederick B. Adams, 10 Jan. 1955. PML
6. Donald Hyde to JWC, 20 Jan. 1955. CA
7. JWC to DR, 6 June 1957. IND
8. JWC, "Sotheby's of London; New York: the Early Days," *Art at Auction 1970-1971,* 1971, p. 37.
9. JWC, reprinted in *BC,* Summer 1956, p. 109.
10. JWC reprinted in Towner, p. 605.
11. JWC, "Sotheby's of London, New York; the Early Days:" *Art at Auction 1970-1971,* p. 41.
12. Ibid., p. 42.
13. JWC, Memorandum in typescript, June 1961. CA
14. Ibid.
15. JWC to Sevellon Brown, Editor of the *Providence Journal,* 1 March 1956. CA
16. DR, p.353.
17. JWC to DR, 10 July 1955. IND

18. Ibid.
19. JWC to DR, 24 Jan. 1956. IND
20. DR to JWC, 5 March 1957. IND
21. JWC to DR, copy to Herman Wells, 22 Oct. 1959. IND
22. JWC to DR, 21 Jan 1960. IND
23. JWC to Herman Wells, 11 Oct. 1960. IND
24. DR to JWC, 27 April 1962. IND
25. Elvis J. Stahr, "Foreword," *Incunabula, American Literary & Scientific Classics - Duplicates from the Lilly Library.* New York: Parke-Bernet, 1962.
26. JWC to DR, 8 Oct. 1962. IND
27. JWC, "Sotheby's of London; New York; the Early Days:" *Art at Auction 1970-1971,* 1971, p. 41.
28. JWC, "Eastward the Course of Empire," *AB Yearbook 1955,* p. 10.
29. JWC, "The Pendulum of Taste," *Atlantic Monthly,* Oct. 1956, p. 69.
30. William A. Jackson to JWC, 15 Oct. 1956. CA
31. JWC, "Playing the Rare Book Market," *Harper's,* April 1960, p. 7.
32. JWC, "Sotheby's of London; New York: the Early Days:" *Art at Auction 1970-1971,* 1971, p. 46.
33. John T. Fleming quoted by Sanka Knox in "Academy of Arts Irks U.S. Dealers," *NYT,* 21 April 1963.
34. JWC, letter to *AB,* 1-8 July 1963, p. 28.
35. JWC to executors of the Ian Fleming estate, 24 Aug. 1964. CA
36. JWC to PM, 10 Dec. 1968. IND
37. JWC to PM, 26 June 1969. IND
38. PM to JWC, 1 July 1969. IND
39. JWC to PM, 17 July 1969. IND
40. DR to JWC, 22 March 1971. IND
41. JWC to PM, 17 July 1969. IND

CHAPTER EIGHT NOTES

1. Herrmann, p. 442.
2. PCW to JWC, 7 March 1960. CA
3. JWC to PCW, 19 March 1960. CA
4. JWC, "Sotheby's of London; New York: The Early Days" *Art at Auction 1970-1971.* 1971, p. 47.
5. Peregrine Pollen to the author, 5 Dec. 2002.
6. JWC to Richard Gimbel, 2 Feb. 1961. CA
7. JWC to Richard Gimbel, 16 Feb. 1961. CA
8. JWC to Frank Herrmann, 27 March 1973. CA
9. JWC, "Two Way Stretch," *AB,* 5 Oct. 1964, p. 2324.

10. JWC, "Transatlantic Traffic in Rare Books," *Books, the Journal of the Book League of London,* June 1961, p. 78. Reprinted in *AB,* 26 June 1961, p. 2425.
11. Richard Wormser, letter to *AB,*17 July 1961, p. 2578.
12. JWC, letter to *AB,* 31 July 1961, p.2704.
13. JWC to Amy Silver, 2 Jan 1964. NL
14. JWC to Warren Roberts, 1 Nov. 1972. TX
15. "Rare Book Dealer Sues Silver Estate," *PW,* 17 Aug. 1964, pp. 24-25.
16. Edmond de Goncourt quoted by JH, *BC,* Summer 1964, p. 142.
17. JWC, "Newberry Books," *Chicago Daily News,* 16 April 1964.
18. JWC to Lawrence W. Towner, 20 May 1964. NL
19. Louis B. Wright quoted by JWC in *Distinguished Printed Books....Property of the Newberry Library of Chicago,* London: Sotheby's 1964. p. 7.
20. JWC to James Wells, 5 Oct. 1970. NL
21. JWC to PCW, 12 Jan. 1966. CA
22. JWC, "Thomas J. Wise at Sotheby's," *AB,* 22 Jan. 1968, p.271.
23. Ibid.
24. The directors originally signed an agreement with Leo Lerman, a well-known feature editor with *Vogue,* to do the history. After working on it for several years and signing a contract with Holt, Reinhart in New York, Lerman abandoned the project and turned over his notes to Carter.
25. JWC to DR, 12 Jan 1966. IND
26. JWC to DR, 11 April 1972. IND
27. Herrmann's contract agreement included the following statement: "It is clearly understood that the book should conform to its title, "Sotheby's an Informal History" and that you will be absolutely free to write it as you see it without regard to any propaganda aspect: though we should hope that you would consult Mr. Carter, or if necessary the Chairman, over any passages about which you had doubts in the matter of delicacy or expediency." Graham Llewellyn to Frank Herrmann, 17 Jan. 1973. CA
28. In the early months of 1971, Carter disposed of a large collection of bibliographies and other volumes from his personal library by turning them over to Bernard Quaritch Ltd. The books were listed and sold anonymously as "reluctant extrusions enforced upon a past president of the Bibliographical Society by a drastic constriction of shelf space." London: Bernard Quaritch Ltd., Catalogue 908, June 1971.

CHAPTER NINE NOTES

1. JWC to DR, 6 June 1957. IND
2. NB, "John Carter," *BC*, Summer 1975, p. 212.
3. JWC to GP, 1 Nov. 1969. BOD
4. JWC quoted by NB in *BC*, Summer 1975, p. 213.
5. *Book Handbook*, Feb. 1947.
6. [JH], *BC*, Winter 1955, p. 265.
7. JWC letter to Richard Wormser, Herman Cohen, Philip Duschnes, George Goodspeed, Robert Barry, Lawrence Whitten, Hamill & Barker, Harry Levinson, Elizabeth McMurray, and David Magee. 1955. CA
8. PM, "John Hayward," *BC*, Winter 1965, p. 459.
9. Andrew Lycett, *Ian Fleming* London: Weidenfeld & Nicolson, 1995, p. 347.
10. JWC, Memorandum, 19 Sept. 1957. CA
11. Ian Fleming to JWC, 24 Sept. 1957. CA
12. JWC, "After Ten Years," *BC*, Winter 1961, p. 407.
13. JH to JWC, 13 Nov. 1962. CA
14. JH, *BC*, Summer 1964, p. 144.
15. JH to JWC, 16 July 1964. CA
16. NB, "Thoughts on Scoring a Century," *BC*, Winter 1990, pp. 449-450.
17. JWC, "John Hayward," *The Sunday Times*, 19 Sept. 1965 and reprinted in *BC*, Winter 1965, pp. 446-448.
18. JWC, "Some Memories of John Hayward," *BC*, Winter 1965.
19 JWC to William A. Jackson, 28 Aug. 1951. CA
20. [Simon Nowell-Smith], "The Soho Recipe," *TLS*, 25 Oct. 1963, p. 876.
21. JWC to Gordon Ray, 2 March 1965. CA
22. JWC to Lord Bernstein, 3 April 1970. CA
23. JWC to J.C. Reynolds, 3 July 1970. CA
24. JWC to William Cagle, 5 Aug. 1970. CA
25. Frank Francis, Stanley Morison, John Carter, "Preface," to *Printing and the Mind of Man*, London: F.W. Bridges & the Association of British Manufacturers of Printers' Machinery, 1963, p. 7.
26. *PPM* I, p.66.
27. *PPM* 3, p. xi.
28. [George Steiner], "Garland for Gutenberg," *TLS*, 22 June 1967, p. 561.
29. Denis Brogan, *Spectator*, 22 June 1967.
30. Interview with Michael Meredith, 11 Oct. 2000.
31. Ibid.
32. To mark the occasion, the library printed one hundred copies of an exhibition catalog, *Twentieth Century Manuscripts and First Editions from the Eton School Library*. Among the items displayed were a copy

of *An Enquiry Into the Nature of Certain Nineteenth Century Pamphlets* and the preliminary draft of Carter's article published in *The Sunday Times Magazine* 8 March 1970 as "How We Got Wise." Carter didn't like the title assigned by the paper - too determinedly catchy - and wrote to the *Times* editor saying it would have been more appropriate to use the straightforward title suggested in the drafts, "Thomas J. Wise, Book Forger."

33. In 1961 the Rampant Lions Press printed a commemorative pamphlet, *The Ceremony of the Lilies and Roses,* "Devised by John Carter . . . and printed by Will Carter . . . in memory of their father Thomas Buchanan Carter, begetter of this ceremony, whose photograph of Francis Bird's statue [of King Henry VI] makes the frontispiece and whose likeness faces this page." The pamphlet contains a brief history of the ceremony, "The Order of Service," and "The Charter of the Lilies."

34. Carter was a member of the Cambridge Bibliographical Society, the Oxford Bibliographical Society, the Edinburgh Bibliographical Society, the Grolier Club of New York and the Rowfant Club of Cleveland, Ohio. In London he was a member of the Garrick Club, the Double Crown Club, the Eton Ramblers, and the Beefsteak Club.

CHAPTER TEN NOTES

1. JWC to WSL, 27 Dec. 1951, YWL
2. WSL to JWC, 2 Jan. 1951. YWL
3. JWC to WSL, 9 Jan. 1952. YWL
4. WSL to JWC, 14 Jan. 1952. YWL
5. JWC to WSL, 5 Jan. 1952. YWL
6. WSL to JWC, 8 Jan. 1952. YWL
7. JWC, *TLS,* 9 May 1952, p.341.
8. WSL, *BC,* Winter 1952, p. 272.
9. WSL to Ernestine Carter, 23 May 1977. YWL Lewis confused the dates, as Carter did not begin working in London until September 1927.
10. DR to JL, 11 Dec. 1936. IND
11. JWC to JL, 14 Dec. 1936. IND
12. Ibid.
13. JWC to JL, 17 May 1938. IND
14. JL to DR, 19 Oct. 1938. IND
15. JWC to JL, 25 April 1939. IND
16. JWC to JL, 27 April 1939. IND
17. JL to DR, 20 Nov. 1945. IND
18. JWC to JL, 22 Feb. 1952. IND

19. JWC to JL, 18 Nov. 1954. IND
20. JL to JWC, 22 Nov. 1954. IND
21. JWC, *Stanley Morison 1889-1967 A Radio Portrait*, London: W.S. Cowell, 1969, p. 31.
22. SM to JWC, 3 June 1953. CA
23. SM to JWC, July 1942. CA
24. JWC in *Stanley Morison 1889-1967 A Radio Portrait.* p. 31.
25. SM in *Handlist*, 1950, p. 12.
26. Ibid., p.10.
27. JWC, "Stanley Morison, Designer and Typographer," *PW*, 3 June 1950, p. 2484.
28. [NB], "Stanley Morison," *BC*, Spring 1968, p. 47.
29. NB, "Introduction," *A.N.L. Munby Essays and Papers.* London: Scolar Press, 1977, p. xiii.
30. PM, p. 94.
31. JH, "Why First Editions?" *Book Collecting Four Broadcast Talks* Cambridge: Bowes and Bowes, 1950. p. 24.
32. James M. Wells, Custodian of the John M. Wing Collection on the History of Printing at the Newberry Library, Chicago, Illinois, remembers Carter's astonishment when a determined soprano launched into a rousing chorus - "Lilly you are the fairest flower in our campus garden." His usual aplomb gave way and his eye-piece fell into his coffee cup. Interview with James M. Wells, 1 May 2002.
33. JWC to DR, 27 July 1965. IND
34. JWC to DR, 20 Sept. 1973. IND
35. JWC to DR, 22 Feb. 1969. IND
36. JWC to DR, 24 Jan. 1956. IND
37. JWC to DR, 15 Nov. 1961. IND
38. MS quoted by JWC in "Remarks Prepared for the Indiana University Printing and the Mind of Man Exhibition." 1973, typescript, p.16. IND
39. JWC, tribute to PM in *PHM 80*, Edited by Laurie Deval., 1974, pp. 43-44
40. JWC, "Percy Muir at Eighty," *BC*, Winter 1974, p. 488.
41. JWC to GP, 7 Sept. 1948. BOD
42. JWC to GP, 20 Jan. 1950. BOD
43. JWC to GP, June 1940. BOD
44. JWC, "Graham Pollard," *Studies in the Book Trade.* Oxford: Oxford Bibliographical Society, 1975. p. 7

CHAPTER ELEVEN NOTES

1. [JWC], "The Heritage of Culture," *TLS,* 18 Dec.1948, p. 705.
2. Ibid., p. 706.
3. [JH], *BC,* Spring 1953, p. 4.
4. Ibid.
5. John J. Rorimer, quoted in *AB,* 10 Feb. 1964, p. 652.
6. JWC, Letter to the editor *AB,* 10 Feb. 1964, p. 652.
7. Ibid.
8. Reviewing Committee Report, quoted by JWC in "The Caxton Ovid," *BC,* Spring 1971, pp. 9-10.
9. Ibid., p. 16.
10. Ibid., p. 17.
11. JWC to Eugene Power, 30 June 1969. CA
12. [JWC], "The Rothschild Collection," *TLS,* 13 March 1955, p. 172.
13. JWC, Letter to the editor *AB,* 26 April 1965, p. 489.
14. JWC, Letter to the editor *AB,* 21 April 1969, p. 1453.

CHAPTER TWELVE NOTES

1. JWC to DR, 10 Oct. 1973. IND
2. JWC to DR, 10 Jan. 1974. IND Randall was also suffering serious health problems at this time.
3. JWC to DR, 12 Feb. 1974. IND
4. Larry McMurtrie, "Mad About the Book," *New York Review of Books,* 20 Dec. 2001, p. 58.
5. JWC, Preface, *A Handlist of the Writings of Stanley Morison,* Cambridge: Cambridge University Press, 1950, p. vii.
6. JWC and JS, Preface, "A. E. Housman An Annotated Check-List," *The Library,* Sept. 1940, p. 31.
7. JWC, "A Hand-List of the Printed Works of William Johnson afterwards Cory," *Transactions of the Cambridge Bibliographical Society.* 1953, p. 69.
8. JWC, *ABC,* 1952, p. 30.
9. Ibid., pp. 98-99.
10. JWC, "Nineteenth Century Books: Some Bibliographic Agenda," Windsor Lecture, University of Illinois, 1951, reprinted in *BBC,* pp. 157-186.
11. JWC, "The Digressive Principle," letter to *TLS,* 21 July 1966, p. 716.
12. Donald C. Gallup, *On Contemporary Bibliography.* Austin, Texas: University of Texas, 1970, p. 12.

13. Keynes, p. 383.
14. Ibid., p. 385.
15. The inscription on Carter's stone, cut by his brother Will, reads "John Waynflete Carter KS 1919 Fellow 1967 Born in this Parish 1905 Lies Here With his Forebears 1975."
16. JWC, "For My Funeral," May 1970. typescript. SC
17. Lord Redcliffe-Maud, "John Carter 1905-1975," Address delivered at Memorial Service 5 May 1975. typescript. KCL
18. Larry McMurtrie, "Mad About the Book," *New York Review of Books* 20 Dec. 2001, p. 58.

SELECTED BIBLIOGRAPHY

This bibliography includes full citations to books given in abbreviated form in the notes. A list of John Carter's publications is provided in a separate CHECKLIST.

Altick, Richard D., "The Case of the Curious Bibliographers," in *The Scholar Adventurers* (New York: Macmillan, 1950), pp. 37-64.

Arnold, Ralph, *Orange Street & Brickhole Lane* (London: Hart-Davis, 1963)

Barker, Nicolas, *Stanley Morison* (London: Macmillan, 1972)

Barker, Nicolas and John Collins, *A Sequel to An Enquiry Into the Nature of Certain Nineteenth Century Pamphlets by John Carter and Graham Pollard* (London: Scolar Press, 1983; New Castle, Delaware: Oak Knoll Press, 1983)

Bertram, Anthony, *Paul Nash, The Portrait of an Artist* (London: Faber and Faber, 1955)

Brownrigg, Philip, "College," in *Eton Portrait* by Bernard Fergusson (London: Miles, 1937), pp. 38-60.

Carter, Ernestine, *With Tongue in Chic* (London: Michael Joseph, 1974)

Collins, John, *The Two Forgers: A Biography of Harry Buxton Forman & Thomas James Wise* (New Castle, Delaware: Oak Knoll Press, 1992)

Connolly, Cyril, *Enemies of Promise* (London: Deutsch, 1973)

Crutchley, Brooke, *To Be a Printer* (London: Bodley Head, 1980)

Davison, Peter, ed.,*The Book Encompassed - Studies in Twentieth Century Bibliography* (Cambridge: Cambridge University Press, 1992)

Fowler, Laurence, ed., *Cambridge Commemorated* (Cambridge: Cambridge University Press, 1984)

Gow, A. S. F., *A.E. Housman* (Cambridge: Cambridge University Press, 1936)

Grant, Michael, *Cambridge* (London: Weidenfeld and Nicolson, 1966)

Green, Henry, *Pack My Bag* (London: Hogarth Press, 1940)

Haber, Tom Burns, *A.E. Housman* (Boston: Twayne, 1967)

Hart-Davis, Rupert, *The Power of Chance* (London: Sinclair Stevenson, 1991)

Herrmann, Frank, *Sotheby's, Portrait of an Auction House* (London: Chatto & Windus, 1980)

_____. *Low Profile* (Nottingham: Plough Press; New Castle, Delaware: Oak Knoll Press, 2002)

Hollis, Christopher, *Eton, a History* (London: Hollis & Carter, 1960)

Howarth, T.E.B., *Cambridge Between the Two Wars* (London: Collins, 1978)

Keynes, Geoffrey, *Gates of Memory* (Oxford: Clarendon Press, 1981)

Lacey, Robert, *Sotheby's — Bidding for Class* (Boston: Little Brown, 1998)

Mackenzie, Faith Compton, *As Much As I Dare* (London: Collins, 1938)

_____. *William Cory, A Biography* (London: Constable, 1950)

May, Derwent, *Critical Times — The History of The Times Literary Supplement* (London: Harper Collins, 2001)

Meyers, Robin, *The British Book Trade* (London: Andre Deutsch, 1973)

Meynell, Francis, *My Lives* (London: Bodley Head, 1971)

Moran, James, *The Double Crown Club* (London: Westerham Press, 1974)

Muir, Percy, *Minding My Own Business, an Autobiography* (London: Chatto & Windus, 1956; New Castle, Delaware: Oak Knoll Press, 1991)

Ollard, Richard, *An English Education, A Perspective of Eton* (London: Collins, 1982)

Orwell, George, *Such, Such Were the Joys* (New York: Harcourt Brace, 1952)

Munby, A.N.L., *Essays and Papers* Edited by Nicolas Barker (London: Scolar Press, 1977)

Page, Norman, *A.E.Housman, A Critical Biography* (London: Macmillan, 1983)

Pariser, Sir Maurice, *Catalogue of the Celebrated Collection Formed by Sir Maurice Pariser of Manchester, of the Notorious Nineteenth Century Pamphlets and Other Important Wiseana - Manuscripts and Printed* (London: Sotheby's, 1967)

Partington, Wilfred, *Forging Ahead* (New York: Putnam's, 1939). Enlarged as *Thomas J. Wise in the Original Cloth* (London: Robert Hale, 1947)

Pfaff, Richard William, *Montague Rhodes James* (London: Scolar Press, 1980)

Pryce-Jones, Alan, *The Bonus of Laughter* (London: Hamish Hamilton, 1987)

Randall, David, *Dukedom Large Enough* (New York: Random House, 1969)

Ratchford, Fannie E., ed., *Between the Lines: Letters and Memoranda Interchanged by H. Buxton Forman and Thomas J. Wise* (Austin: University of Texas Press, 1945)

_____. *Letters of Thomas J. Wise to John Henry Wrenn* (New York: Knopf, 1944)

Rota, Anthony, *Books in the Blood* (London: Private Libraries Association, 2002; New Castle, Delaware: Oak Knoll Press, 2002)

Scribner, Charles Jr., *In the Web of Ideas* (New York: Scribner's, 1993)

_____. *In the Company of Writers: A Life in Publishing* (New York: Scribner's 1990)

Symons, Julian, *A.J.A. Symons - His Life and Speculations* (London: Eyre & Spottswoode, 1950)

Tarling, Alan, *Will Carter. Printer* (London: Galahad Press, 1968)

Todd, William B., ed., *Thomas J. Wise Centenary Studies* (Austin: University of Texas Press, 1959)

Towner, Wesley, *The Elegant Auctioneers* (New York: Hill & Wang, 1970)

Treglown, Jeremy, *Romancing - The Life and Work of Henry Green* (London: Faber and Faber, 2000)

Wells, Gabriel, *The Carter-Pollard Disclosures* (New York: Doubleday Doran, 1934)

Wilkinson, L. P., *A Century of Kings 1873-1972* (Cambridge: King's College, 1980)

_____. *Kingsmen of a Century 1873-1972* (Cambridge: King's College, 1981)

CHECKLIST OF THE
WRITINGS OF JOHN CARTER

This Checklist is chronologically arranged and divided into four parts: (A) Separate Works, (B) Books and Pamphlets Edited or with Contributions by Carter, (C) Periodical Contributions, (D) Publications about John Carter.

The purpose of the Checklist is to supply a when and where approach to Carter's major publications and to demonstrate the range of his interests. While errors and gaps are sure to be found, certain omissions are deliberate. I made no attempt to include Carter's book reviews, catalog notes, letters to editors (he was a prolific and lively contributor to a variety of journals and newspapers) or his many contributions to the query and answer sections of *Bibliographic Notes & Queries* and *The Book Collector*. An examination of the web site, *The Times Literary Supplement Centenary Archive 1902-1990*, will provide an approach to Carter's reviews, letters to the editor and notes in that source. A full-scale bibliography of Carter's work would be a worthwhile and ambitious undertaking.

The content and scope of information included in the entries is intended for the interested amateur rather than the bibliographic or literary specialist. Abbreviations correspond to those listed on pp. 339-340.

(A) Separate Works

1932 –
A1 BINDING VARIANTS IN ENGLISH PUBLISHING 1820-1900
a. First edition:
Binding variants in English publishing 1820-1900. London: Constable;
New York: R. Long and R. R. Smith, 1932. Parchment-backed marbled
boards, xvii, 172p., 16 collotype plates.
Limited to 500 copies. Portions appeared originally in *The Colophon* and
The Book Collector's Quarterly.
Bibliographia series no. 6

b. Reprint edition:
_____. With *More binding variants.* Introduction by Robert D.
Fleck. New Castle, Delaware: Oak Knoll Press, 1989, cloth, dust jacket,
xvii, 172, x, 52 p.

A2 THE INIQUITY OF OBLIVION FOIL'D
*The iniquity of oblivion foil'd or a discource of certain copies, lately found, of
Urne buriall* and *The garden of Cyrus by Thomas Browne. The Whole
Palaeographically, Textually, Bibliophilcally Considered with Sundry
Observations. By a Gentleman, lately scholar of King Henry the Sixth's
Foundations of Eton College, & King's College at Cambridge.* [Campden,
Gloucestershire: Alcuin Press], 1932, wrappers, [11] p, 1 plate.
Limited to 50 copies. "Reprinted from *The Colophon* for the author, and
to be had of no booksellers."

1934 –
A3 AN ENQUIRY INTO THE NATURE OF CERTAIN NINE-
TEENTH CENTURY PAMPHLETS
a. First edition:
An enquiry into the nature of certain nineteenth century pamphlets, with
Graham Pollard. London: Constable; New York: Scribner's, 1934, cloth,
dust jacket, xii, 400p., 4 plates.

b. Reprint edition:
_____. New York: Haskell House, 1971, cloth, xii, 400p., 4 plates.

c. Second edition:
_____. Second edition, with an Epilogue by John Carter and Graham
Pollard, edited by Nicolas Barker and John Collins. London: Scolar
Press; 1983, cloth, dust jacket, 10, xii, 400, 41p., 6 plates.

1935 –
A4 PUBLISHER'S CLOTH
a. First edition:
Publisher's cloth, an outline history of publisher's binding in England 1820-1900. New York: Bowker; London: Constable, 1935, wrappers, 48p. Produced in conjunction with an exhibition at the New York Public Library.

b. Reprint edition:
_____. New York: Bowker; London: Constable, 1938, wrappers, 48p. *Aspects of Book-Collecting* series.

1938 –
A5 MORE BINDING VARIANTS
a. First edition:
More binding variants, with contributions by Michael Sadleir. London: Constable, 1938, wrappers, x, 52p. Also in cloth, interleaved. *Aspects of Book-Collecting* series.

b. Reprint edition:
_____. With *Binding Variants in English Publishing 1820-1900*. Introduction by Robert D. Fleck. New Castle, Delaware: Oak Knoll Press, 1989, cloth, dust jacket, xvii, 172, x, 52p.

A6 COLLECTING DETECTIVE FICTION
Collecting detective fiction. London: Constable, 1938, wrappers, pp. 32-62. *Aspects of Book Collecting* series.
Previously published in *New Paths in Book Collecting*, B6.

1945 –
A7 VICTORY IN BURMA
Victory in Burma, New York: British Information Services, July 1945, wrappers. Carter served as director of the general division of the British Information Services in New York from late 1943 to 1945. He discussed the publication program in "Publishing-But for Free," in *PW*, 10 November1945. He is frequently identified as the author of this publication although it does not carry his name.

1948 –
A8 TASTE & TECHNIQUE IN BOOK-COLLECTING
a. First edition:
Taste & technique in book-collecting, a study of recent developments in

Great Britain and the United States. The 1947 Sandars Lectures in Bibliography. Cambridge: Cambridge University Press, 1948, cloth, dust jacket, [xii], 201p.

b. American edition:
_____. New York: R. R. Bowker, 1948, cloth, dust jacket, [xxii], 203p.

c. Second impression corrected:
_____. Cambridge: Cambridge University Press, 1949, cloth, dust jacket, xii, 203p.

d. Third impression corrected:
_____. With an epilogue, "Taste & Technique in Book Collecting 1928-1968," An address delivered to the Bibliographical Society 18 November 1969. London: Private Libraries Association, 1970, cloth, dust jacket, xiv, 242p.

A9 THE FIRM OF CHARLES OTTLEY, LANDON & CO.
a. First edition:
The firm of Charles Ottley, Landon & Co., footnote to An Enquiry, with Graham Pollard. London: Hart-Davis; New York: Scribner's, 1948, wrappers, 95p. 3 plates.
"Part of this monograph was read as a paper to the Bibliographical Society." Prefatory Note.

1950 –
A10 A HANDLIST OF THE WRITINGS OF STANLEY MORISON
a. *A handlist of the writings of Stanley Morison*, with some notes by Mr. Morison and indexes by Graham Pollard. Cambridge: Cambridge University Press, for private distribution, 1950, printed paper over boards, x, 48p.
The Handlist was completed as a tribute to Morison on his sixtieth birthday, 6 May 1949.

b. Extended as "Stanley Morison, a Second Handlist 1950-1959" by P.M. Handover, in *Motif 3* 1959, pp. 52-57. Includes corrections and additions by Carter to his original 1950 *Handlist.*
Reprinted in blue wrappers. London: Shenval Press, 1959.

c. Extended as *The writings of Stanley Morison* compiled by Tony Appleton, with a biographical and typographical supplement and essays by Brooke Crutchley and John Dreyfus. Includes corrections and additions by Carter to his original 1950 *Handlist.* Brighton: Tony Appleton, 1976, cloth, xix, 117p.
Limited to 600 copies.

1952 –

A11 A. E. HOUSMAN AN ANNOTATED HAND-LIST
a. First edition: .
A. E. Housman an annotated hand-list, with John Sparrow. London: Hart-Davis, 1952, cloth, 54p.
Corrected and revised from original publication in *The Library* n.s., No. 2, 1940, "A E. Housman, An Annotated Check-List."
Soho Bibliography, no. 2.

b. Second edition:.
A. E. Housman, a bibliography, with John Sparrow and William White. Second edition revised by William White. Godalming, Surrey: 1982, cloth, xvii, 94p.
St. Paul's Bibliography, no. 6.

A12 ABC FOR BOOK-COLLECTORS
a. First edition:
ABC for book-collectors. London: Hart-Davis; New York: Knopf, 1952, cloth, dust jacket, 191p.

b. Second edition:
_____. London: Hart-Davis; New York: Knopf, 1953, cloth, dust jacket, 196p.

c. Third edition:
_____. London: Hart-Davis; New York: Knopf, 1961, cloth, dust jacket, 208p.
"Completely reset and extensively revised" Preface

d. Third edition, reprint.
_____.London: Mercury Books, 1961, paper wrappers, 208p.
Mercury Books No. 12.

e. Fourth edition:
_____. London: Hart-Davis; New York: Knopf, 1966, cloth, dust jacket, 210p.
Reprinted with corrections 1967.

f. Fifth edition:
_____. London: Granada; New York: Knopf, 1972, cloth, dust jacket, 211p.
Last edition revised by Carter.
Reprinted with corrections 1974, reissued by Granada, 1978.

g. Sixth edition:
_____. London: Granada; Revised by Nicolas Barker, 1980, cloth, dust jacket, 219p.
Reprinted 1982, 1985. Reissued New Castle, Delaware: Oak Knoll Press, 1992, reprinted 1993, 1994, cloth, dust jacket, 219p.

h. Seventh edition:
_____. London: Werner-Shaw; New Castle, Delaware: Oak Knoll Press, With corrections, additions and an introduction by Nicolas Barker, 1995, cloth, dust jacket, 223p.
Reprinted 1997, 1998, 2002.

i. Eighth edition:
_____. New Castle, Delaware: Oak Knoll Press; London: The British Library, With corrections, additions and an introduction by Nicolas Barker, 2004, cloth, dust jacket.

1956 –
A13 BOOKS AND BOOK-COLLECTORS
a. First edition:
Books and book-collectors. London: Hart-Davis; Cleveland, Ohio: World, 1956, cloth, dust jacket, 196p.
Contents: Thomas J. Wise - Two Beckford Collections - Carroll A. Wilson - Michael Sadleir - Wilmarth S. Lewis - Lord Rothschild - D. B. Updike - Stanley Morison - Collecting Detective Fiction - Off-Subject Books - Collecting A. E. Housman - Bentley Three-Deckers - Fashions in Book-Collecting - Thomas J. Wise and his Forgeries - Thomas J. Wise and H. Buxton Forman - Nineteenth-Century English Books: Some Bibliographical Agenda - Operation Shuckburgh - ABC for Book-Collectors.

1959 –
A14 WILLIAM JOHNSON CORY
William Johnson Cory: a great Eton master 1823-1892. Cambridge: Rampant Lions Press, 1959, wrappers, [8] p.
No statement of limitation.
Originally appeared in *TLS*, 2 June 1950 as "A Great Eton Master," as Carter's review of Faith Compton Mackenzie's *William Cory, a Biography.*

1961 –
A15 CEREMONY OF THE LILIES AND ROSES
The ceremony of the lilies and roses, 21st May at 6:30 p.m. H.M. Tower of London. Cambridge: Rampant Lions Press, 1961, wrappers, [16] p. 2 plates.

No statement of limitation.

Includes a reproduction of a photograph of Thomas Buchanan Carter, "begetter of this ceremony."

"Devised by John Carter/ sometime scholar of Eton and King's/London Rose Bearer/and printed by Will Carter/ father of a Kingsman."

1963 –

A16 THE DRY MARTINI

The dry martini. Worcester: privately printed, 1963, wrappers.
Reprinted from Ernestine Carter's, *Flash in the pan.* London: Hamish Hamilton, 1963.
Limited to 200 copies.

1965 –

A17 THE JOHN CARTER COLLECTION OF A. E. HOUSMAN

The John Carter collection of A. E. Housman. Bloomington: The Lilly Library Indiana University [1965], wrappers, [8] p.
A description of Carter's collection purchased by the Lilly Library in 1965.
"Five hundred copies printed for bookmen of Indiana and friends of the Lilly Library; 100 copies printed for John Carter." Colophon.

1967 –

A18 PRECIS OF PADEN

Precis of Paden or the sources of 'The New Timon,' with Graham Pollard.
Working paper No. 1, Oxford: B.H. Blackwell, 1967, wrappers, 24p.
96 copies for sale, reprinted July 1967, 200 copies for sale.

A19 FORGERIES OF TENNYSON'S PLAYS

The forgeries of Tennyson's plays, with Graham Pollard. Working paper No. 2, Oxford: B.H. Blackwell, 1967, wrappers, 21p.
96 copies for sale, reprinted July 1967, 200 copies for sale.

1969 –

A20 GOLD MEDAL OF THE BIBLIOGRAPHICAL SOCIETY

The gold medal of the Bibliographical Society: Graham Pollard; Fredson Bowers. Oxford: Oxford University Press, 1969, wrappers.
Carter presented the medals on 6 May 1969.

A21 MYSTERY OF 'THE DEATH OF BALDER'

The mystery of 'The Death of Balder,' with Graham Pollard. Working paper No. 3, Oxford: B.H. Blackwell, 1969, wrappers, 21p.
200 copies for sale.

1970 –
A22 GORFIN'S STOCK
Gorfin's stock, with Graham Pollard. Working paper No. 4, Oxford: B.H.
Blackwell, 1970, wrappers, 36p.
400 copies for sale.

(B) Books and Pamphlets Edited or with Contributions by Carter

1932 –

B1 RARE BOOKS IN ENGLISH LITERATURE
Rare books in English literature. London: Elkin Mathews, Catalogue 48,
September 1932.
Introduction by John Carter entitled, "Publishing History and the Collector
with Special Reference to *Binding Variants,*" wrappers, pp. 3-5. Includes a
note: "I am permitted to give, overleaf, a few additional notes to my book on
Binding Variants. To any who have read it, I hope they may be of interest,
to those who have not, I can only say "To them that hath, more is given."
What follows on pp. 6-8 is entitled "Addenda to Binding Variants."

B2 RARE BOOKS IN ENGLISH LITERATURE
Rare books in English literature. London: Elkin Mathews, Catalogue 49,
October 1932.
Introduction by John Carter entitled, "Additional Notes to *Binding
Variants,*" wrappers, pp. 2-3.

B3 URNE BURIALL AND THE GARDEN OF CYRUS
a. First edition:
Sir Thomas Browne. *Urne buriall* and *the garden of Cyrus.* London:
Cassell, London, 1932, bound in morocco and vellum, tooled in gold,
[126] p., 30 collotype color illustrations by Paul Nash. Printed at the
Curwen Press.
Edited by John Carter. Limited to 215 copies. "One copy consisting of
two volumes, the first *Urne Buriall* and *The Garden of Cyrus,* the second a
portfolio of all Mr. Nash's original drawings, both specially bound, at
350 guineas." Advertising prospectus.

b. Revised edition:
_____. Cambridge: Cambridge University Press, 1958, cloth, dust
jacket, viii, 120p.
Edited by John Carter.

c. Partial reprint:
The Last Chapter of Urne Buriall. Cambridge: Rampant Lions Press, 1946.
Pamphlet sewn into wrappers, [16] p.
Edited by John Carter.
Cover and title page designs by John Piper. Limited to 175 copies of
which 125 were for sale.

1933 –

B4 INTRODUCTORY LECTURE

A. E. Housman. *Introductory lecture,* delivered before the Faculty of Arts and Law and of Science in University College, London, 3 October 1892. Cambridge: Cambridge University Press, 1933, stitched without wrappers, [7] p. Unsigned preface attributed to John Carter. 100 copies printed for Carter and John Sparrow, 25 of which were reserved for the author. None were for sale. Two copies were printed on blue paper.

On December 5, 1933 Housman wrote to Carter, "I should like to have it stated that the Council of University College, not I, had the lecture printed. I consented, because it seemed churlish to refuse. This is the purport of *Nescit Vox Missa Reverti* as printed on the title page."

1934 –

B5 POEMS OF CAIUS CATULLUS

Caius Catullus. *The poems of Caius Catullus.* Translated into English by Robert Gathorne-Hardy. Stanford Dingley: Mill House Press, 1934, wrappers, 80p.

Edited by John Carter.

Parts one and two only of a projected six part issue. Latin and English on facing pages.

B6 NEW PATHS IN BOOK COLLECTING

a. First edition:

"Detective Fiction," in New paths in book collecting. Essays by various hands. London: Constable; New York: Scribner's, 1934, cloth, dust jacket, [vi], 294p. Edited and with an Introduction by John Carter.

Contents: John T. Winterich, "The Expansion of an Author Collection," - John Carter, "Detective Fiction," - P. H. Muir, "Ignoring the Flag," - C. B. Oldman, "Musical First Editions," - Michael Sadleir, "Yellow-Backs," - T. Balston, "English Book Illustrations, 1880-1900," - David A. Randall, "American First Editions, 1900-1933," - P. H. Muir, "War Books," - Graham Pollard, "Serial Fiction."

b. Reprint edition:

_____. Freeport, New York: Books for Libraries, 1968, cloth, vi, 294p.

In "An Unsolicited Review," in *BC,* Spring 1969, Carter identified this as an unauthorized reprint.

B7 A CATALOGUE OF AN EXHIBITION ARRANGED TO ILLUSTRATE 'NEW PATHS IN BOOK COLLECTING'

"First Editions of Detective Fiction" in *Catalogue of an exhibition*

arranged to illustrate 'New Paths in Book Collecting.' London: J. & E.
Bumpus, 1934, wrappers, pp. 32-36.
Based on Carter's chapter, "Detective Fiction," in *New Paths in Book Collecting.*

B8 COLLECTION OF DETECTIVE FICTION
Collection of detective fiction. New York: Scribner's Catalogue 98, 1934,
wrappers.
Introduction and notes unsigned but attributed to Carter.
Carter described the origin and final disposition of the collection in
"Hawkshaw Rides Again," in *BC*, Summer 1963.

1938 –
B9 CLERIHEWS
a. First edition:
Clerihews, an unofficial supplement to "Biography for Beginners."
Cambridge: Rampant Lions Press, 1938, stiff paper wrappers, [34] p.
Edited by John Carter.
Edition of about 500 copies.

b. Second edition:
Clerihews, by various hands. Cambridge: Rampant Lions Press, 1946, stiff
paper wrappers, [60] p.
Edited by John Waynflete, B.A. [Carter]
Edition of about 275 copies. Contains eighteen verses from the 1938
printing together with twenty-two new to this edition.

1939 –
B10 COLLECTED POEMS OF A. E. HOUSMAN
a. First edition:
The collected poems of A. E. Housman. London: Cape, 1939, cloth, dust
jacket, 254p.
Edited by John Carter.

b. American first edition:
_____. New York: Holt, 1940, cloth, dust jacket, 254p.
A description of the complicated publishing history of both the English and
American printings is provided in *A. E. Housman A Bibliography*, by John
Carter, John Sparrow and William White. St. Paul's Bibliographies, 1982,
pp. 23-24.

1941 –
B11 THE PRINTED BOOK
a. Second edition:
Harry G. Aldis, *The printed book*, second edition, Cambridge: Cambridge

University Press, 1941, cloth, dust jacket, x, 142p.
Edited by John Carter and Brooke Crutchley.
First edition published in 1916.

b. Reprint edition with corrections:
_____. Cambridge: Cambridge University Press, 1947, cloth, dust jacket, [x], 141p.

c. Third edition:
_____. Cambridge: Cambridge University Press, 1951, cloth, dust jacket, [vi], 141p.

1945 –

B12 NINETEENTH CENTURY PAMPHLETS
Nineteenth century pamphlets: with an appendix of Wiseana. New York: Scribner's Catalogue 113, 1945, wrappers, 30p.
Made up of Wise forgeries from the library of Walter B. Slater.
Introduction and notes unsigned but attributed to Carter.

1947 –

B13 VICTORIAN FICTION
a. First edition:
Victorian fiction, an exhibition of original editions at 7 Albemarle Street, London, January to February 1947, published for The National Book League by the Cambridge University Press, 1947, wrappers, 50p.
Arranged by John Carter with the collaboration of Michael Sadleir.

b. Illustrated edition:
_____. cloth, dust jacket, 50p. followed by 16 plates.

1950 –

B14 BOOK COLLECTING - FOUR BROADCAST TALKS
"The Technical Approach," in *Book collecting - four broadcast talks.*
Cambridge: Bowes and Bowes, 1950, wrappers, 45p.
Preface by John Carter.
Contents: R. W. Chapman, "The Sense of the Past," - John Hayward, "Why First Editions?" - John Carter, "The Technical Approach," and Michael Sadleir, "Bookshop and Auction Room."
First broadcast on the BBC Third Programme in the summer of 1950.

1951 –

B15 MODERN BOOKS AND WRITERS
Modern books and writers. The catalogue of an exhibition held at 7 Albemarle Street, London, April to September 1951, published for The National

Book League by the Cambridge University Press, 1951, wrappers, vi, 69p.
Carter was chairman of the exhibitions subcommittee and wrote the preface.

B16 LUCRETILIS
William Johnson Cory, *Lucretilis*. Cambridge: Rampant Lions Press,
1951, quarter brown cloth with a paper label, xii, [58] p.
Edited by John Sparrow and with bibliographic note signed JWC.
175 copies printed.

1952 –

B17 NINETEENTH-CENTURY ENGLISH BOOKS - SOME PROBLEMS
"Some Bibliographical Agenda," in *Nineteenth-century English books, some
problems in bibliography*. Windsor Lecture in Bibliography. Urbana,
Illinois: University of Illinois Press, 1952, cloth, pp. 53-81.
Contents: Gordon Ray, "The Importance of Original Editions," Carl
Weber, "American Editions of English Authors," John Carter, "Some
Bibliographical Agenda."

B18 TALKS ON BOOK COLLECTING
"Fashions in Book Collecting," in *Talks on book collecting*, delivered
under the authority of the Antiquarian Booksellers' Association. London:
Cassell, 1952, cloth, pp. 53-73.
Contents: P.H. Muir, "The Nature and Scope of Book Collecting," - E. P.
Goldschmidt, "The Period Before Printing," - Simon Nowell-Smith, "The
Language of Book Collecting," - John Carter, "Fashions in Book-Collecting,"
- Howard M. Nixon, "Binding and Binders," - Ernest Weil, "Milestones of
Civilization," - Ifan Kyrle Fletcher, "The Theatre for Collectors."
Carter's talk was originally published in the *Virginia Quarterly Review*,
Fall 1950.

1953 –

B19 THE DRY MARTINI
a. First edition:
"The Dry Martini," in *Flash in the pan* by Ernestine Carter, London:
Hamish Hamilton, 1953, cloth, dust jacket, pp. 129-133.

b. Revised edition:
_____. London: Hamish Hamilton, 1963, cloth, dust jacket, pp. 123-126.

1954 –

B20 CONCISE ENCYCLOPEDIA OF ANTIQUES
"Book Collecting," in *Concise encyclopedia of antiques*. London: The
Connoisseur, 1954, cloth, pp. 199-205.

1955 –

B21 BOUILLABAISSE FOR BIBLIOPHILES

"Definition of a Book Collector," in *Bouillabaisse for bibliophiles,* Edited by William Targ. Cleveland, Ohio: World, 1955, cloth, dust jacket, pp.19-30.

1956-1959 –

B22 SOTHEBY'S SEASONS

Sotheby's 213th season, 1956-1957; Sotheby's 214th season, 1957-1958, Sotheby's 215th season, 1958-1959. London: Sotheby's, 1956-1959, wrappers.

Carter described the creation and development of these reports in "Sotheby's of London: the early days. Some egotistical reminiscences," in *Art at Auction 1970-1971*, pp. 45-46.

1958 –

B23 MONEY AT WORK

"The Auction Room," in *Money at work.* Edited by Milton Grundy. London: Sweet & Maxwell, 1958, cloth, dust jacket, pp. 132-155.

Second edition:

_____. Second edition, London: Sweet & Maxwell, 1960, cloth, dust jacket, pp.147-170.

1959 –

B24 TYPOGRAPHIC DESIGN

Stanley Morison, *Typographic design in relation to photographic composition.* San Francisco: Book Club of California, 1959, quarter parchment with marbled boards.

Introduction by John Carter.

400 copies printed by the Black Vine Press.

B25 THOMAS J. WISE CENTENARY STUDIES

"Thomas J. Wise in Perspective," in *Thomas J. Wise centenary studies.* Edited by William B. Todd. Austin, Texas: University of Texas Press, 1959, cloth, dust jacket, pp. 3-19.

Contents: John Carter, "Thomas J. Wise in Perspective," Graham Pollard, "The Case of *The Devil's Due* and "The Scope for Further Typographical Analysis," - William B. Todd, "Handlist of Thomas J. Wise," and reprints of Wise's letters to J. E. Cornish and Sir Edmund Gosse, and his Introduction to the *Browning Library.*

B26 A.E. HOUSMAN: CATALOGUE OF AN EXHIBITION
A. E. Housman: A catalogue of an exhibition on the centenary of his birth.
London: University College, 1959, wrappers.
Compiled by John Carter.

B27 GROLIER 75
"John Henry Wrenn." in *Grolier 75*, a biographical retrospective to celebrate the seventy-fifth anniversary of the Grolier Club in New York.
New York: The Grolier Club, 1959, cloth, pp. 31-34.
On 16 July 1958, Alexander Davidson wrote to Carter and asked if he
would prepare a brief biographical sketch of John Henry Wrenn for the
forthcoming Grolier Club volume, *Grolier 75*. Carter was unenthusiastic,
as shown in his reply of 7 August 1958. "I am afraid, that I can not
undertake the assignment proffered in your letter of July 16. You say that
you (plural) feel that I am the man to do John H. Wrenn. Unfortunately
all I know about Wrenn is derived from Miss Ratchford's edition of his
correspondence with Wise, and what little I ever heard about him outside
that made me think he must have been a very dull fellow, though rich. . .
. . Was Wise ever a member of the Grolier Club? I would not mind doing
him, even with such a tough deadline as November 1." Eventually,
Carter did the Wrenn sketch in spite of his stated reluctance.

1961 –
B28 ENGLISH PRIVATE PRESSES
English private presses 1757-1961. London: Times Bookshop, 1961, wrap-
pers, 64p.
Introduction by John Carter.
Special printing of 100 copies on handmade paper.

B29 A. E. HOUSMAN SELECTED PROSE
a. First edition:
A. E. Housman selected prose. Cambridge and New York: Cambridge
University Press, 1961, cloth and stiff paper wrappers, xv, 204p.
Edited and with a preface by John Carter.

b. Corrected edition:
_____. Cambridge and New York: Cambridge University Press, 1962,
cloth and stiff paper wrappers, xv, 208p.

c. American revised edition:
The name and nature of poetry and other selected prose. New York: New
Amsterdam Press, 1989, cloth.

B30 A. E. HOUSMAN, A COLLECTION OF MANUSCRIPTS, LET-
TERS . . .
"A Footnote," in *A. E. Housman a collection of manuscripts, letters, proofs,
first editions, etc.* Formed by H. B. Collamore of West Hartford,
Connecticut and presented to the Lilly Library Indiana University.
Bloomington: The Lilly Library, 1961, pp. 33-37.
The publication was designed to go with the exhibition held in the
library April 1-30, 1961.
Carter's account of the sale of books from Housman's library in the fall
of 1936.

1963 –
B31 PRINTING AND THE MIND OF MAN
a. First edition:
Printing and the mind of man, catalogue of the exhibition at the British
Museum and at Earls Court, London 16-27 July 1963. London: F. W.
Bridges and the Association of British Manufactures of Printing
Machinery, 1963, stiff paper wrappers. Part 1, The exhibition at Earls
Court, 125p., 32 plates; Part 2, The exhibition of fine printing in the
British Museum, 64p., 16 plates.
Preface by Frank Francis, Stanley Morison and John Carter.

b. Revised edition:
_____. *A descriptive catalogue illustrating the impact of print on the evo-
lution of western civilization during five centuries.* London: Cassell; New
York: Holt, 1967, cloth, dust jacket, xxxvi, 280p.
Edited by John Carter and Percy Muir, with an essay by Denys Hay.
Title page engravings by Reynolds Stone. Printed at the University
Printing House, Cambridge under the direction of John Dreyfus

c. Second edition:
_____. Revised and enlarged, Munich: Karl Pressler, 1983, cloth, dust
jacket, xxv, 280p.

d. German translation:
Bücher die die welt verandërn. Munich: Prestel Verlag, 1968, cloth. dust
jacket, 788p.

e. German reprint:
_____. Munich: Taschenbuch Verlag, 1976, paper wrappers, 788p.

f. Japanese translation:
Seiyo o kizuita shomotso Toyko: Yushodo Shoten, 1977, 345p.

1964 –

B32 EDUCATION OF THE REASONING FACILITIES
William Johnson Cory, *The education of the reasoning facilities.*
Halcyon Booklet No. 2. Cambridge: Cambridge University Press,
1964, wrappers, 8p.
Preface by John Carter.
A reprint of Cory's 1867 essay originally published in his *Essays on a
Liberal Education.*
Carter was General Editor of the Halcyon Booklets for the Halcyon-
Commonwealth Foundation in New York.

B33 WISE AFTER THE EVENT
Wise after the event. A catalogue of books, pamphlets, manuscripts and
letters relating to Thomas James Wise displayed in an exhibition in the
Manchester Central Library. Manchester: Libraries Committee.
September 1964, wrappers, 67p.
Edited by G. E. Haslam with a Foreword by John Carter.
The collection of Maurice P. Pariser, Alderman of Manchester.

B34 PRINTING AND DEMOCRACY
Robert Birley, *Printing and democracy.* London: Privately Printed for the
Monotype Corporation, 1964, wrappers. 32p., 8 plates.
Preface by Frank Francis, Stanley Morison and John Carter.
"Designed as a pendant to *Printing and the Mind of Man.*" Preface

1966 –

B35 VICTORIAN DETECTIVE FICTION, A CATALOGUE
Dorothy Glover and Graham Greene. *Victorian detective fiction, a cata-
logue of the collection made by Dorothy Glover and Graham Greene.*
London: Bodley Head, 1966, cloth, dust jacket, xviii. 149p.
Bibliographically arranged by Eric Osborne and Introduced by John Carter.
Limited to 500 copies; 475 numbered copies for sale signed by Glover,
Greene and Carter.

1967 –

B36 CATALOGUE OF THE CELEBRATED COLLECTION
FORMED BY MAURICE PARISER . . .
*Catalogue of the celebrated collection formed by Sir Maurice Pariser of
Manchester of the notorious nineteenth century pamphlets and other impor-
tant Wiseiana manuscripts and printed books,* 4, 5 December 1967.
London: Sotheby's, 1967, paper wrappers, 139p.
25 copies printed on green paper.

Compiled by John Carter.
Carter described the arrangements for the sale and the results in "Thomas
J. Wise at Sotheby's," *AB*, 22 January 1968, pp. 271-273.

1968 –

B37 GOVERNMENT BY CONTEMPT
John Redcliffe Maud. *Government by contempt*, Whitehall's way with
Parliament and people. London: Chatto and Windus, 1968, wrappers, 32p.
Preface by John Carter.
A speech delivered in the House of Lords on the government's "dishonest
decisions" surrounding the proposed relocation of the British Library.
Reprinted from a letter to *The Times* 31 October 1967.

1969 –

B38 STANLEY MORISON 1889-1967
Stanley Morison 1889-1967, a radio portrait compiled by Nicolas Barker
and Douglas Cleverdon from recollections by T. F. Burns, John Carter,
Arthur Crook, Brooke Crutchley, Francis Meynell, Graham Pollard,
Janet and Reynolds Stone, and Beatrice Ward. Ipswich: W. S. Cowell,
1969, cloth, 38p.
Carter's remarks, p. 13, 31, 35.
Initials on the cover designed by Reynolds Stone and frontispiece photo-
graph by Janet Stone. Profits of the publication to be expended on an
appropriate acquisition for the library of St. Bride's Foundation Institute.
Limited to 800 copies of which 550 were for sale.

B39 THE CONFINES OF CRITICISM
A. E. Housman. *The confines of criticism: the Cambridge inaugural 1911.*
Cambridge: Cambridge University Press, 1969, cloth, 54p.
Edited by John Carter.
Contains an appendix "Shelley, Swinburne and Housman," taken from a
TLS article by Carter and John Sparrow, 21 November 1968. "The
Cambridge Inaugural" minus a short paragraph was first published in the
TLS on 9 May 1968 followed by a note by Carter.
25 copies printed for private distribution.

1970 –

B40 CATALOGUE OF A COLLECTION OF VICTORIAN FICTION
*Catalogue of a collection of Victorian fiction mainly three-deckers and auto-
graph letters.* The library of Douglas Ewing. London: Sotheby's, 1970,
wrappers, 66p., 1 plate.
Compiled by John Carter.

1974 –

B41 PHM [Percy Muir] 80
PHM 80. A collection of tributes to Percy Muir on his eightieth birthday.
Introduction and arrangement by Laurie Deval, December 1974, stiff
paper wrappers, 50p.
Carter's remarks pp. 43-45.
Photograph of Muir opposite title page by Anton Roth.
Limited to 100 copies.

1975 –

B42 STUDIES IN THE BOOK TRADE
"Graham Pollard," in *Studies in the book trade in honour of Graham
Pollard.* Oxford: Oxford Bibliographical Society, N.S. xviii, 1975, linen-
backed boards, pp. 3-9.

(C) Periodical Contributions

1930 –
C1 "Original Condition," *PW*, 15 Nov. 1930, pp. 2277-2279.

1931 –
C2 "The Origins of Publishers' Cloth Binding," *The Colophon*, pt. 8, 1931.
Reprinted by William Rasmussen, Orange, California: Rasmussen Press, 1972, wrappers [15] p. "Limited edition for friends."

C3 "Personality in Notepaper," *The Queen*, 12 Aug. 1931.

C4 "Looking Backward," *PW*, 17 Jan. 1931, pp. 330-332.

C5 "Looking Forward," *PW*, 20 June 1931, pp. 2889-2891.

1932 –
C6 "Notes on the Early Years of Cloth Binding," *BCQ*, April 1932, pp. 46-56.

C7 "The 'Edition or Impression' Controversy," *PW*, 16 April 1932, pp. 1733-1736.

C8 "Bibliography and the Collector," *PW*, 19 Nov. 1932, pp.1923-1926.

1933 –
C9 "The Iniquity of Oblivion Foil'd," *The Colophon*, pt. 13. 1933.
Account of the history and ownership of six author-corrected copies of Sir Thomas Browne's *Urne Buriall* and *The Garden of Cyrus*.
Published as a separate - A2.

C10 "Notes on the Bibliography of Byron," *TLS*, 27 April 1933, p. 300, continued in *TLS*, 4 May 1933, p.316.

1935 –
C11 "The 19th Century Pamphlet Forgeries," *PW*, 9 Feb. 1935, pp. 719-721.

C12 "Publisher's Cloth, An Outline History of Publisher's Binding in England 1820 -1900," *PW*, 16 Feb. 1935, pp. 807-809, and 23 Feb. 1935, pp. 901-904.

C13 "Off-Subject Books," *The Colophon,* vol. 1 no. 2, 1935, pp. 201-206.
Reprinted in *BBC,* pp. 94-100.

1936 –
C14 "Mrs. Browning's *Poems* 1850," *TLS,* 30 May 1936, p. 464.

1937 –
C15 "The Lausanne Edition of Beckford's 'Vathek,'" *The Library,* 5th
series, March 1937, pp. 369-394.

C16 "Bentley Three-Deckers," *The Spectator,* 7 May 1937, pp. 856-857.
Reprinted *PW,* 30 Oct. 1937, pp. 1738-1740 and in *BBC,* pp. 112-116.

C17 "The Puzzle of Thomas J. Wise," *PW,* 29 May 1937, pp. 2213-2214.

C18 "Thomas J. Wise," *The Spectator,* 21 May 1937, pp. 954-955.
Reprinted in *BBC,* pp. 15-21.

1938 –
C19 "Cheap Reprints," *Typography,* 1938.
Originally given as a talk to the Double Crown Club, 28 Feb. 1938.

C20 "On Collecting A. E. Housman," *The Colophon,* vol. 3 no. 1, 1938,
pp. 54-62.

C21 "The Hanging Judge Acquitted," *The Colophon,* n.s. vol. 3 no. 2,
1938, pp. 238-242.

C22 "Publisher's Binding in America," *PW,* 19 Nov. 1938, pp. 1823-
1824.

C23 "Best Sellers and the Atlantic," *The Spectator,* 16 Sept. 1938, p. 446-
447.
Reprinted in *Living Age,* Nov. 1938, pp. 274-276.

1939 –
C24 "Two Beckford Collections," *The Colophon,* n.s. vol. 1 no. 1, 1939,
pp. 67-74.
Reprinted in *BBC,* pp. 22-31.

C25 "News in America," *The Spectator,* 3 Feb. 1939, pp. 172-173.

C26 "The Library at Dormy House," *The Colophon*, n.s. vol. 1 no. 2, 1939, pp. 25-36.
The library of Morris L. Parrish.

C27 "The Library of Frank Hogan," *The Colophon*, vol. 1 no. 3, 1939, pp. 55-66.

1940 –
C28 "The Rare Book Trade in London," *PW*, 13 Jan. 1940, pp. 129-132.

C29 "London Rare Book Notes," *PW*, 27 April, 1940, pp. 1689-1692; 15 June 1940, pp. 2296-2298.
By "Waynflete." Continued in 1941 and 1942.

C30 "A Bookseller's Day in London," *PW*, 2 Nov. 1940, pp. 1764-1765.

C30b "A. E. Housman an Annotated Check-List" *The Library* N.S. No. 2 1940, pp. 160-191.

1941 –
C31 "London Rare Book Notes," *PW*, 19 April 1941, pp. 1677-1678.

C32 "Clough to Churchill," *PW*, 2 Aug. 1941, pp. 311-312.

C33 "Stocktaking, 1941," *PW*, 20 Dec. 1941. pp. 2241-2245.
Survey of trends in bibliography and book-collecting 1927-1940.

1942 –
C34 "London Rare Book Notes," *PW*, 21 Feb. 1942, pp. 896-897 and 15 Aug. 1942, pp. 487-488.

C35 "The British Book Trade in the Third Year of War," *PW*, 9 May, 1942, pp. 1744-1746.

1945 –
C36 "Thomas J. Wise and his Forgeries," *Atlantic Monthly*, Feb. 1945, pp. 93-100.

C37 "Publishing - But for Free," *PW*, 10 Nov. 1945, pp. 2136-2139.
The work of the British Information Service in New York.

1946 –
C38 "Fifty Years of the Bibliographical Society," *PW*, 20 April 1946, pp. 2219-2220.

C39 "Celebrations at Yale," *PW*, 23 Nov. 1946, pp. 2898-2900.
The return of the Yale collections to peacetime use.

1947 –
C40 "Browne's Urne Buriall," *The Library*, 5th series, Sept. 1947, pp. 191-192.
Identifies 11th author hand-corrected copy.

C41 "Condition; A Highly Controversial Subject," *PW*, 22 Nov. 1947, pp. 2384-2389.
Modified text taken from Carter's Sandars lecture, as printed in *Taste & Technique in Book-Collecting*.

C42 "Disequilibrium in the Rare Book Market," *PW*, 20 Dec. 1947, pp. 433-436.
Comparison of the 1946-1947 auction season in London and New York.

1948 –
C43 "Limelight on Bibliographers," *AB*, 24 April 1948, p. 677.
Bibliographical Society Gold Medals to Stanley Morison and Strickland Gibson.

C44 [Anon.] "Daniel Berkeley Updike" *TLS*, 20 March 1948, Review of *American Printer* by Peter Beilenson. Reprinted in *BBC*, pp. 63-66.

C45 "Bookseller and Auctioneer," *Atlantic Monthly*, July 1948, pp. 96-99.

C46 "Reflections on Rarity," *The New Colophon*, n.s. vol. 1 no. 2, 1948, pp. 134-150.
Modified text taken from Carter's Sandars lecture as printed in *Taste & Technique in Book-Collecting*.

C47 "The ABA Lectures on Book Collecting and Bibliography," *AB*, 6 Nov. 1948, pp. 822.

C48 [Anon.] "The Heritage of Culture," *TLS*, 18 Dec. 1948, pp. 705-706.

1949 –
C49 A Hand-List of the Printed Works of William Johnson, Afterwards Cory," *Transactions of the Cambridge Bibliographical Society*, vol. 1, 1949, pp. 69-87.

C50 "The National Book League," *The Penrose Annual*, 1949, pp. 39-41.

1950 –
C51 "Stanley Morison, Designer and Typographer," *PW,* 3 June 1950, pp. 2481-2486.
Reprinted in *BBC*, pp. 67-76.
Swedish translation: *Bogvännen* No. 8, 1951.
German translation: *Schweizer Graphischer Mitteilungen*, 1950.

C52 "Fashions in Book-Collecting," *Virginia Quarterly Review*, Fall 1950, pp. 382-392.

C53 "British Book Illustration," *AIGA Journal*, June 1950, pp. 31-32.
Reprinted from *TLS*, 25 Aug. 1950.

1951 –
C54 [Anon.] "Carroll Atwood Wilson," *TLS*, 12 Jan. 1951, p. 28.
Review of Wilson's *Thirteen Author Collections*.
Reprinted in *BBC*, pp. 32-38.

C55 "Operation Shuckburgh," *The Bookseller*, 17 Feb. 1951.
Bringing the Gutenberg Bible to the United States.
Reprinted in *BBC*, pp. 187-192.

C56 [Anon.] "Michael Sadleir," *TLS*, 13 April 1951 p. 234.
Review of Sadleir's *XIX Century Fiction*.
Reprinted in *BBC*, pp. 39-50.

1952 –
C57 [Anon.] "Wilmarth S. Lewis," *TLS*, 9 May 1952, p. 320.
Review of Wilmarth S. Lewis' *Collector's Progress*.
Reprinted in *BBC*, pp. 51-55.

1954 –
C58 "Bibliography an the Rare Book Trade," *PBSA*, 3rd quarter 1954, pp. 219-229.
Reprinted in *The Bibliographical Society of America 1904-1979, A Retrospective Collection*, pp. 307-317.

1955 –
C59 [Anon.] "Lord Rothschild." *TLS*, 18 March 1955, p. 172.
Review of *The Rothschild Library*.
Reprinted in *BBC*, pp. 56-62.

C60 [Anon.] "Parkinson's Law," *The Economist,* 19 Nov.1955, pp. 635-637.

C61 "Eastward the Course of Empire?" *AB Yearbook, 1955,* pp. 9-10.

C62 "The A.E. Housman Manuscripts in the Library of Congress," *BC,* Summer 1955, pp.110-114.

1956 –
C63 "The Pendulum of Taste," *Atlantic Monthly,* Oct. 1956, pp. 67-69.

C64 "Busy Market in Rare Books," *Financial Times,* July 1956.

C65 "Sidelights on American Bibliophily," *BC,* Winter 1956, pp. 357-367. Originally given as an address at the annual meeting of the Oxford Bibliographical Society, 14 March 1956.

1957 –
C66 "George Eliot's '*Agatha'*" *BC,* Autumn 1957, pp. 244-252.

C67 "Works of Art as Property," *The Trust Bulletin,* May 1957, pp. 2-7.

C68 "Paperback Revolution," *TLS,* paperback section, 12 July 1957, p. ii-iii.
Comparison of the development of the paperback market in England and the United States.

C69 "Investing in Rare Books," *Financial Times,* Dec. 1957.

C70 "A Book Collector's Bookshelf," *Books* [National Book League], 1957.

C71 "The Hub of the Fine Arts Market," *Vogue,* Dec. 1957, pp. 54-57.

1958 –
C72 "Realization on Estate Assets, the International Market in Works of Art," *Trusts and Estates,* Jan. 1958, pp. 527-530.

C73 "Bookshelves," *House and Garden,* 22 March 1958, pp. 67-68.

C74 "Rare Book Market, Still Buoyant," *Financial Times,* Aug. 1958.

1959 –
C75 "Bibliomania in Bond Street," *The Queen*, 1959.

1960 –
C76 "Playing the Rare Book Market," *Harper's Monthly*, April 1960, pp. 74-76.

C77 "What Happens to Authors' Manuscripts?" *Atlantic Monthly*, July 1960, pp. 76-80.

C78 "William Ged and the Invention of Stereotype," *The Library*, 5th series, Sept. 1960, pp. 161-192.

C79 "Farewell, Catullus," *Texas Quarterly*, Autumn 1960, pp. 274-284.

1961 –
C80 "William Ged and the Invention of Stereotype, a Postscript," *The Library*, 5th series, June 1961, pp. 143-145.

C81 "Transatlantic Traffic in Rare Books," *Books* [National Book League], June 1961.
Reprinted in *AB*, 26 June, pp. 2435.2436, and in *AB Bookman's Yearbook*, 1973-74, pp. 24-25.

C82 "Book Auctions," *Library Trends*, April 1961, pp. 471-482.

1962 –
C83 "The Hastings Rarities," *NSN*, 24 Aug. 1962, pp. 224, 226.
Account of a hoax involving a taxidermist who claimed to have found more than thirty birds previously unknown in the Hastings area. Comparison with the T. J. Wise forgeries.

C84 [Anon.] "Chrysler's Controversial Century, or What Price the Name on the Frame," *NSN*, 14 Dec. 1962, pp. 865-866.
Examines the furor that greeted the opening of the exhibition in Ottawa when a large number of painting were condemned as fakes.

1963 –
C85 "The Framed Dollar," *Harper's Montly*, July 1963, pp. 23-29.

C86 "Hawkshaw Rides Again," *BC*, Summer 1963, pp. 178-183.
An account of Carter's interest in detective fiction.

C87 "Housman, Shelley and Swinburne," *TLS*, 6 Sept. 1963, p. 680.

C88 "Beckford and 'Vathek,'" *The Library*, 5th series, Dec. 1963, pp.308-309.

1964 –
C89 "The 'Battle of Life:' Round Three," *AB*, 18 May 1964, pp. 2203-2205.
Establishing the priority of the first edition of Dickens' *The Battle of Life*.

C90 "The Two-Way Stretch," *AB*, 5 Oct. 1964, pp. 1363-1364.
Originally given as an address to the Baltimore Bibliophiles, 23 Sept. 1964
under the title "Recent Trends in American Book-Collecting." Discussion
of the acquisition of Parke-Bernet Galleries by Sotheby's.

C90b "Wise After the Event," *The Bookseller*, 5 Sept. 1964, pp. 43-44.
Account of the M. P. Pariser exhibition of Wiseiana held in Manchester
May 4-3, 1964.

1965 –
C91 "The Art of Book Collecting," *The Director*, 18 Aug. 1965, pp. 258-260.

C92 "A Valediction," [for John Hayward] *BC*, Winter 1965, pp. 446-448.
Reprinted from *The Sunday Times*, 19 Sept. 1965.

1966 –
C93 "The Iniquity of Oblivion Foil'd," *BC*, Autumn 1966, pp. 279-282.
Account of growth of Carter's collection of author hand-corrected copies
of Sir Thomas Browne's *Urne Buriall* and *The Garden of Cyrus*.
Reprinted in *The Pleasures of Bibliophily*. London: The British Library;
New Castle, Delaware: Oak Knoll Press, 2004, pp. 100-106.

1967 –
C94 "Addenda and Corrigenda to 'A Handlist of the Printed Works of
William Johnson, Afterwards Cory,'" *Transactions of the Cambridge
Bibliographical Society*, vol. 4, 1967, pp. 318-320.

C95 "Thomas J. Wise and his Forgeries," *Auction*, Dec. 1967, pp. 2-3.

1968 –
C96 "Thomas J. Wise at Sotheby's," *AB*, 22 Jan. 1968, pp. 271-273.
The auction, 4-5 Dec. 1967, of the Maurice Pariser collection.

C97 "Shelley, Swinburne and Housman," with John Sparrow, *TLS*, 24
Nov. 1968, pp. 1318-1319.

1969 –

C98 "Thomas J. Wise's Verses, 1882-1883," *The Library*, 5th series, Sept. 1969, pp. 246-249.

C99 "The Rainbow Prosecution," *TLS*, 27 Feb. 1969, p. 216.
Documents involved in the 1915 suppression of *The Rainbow* by D. H. Lawrence.

C100 "Is This a Record?" *BC*, Autumn 1969, pp. 353-359.
Highest price paid for broadsides and pamphlets.

1970 –

C101 "The Rare Book Market, 1928-1968," *AB*, 2-9 Feb. 1970, pp. 339-344.

C102 "How We Got Wise," *Sunday Times Magazine*, 8 March 1970, pp. 38-43.
Carter's original title, "Thomas J. Wise, Book Forger," was dropped by the editor in favor of what Carter sarcastically called a more "trendy" title.

C103 "Sadleir Rides Again," *TLS*, 30 Oct. 1970, p. 1280.
Describes Sotheby's sale of Victorian fiction, 12-13 Oct. 1970.

1971 –

C104 "Sotheby's of London, New York: The Early Days - Some Egotistical Reminiscences," *Art at Auction, 1970-1971*, pp. 34-47.

1972 –

C105 "I.R. Brussel, L.O.G.S.," *BC*, Autumn 1972, pp. 402-405.
Reprinted in *AB*, 25 Dec. 1972, p. 2096.

1973 –

C106 "The Private Library in America," *American Libraries*," Dec. 1973, pp. 665-667.

C107 "Robert Gathorne-Hardy," *BC*, Summer 1973, pp. 229-230.

1974 –

C108 "Percy Muir at Eighty," *BC*, Winter 1974, pp. 479-488.

(D) Publications about John Carter

1950 –
D1 Richard D. Altick, "The Case of the Curious Bibliographers," in *The Scholar Adventurers*. New York: Macmillan, 1950, pp. 37-64.

1953 –
D2 [Anon.] "John Carter," *PW*, 3 Jan. 1933, pp. 31-33.

1959 –
D3 [Anon.] "John Carter," *Current Biography*. New York: Current Biography 1959, pp. 57-59.

1961 –
D4 Dwight Macdonald, "The First Editions of T. J. Wise," *New Yorker*, 10 Nov. 1961, pp. 168-205.

1975 –
D5 [Nicolas Barker] "John Carter," *BC*, Summer 1975, pp. 202-216. Obituary.

D6 Lord Redcliffe-Maud, "John Carter 1905-1975." Memorial service address, Eton College, 5 May, 1975, 6 page typescript.

D7 Percy Muir, "John Carter," *BC*, Summer 1975, pp. 271-276. Obituary.

D8 [A.N. L. Munby] "John Carter, Bibliographer and Man of Taste," *The Times*, 19 March 1975, p. 19. Obituary.

1976 –
D9 Sotheby Parke Bernet, *Catalogue of the Valuable Collection of Printed Books, the Property of the Late John Carter. Esq., C.B.E.*, London: Sotheby Parke Bernet, 24 March 1976, wrappers, 78p. 356 lots.

1980 –
D10 Frank Herrmann, "John Carter," *Dictionary of National Biography* 1971-1980, Oxford: Oxford University Press, 1980, pp. 124-125. Condensed in *The Concise Dictionary of National Biography*, Oxford: Oxford University Press, vol.1, 1992, p. 485.

1999 –
D11 Virginia T. Bemis, "John Carter," *Dictionary of Literary Biography,* vol. 201, Detroit: Gale Research, 1999, pp. 30-39.

2001 –
D12 Milton McC. Gatch, "John Carter," *Grolier 2000,* New York: Grolier Club, 2001, pp. 63-65.

INDEX

(Page numbers in *italic* indicate illustrations)